The Russell/Bradley Dispute and its Significance for
Twentieth-Century Philosophy

The Russell/Bradley Dispute and its Significance for Twentieth-Century Philosophy

Stewart Candlish

© Stewart Candlish 2007

First published 2007 by
PALGRAVE MACMILLAN
Houndmills, Basingstoke, Hampshire RG21 6XS and
175 Fifth Avenue, New York, N.Y. 10010
Companies and representatives throughout the world

PALGRAVE MACMILLAN is the global academic imprint of the Palgrave Macmillan division of St. Martin's Press, LLC and of Palgrave Macmillan Ltd. Macmillan® is a registered trademark in the United States, United Kingdom and other countries. Palgrave is a registered trademark in the European Union and other countries.

ISBN 13: 978–0–230–50685–5
ISBN 10: 0–230–50685–2

This book is printed on paper suitable for recycling and made from fully managed and sustained forest sources.

A catalogue record for this book is available from the British Library.

Library of Congress Cataloging-in-Publication Data
Candlish Stewart.
    The Russell/Bradley dispute and its significance for twentieth-century philosophy / Stewart Candlish.
       p. cm.
    Includes bibliographical references (p. #) and index.
    ISBN 0-230-50685-2 (cloth)
       1. Russell, Bertrand, 1872–1970. 2. Bradley, F.H. (Francis Herbert),
    1846–1924. 3. Analysis (Philosophy)–History–20th century. 4. Idealism–
    History–20th century. I. Title.
    B1649.R94C37 2006
    192–dc22
                                                                    2006044842

10   9   8   7   6   5   4   3   2   1
16   15   14   13   12   11   10   09   08   07

Printed and bound in Great Britain by
Antony Rowe Ltd, Chippenham and Eastbourne

'For *this* is what disputes between Idealists, Solipsists and Realists look like. The one party attack the normal form of expression as if they were attacking a statement; the others defend it, as if they were stating facts recognized by every reasonable human being.'

—Wittgenstein, *Philosophical Investigations*,
trans. G.E.M. Anscombe
(Oxford: Blackwell, 1953), §402

'The basic colours of history are not black and white, their basic pattern not the contrast of a chess-board; the basic colour of history is grey, in endless variations.'

Thomas Nipperdey, *Deutsche Geschichte 1866–1918*,
2 vols (Munich: C.H. Beck, 1990–92); vol. ii, p. 905;
the translation is presumably that of Ian Kershaw,
who quotes the remark in the first volume of
his biography of Hitler

Contents

Preface and Acknowledgments

A distinguished philosopher of the present day, whose name would be immediately recognized by most of the likely readers of this Preface and who is to my knowledge extremely well-acquainted with the work of Russell, said to me a few years ago after hearing a talk on Bradley and Russell, 'That was most interesting. I had always thought that Bradley was a lot of nonsense.' In the later years of his career, the Russell scholar Leonard Linsky made in print a comparable, though more discreetly phrased, admission (Linsky 1992, p. 247n).

How is it possible for Russell experts to be so ignorant of Bradley, when Bradley, the major figure in British Idealism, loomed so large for Russell himself, and the dispute between them formed one of the major turning points in twentieth-century philosophy?

Part of the answer to this question lies in Russell's eventual success in this dispute: the picture which he, together with G.E. Moore, drew of Bradley for the purpose of controversy and polemic, was so far absorbed by generations of subsequent philosophers that it became impossible to see him as worth the trouble spent on his refutation. Observing the past from this perspective is like looking through the wrong end of a telescope with a charcoal-tinted lens and finding only the Dark Ages, curiously diminished.

In this book I try to turn the telescope around, substitute a lens as far as possible free of all tinting (especially the rosy) and re-examine this significant episode in the recent history of philosophy. Although, as we shall see, characterizing it in this way is already to enter into controversy, at this point we can think of the dispute as that between the British Idealists and the founders of the movement which eventually became known as 'analytic philosophy'.

One understandable reaction at this point, especially given recent interest in Russell's move away from Idealism, would be to wonder whether the job had already been done.[1] A brief description of how I have approached these matters should make clear that what I am attempting here is unusual:

1 I have focused on both philosophers, and have given Bradley at least as much attention as Russell (indeed, Chapters 2 to 6 of this book alternate in taking one philosopher or the other as their protagonist).

2   I have chosen an apparently idiosyncratic set of themes around which to construct the book; this is partly because the standard themes are already well-discussed, but mainly because I think that on occasion matters of real importance have been missed.

3   I have paid attention to the dialectical interplay of Bradley and Russell's mutual criticism.

4   Because of this, I have allowed, to some extent, their conception of each other's work to shape the content of my own discussion. One result is that I have said nothing directly about the details of Russell's logic, and relatively little about his attempts to find technical solutions to philosophical problems; this has already been done by others, and in any case Bradley's concern, like Wittgenstein's, was with the philosophical assumptions underlying technical solutions. Likewise, I have said very little about Bradley's notion of 'feeling'; although commentators often attach great importance to this, it was ignored by Russell.

5   I have extended the discussion of both philosophers into the 1920s, roughly to the point of Bradley's death. This is partly to take into account some of Wittgenstein's influence on Russell, and partly because the interplay of criticism continued up to that point (and even beyond, with some retrospective criticism by Russell and some posthumous publication of Bradley essays).

6   One of my concerns has been to illustrate how subsequent English-language philosophy has been subject to false conceptions of its own history.

For the record: I have *not* tried to give complete and systematic outlines of the views of any of the philosophers on whom I have focused (though, because of its relative unfamiliarity, both in content and in expression, I have in Chapter 2 tried to provide a way into Bradley's thought which identifies some of its crucial features, and, for these are not always the most salient ones, to make that thought intelligible to a readership to whom the original texts are now largely alien). While I have not refrained from criticism and verdict, I *have* tried to avoid identifying with either side; instead, I have preferred to uncover, explain and correct misrepresentations and to highlight matters which have been overlooked – often this on its own makes clear which side, if either, should be taken. If misrepresentation is not equally balanced, that is a matter of history, not of my bias.

Some readers may already be losing interest. They will include those for whom philosophy is in some sense a timeless discipline, and who want to know, reasonably enough, whether the coherence theory of truth can be rationally defended; or whether there is better reason to accept, say, pluralism or monism; or, if one *must* sit with one's back to the locomotive of progress and accordingly notice that two philosophers of the past were in disagreement, then who was right, not whether or not this one misunderstood that one. Such readers may be reassured to learn that in Chapter 6 of this book I conclude that, on the central matter of relations, Bradley was 'unanswerably correct'. But to confine oneself to this sort of straightforward approach to the matter in hand would be to risk overlooking two ways in which this dispute is of great importance to that approach itself. One is that the dispute's outcome shaped the way in which the discipline has since developed; the currency of this conception of philosophy as timeless is itself an historical product of the events I describe. The second is that the dispute is *representative*: and I shall try to provide, with the detachment that hindsight affords, a case study of major philosophers in action and of how the process – no matter who is right about what – can affect the historical understanding of later generations who all proclaim an attachment to truth and would disdain resting their ideas upon a baseless myth. Setting the record straight can open up possibilities that may wrongly be thought to have been closed off. The tenseless approach is also associated with another conception of philosophy: as autonomous, occupying the Archimedean point. But this conception makes it easy to overlook another way in which the dispute is important: it is in a curious way emblematic of a range of struggles of its period. These include the historical/cultural (Victorian versus Edwardian), the political (conservative versus liberal), the academic (literary/classical versus mathematical/ scientific), the institutional (Oxford versus Cambridge), and even the national (Germany versus Britain). To take sides in this dispute was not just a metaphysical commitment. I do not – of course – intend by this the absurd suggestion that, say, to be a Russellian atomist in metaphysics requires, or is required by, being a Russellian liberal in politics; what I mean concerns matters of association, not of logic. The point is rather that, depending on the side taken, one might, for example, look progressive, or conservative (even reactionary) – certainly to others, even perhaps to oneself.[2]

Despite what I have just said, this book will undoubtedly be read as an attempted vindication of Bradley. I cannot stop that happening. But I do protest against such a reading; and, indeed, a careful reader will notice that I reject some of Bradley's most fundamental arguments. Still, I can explain how the impression will arise in some minds. The explanation is fairly simple. It is a truism to say that history is written by the victors; and the fact is that, historically speaking – let us reserve judgment, for the time being, about the philosophy – Russell was the victor. There are many reasons for this. Here I shall remark just one of the most obvious: Russell is immensely more readable, and more read; and he survived to write the history of the events with which I shall deal. Now, most philosophers, still more or less content with the Russellian account of it, do not look back on this matter at all; and most of those who do look back on it do so through Russellian eyes. To such philosophers, any attempt to set the historical record straight is bound to look like an attempt to vindicate Bradley, if only because the conventional history displays Bradley as wrong, perverse, even muddle-headed, at every turn, who, from the timeless perspective, is now worth reading, if at all, only for his classic critique of hedonistic utilitarianism.

*   *   *

So much for what I am trying to do. But how did this project come about? I had originally conceived this book as the first part of a longer work for which I had no definite title but had begun to think of as *Russell's Critics* or *Russell's Century*, though neither would have been satisfactory. The idea was to look at the reactions of what one might think of as a philosopher from the past, and one from the future, to that part of Russell's intellectual career which had such an impact on twentieth-century philosophy – roughly the period from 1903 (*The Principles of Mathematics*) to 1921 (*The Analysis of Mind*). These philosophers are, of course, Bradley, on matters of metaphysics and logic, and (the so-called 'later') Wittgenstein, on matters of metaphysics and philosophy of mind. It seemed to me that, while books on philosophers are innumerable, books on their interactions – although these are of great importance – are comparatively rare, and that the display of these two philosophers' interactions with Russell sheds new light on all three. But this 'first part' has grown in the writing sufficiently for the intended whole to begin to look unwieldy, while the second remains incomplete. Had I more confidence that I could finish that second part, I should call this 'Volume I'.

Volume I or not, I came to write it through a series of events so utterly contingent that it is ironic that one of its two subjects should be a philosopher notorious for his opposition to contingency. The first draft was written in a period of unpaid leave resulting from a co-operative effort to mitigate the effects of cuts in per capita government education funding; poorer but happier (having helped save a colleague's job), for once I was able to do as I pleased, without even having to write a self-justificatory report. But initially, and many years earlier, there was the bizarre way in which I had turned from chemistry to philosophy: a teenage interest in witchcraft had led me surprisingly quickly, via the vagaries of the Dewey decimal system, from left to right along the shelves of the public library through the trials of the Lancaster witches until I happened upon Russell's *History of Western Philosophy*, never to retrace my steps. Subsequently there was the juxtaposition, in my final year as an undergraduate, of two courses which I am sure had been independently devised. In one of them ('Metaphysics'), I studied, amongst other things, books by Leibniz and Bradley; in another ('Special Author'), I studied Russell and Moore who, as well as seeming mysteriously to count as one author, had between them a good deal to say in criticism of these two philosophers. Even the profound incomprehension with which I dutifully scanned every word of *Appearance and Reality* did not entirely obscure the fact that there was room for doubt about the justice of some of what these critics had said of it. But this was of no particular concern to me until, many years later, having been in the vulnerable position of absence on sabbatical leave, I returned to find that I had been assigned to teach a final-year course entitled 'Twentieth Century British Philosophy' which no one else wanted to do and had to be prepared from scratch. At this stage I had no special interest or expertise in the history of philosophy, but I chose to go back close to the turn of the century and focus on the development of Logical Atomism, for what in these more straitened times would be the quixotic reason that I had never formally studied the *Tractatus Logico-Philosophicus*. While I still feel uneasy about the students who were the unwitting victims of my attempt at overdue self-education, recollections of my own student experience prompted me at least to make a very serious effort to avoid one of the major shortcomings in the kind of teaching that had been offered to me in my own student days: being told to read various historical texts for which at that time, apart from those by much worked-over philosophers like Plato and Descartes, little accessible contextual guidance was available, and still less provided or even identified. For instance, I decided to fill in some historical background, including primary sources, so that the students could begin to understand what was being asserted by looking directly at what was being denied. Given the frequency of Russell's explicit criticisms of him, Bradley was the obvious choice. One result was that the Whiggish confidence (matching my undergraduate relief on learning from my reading that whatever the

turgid and incomprehensible Bradley had meant, it had been definitive-
ly refuted) with which I had initially approached the displacement of
idealism by the early forerunners of what we have come to think of as
analytic philosophy soon began to come under pressure. And as the participants in these seminars increasingly found that what was being said
about this background seemed not to match what we could see, however indistinctly, for ourselves, it did not take long for the 'background'
to expand into the foreground, so that for us the beginning of the twentieth century slipped back to 1883 and I had to force myself not to let
it slip further so that we could study Mill's logic directly rather than rely
on what Bradley and Frege had said about it. I must have taught this
course about a dozen times in various forms and guises before diverse
restructurings eventually led to its emasculation. If there is anything
worthwhile in this book, it is probably because my students were constantly asking me questions to which I had to work out answers.
Although I was lucky enough to have in the main students of great ability, nearly everyone worked very hard, and sometimes the most naive
of these questions were just as difficult to answer as the most sophisticated. I am genuinely grateful to all those who took part in what was,
for me, perhaps the most rewardingly co-operative classwork I have ever
experienced, and, for them, as many told me, the most challenging of
all the courses they undertook in their entire undergraduate career.
(One participant, I learned later, used to take a prophylactic aspirin
before each seminar.)

It is as a result of some of these events that I have done something
unusual for writers of philosophical monographs: I have devoted, mostly in Chapter 1, a good deal of space to introductory texts and works of
reference. I have done this because these have become the chief means
by which formative philosophical impressions are transmitted to the
next generation. Their contents thus deserve more attention from professional philosophers than, I suspect, they usually receive. For related
reasons, while this book is by no means an introduction or a textbook,
I have tried to write in such a way that it is accessible to advanced
undergraduates and usable in a seminar programme. It would not have
been possible to explain from scratch everything necessary to grasp the
issues with which it deals, but it has been my aim that even a comparatively non-specialist reader who can consult the various good reference
works in philosophy which are now widely available should be able to
follow the principal threads even if some of the allusions remain
unclear. With such ease of use in mind, I have often given multiple citations so that, for instance, both a scholar who is working with the splen-

did edition of Russell's Collected Papers and a reader who is relying on one of the budget-priced volumes of his essays can readily locate the passage to which I refer. I have not done this with Bradley, for there are far fewer variant editions, and in any case much of the material I have cited has been reprinted in Allard and Stock's useful compilation, *F.H. Bradley: Writings on Logic and Metaphysics*, where the original pagination is provided so that, for instance, a passage from *Essays on Truth and Reality*, if present at all, can be quickly found. Further, although this book is intended to be read from front to back – it has, after all, an accumulating story to tell – I have tried to make it possible to refer a student to a single chapter which accordingly must, as far as possible, be intelligible as it stands. Inevitably, this has made for a certain amount of repetition and cross-referencing, for example as some crucial doctrine is re-illustrated. (In general, the overall sketches of Chapter 2 are replaced by subsequent more detailed treatments.) While I have done my best to keep these annoyances to a minimum, I know that they are there and I must ask the indulgence of those who do read the entire work.

I said that I have tried to make this book accessible even to 'a comparatively non-specialist reader'. This awkward phrase may be interpreted in terms of beginners in philosophy. But I mean to include both those who have a background in philosophy but perhaps neither the time nor the inclination to keep up with the professional literature, and, especially, educated readers in other fields, particularly intellectual history. One very common criticism of modern professional philosophy – the unseemly and ill-informed complaints that spilled into the public press in more than one country recently, after the death of Quine, illustrate the point – is that it has lost touch with the wider public. Aware of this, I have presented these apparently narrow technical issues in as lively, clear and informal prose as the subject – and my ability to expound it – permits, and in a way that will help to illustrate just how they can be connected with matters of wider concern. In particular, and although the matters I discuss concern the rise of formal logic, I have avoided writing in a manner whose very intelligibility requires a training in formal techniques. Such a non-specialist reader will nevertheless need patience and persistence as positions, theories and concepts at first merely alluded to, especially in Chapter 1, are gradually unfolded.

The non-specialist readership which I hope to reach may be put off by the plethora of endnotes. Here I can plead only that the subject matter of such a book as this demands constant citing of evidence; I have tried not to make any significant claim about what someone has said, without providing a method of verification. It also demands, for the sake of accuracy, qualifications which would obscure the main points if at least many of them were not relegated to notes. But I hope that my endnotes will not be ignored. They are not all dull reading.

*   *   *

I have chosen to use a modified version of the author/date system for referencing. The result in the main text is sometimes regrettably clumsy (though I have taken steps to obviate this), but the decision is deliberate. It makes explicit the date when the author was expressing the views displayed. This can be important. It has served as a regular reminder to me to ensure that my account is historically possible: for instance, it has helped me to resist the temptation to attribute fictitious arguments to philosophers by yoking together widely separated statements (a practice that is not as uncommon as it should be). It is also a regular reminder to the reader. If a philosopher is restlessly changing his mind, trying out new ways of solving problems, as Russell did, it is essential to know what was happening when. If a philosopher's views are relatively stable, as Bradley's were, it is essential to be able to see both where there is constancy across time, and the occasions of instability, where something appears (such as in his additions to later editions) – and maybe disappears again.

My non-standard system of citation has arisen from this concern for historical accuracy, and is as follows: in the main text and final bibliography, the citation date shown following the author's name is the date of original publication (or, occasionally, of composition). A separate date is shown in the bibliography for the edition cited only where this differs from the original. The modification avoids the anachronistic absurdities displayed in thoughtless use of the system, such as 'Kant 1991'. Page references in both main text and endnotes are, unless otherwise stated, to the latest edition cited. In addition, to alleviate the strain on the reader imposed by the author/date system, I have used some standard and immediately intelligible abbreviations to refer to well-known or frequently mentioned works by Bradley and Russell. For ease of access, these are set out on a preliminary page, and again in the final bibliography.

*   *   *

At this point I should list my acknowledgments. To some extent, these are conventional. I have freely drawn upon some of my previously published essays, which in order of original publication are:

1 'Scepticism, Ideal Experiment and Priorities in Bradley's Metaphysics', in A. Manser and G. Stock (eds), *The Philosophy of F. H. Bradley*. Oxford: Clarendon Press, 1984: 243–67.
2 'The Truth about F.H. Bradley', *Mind*, 98: 1989: 331–48.
3 'The Unity of the Proposition and Russell's Theories of Judgement', in R. Monk and A. Palmer (eds), *Bertrand Russell and the Origins of Analytical Philosophy*. Bristol: Thoemmes, 1996: 103–35.
4 'The Wrong Side of History: Relations, the Decline of British Idealism, and the Origins of Analytic Philosophy', in G. Stock (ed.), *Appearance versus Reality*. Oxford: Clarendon Press, 1998: 111–51.
5 'A Prolegomenon to an Identity Theory of Truth', *Philosophy*, 74: 1999: 199–220.
6 'There is Nothing Like a Fact', *The Philosophers' Magazine*, 12: Autumn 2000: 17–19.
7 'Grammar, Ontology, and Truth in Russell and Bradley', in R. Gaskin (ed.), *Grammar in Early Twentieth-Century Philosophy*. London: Routledge, 2001: 116–41.
8 'Francis Herbert Bradley', *The Stanford Encyclopedia of Philosophy* (Fall 2002 Edition), Edward N. Zalta (ed.), URL = <http://plato.stanford.edu/archives/fall2002/entries/bradley/>

The reader is warned that not only did I find it necessary to considerably revise many of the ideas expressed in those essays, but also there is no neat mapping between them and the following chapters. In the cases where it is not clear that I am the copyright holder: I am appropriately grateful to Oxford University Press for this freedom with respect to item 1, to Oxford University Press and the Mind Association for item 2, to the Royal Institute of Philosophy for item 5, and to the Editor of *The Philosophers' Magazine* for item 6. I should also acknowledge partial funding (direct or indirect) of the work involved by the Australian Research Council (items 1, 2, 4 and 5), the Rockefeller Foundation (item 1), and the British Academy (item 4).

Acknowledgments of assistance apart from what is stated in the various citations and endnotes are most emphatically not conventional with respect to a number of individuals, who even if they do not recall the fact, or did not recognize it at the time, and may even be very surprised to learn of it, have all helped in one way or another. To a few, the debt is very great: it could be said that without them there would have been no book at all. Here is what I hope is a complete list, in alphabetical order of surname: Jim Allard, David Armstrong, Tom Baldwin, Ken Blackwell, Max Cresswell, Nic Damnjanovic, Richard Gaskin, the late

S. A. Grave, Nick Griffin, Bernard Harrison, Jane Heal, Lloyd Humberstone, Peter Hylton, Jamie Kassler, Carol Keene, Jonathan Lowe, Mary Mannison, the late Tony Manser, Hugh Mellor, Michael Morris, Charles Pigden, Michael Potter, Graham Priest, Ian Proops, Anonymous Readers, Mark Sainsbury, Carl Spadoni, Guy Stock and the late David Stove. Finally: my wife, Bianca, has had to put up with, amongst many other things, periods of several weeks when I would spend days in succession locked away, failing to write more than a few lines which I would then destroy before emerging despondent, frustrated and prepared to undertake only activities which allowed me to brood on the matters perplexing me. These activities did not usually include conversation. I don't know how she did it, nor why this early experience did not discourage her from persuading me to start, and complete, this book.

The University of Western Australia   STEWART CANDLISH

Notes

1 For example, by Nicholas Griffin or Peter Hylton, in two ground-breaking books: *Russell's Idealist Apprenticeship* (Griffin 1991) and *Russell, Idealism, and the Emergence of Analytic Philosophy* (Hylton 1990) – books for whose existence anyone working in this area should be very grateful. 'Ground-breaking', but not definitive, however. Roughly speaking, Griffin's position on the Russell/ Bradley dispute exemplifies that which I aim to displace. And although Hylton's view of Bradley himself is broadly similar to mine, there are material differences on the dispute and its significance; furthermore, Gideon Makin, in an impressive though more narrowly focused study (Makin 2000), argues that there are major shortcomings in Hylton's treatment of issues surrounding the interpretation of 'On Denoting' (Russell 1905b).
   But, quite apart from whether they get the story right, neither Griffin nor Hylton tells the whole of it. Griffin concentrates on the detail of Russell's views in his idealist period. Hylton gives Bradley more attention. But, as he says himself, very precisely, 'This book is a historical study of the influence of British Idealism on Bertrand Russell, of the rejection of Idealism by Moore and Russell, and of the subsequent development of Russell's thought to about 1913' (1990, p. 1). And his focus too is, naturally, on Russell, the major figure. It should be emphasized that even the amount of discussion Hylton gives Bradley (about 8 per cent of the pages) is unusually large for a book on Russell. And, *mutatis mutandis*, the situation is similar with books on Bradley.
2 A more recent example might be endorsing certain sorts of French philosophy because it is *chic*, or perhaps politically useful. A very striking case of overt political influence on American metaphysics is cited by Passmore (1957 p. 74n).

List of Abbreviations

Bradley's writings

AR   *Appearance and Reality*, the so-called 'ninth impression'. Oxford: Clarendon Press, 1930.*

CE   *Collected Essays*. Oxford: Clarendon Press, 1935.

ETR   *Essays on Truth and Reality*. Oxford: Clarendon Press, 1914.

PL   *The Principles of Logic* (second edition, revised, with commentary and terminal essays). London: Oxford University Press, 1922.

WLM   *Writings on Logic and Metaphysics*, ed. James W. Allard and Guy Stock. Oxford: Clarendon Press, 1994.

* For the mildly comic history of the origins and status of this 'ninth impression', see the note at the end of the Bibliography.

Russell's writings

CP1   *The Collected Papers of Bertrand Russell*, Vol. 1: *Cambridge Essays 1888–99*. London: George Allen and Unwin, 1983.

CP4   *The Collected Papers of Bertrand Russell*, Vol. 4: *Foundations of Logic 1903–05*. London: Routledge, 1994.

CP6   *The Collected Papers of Bertrand Russell*, Vol. 6: *Logical and Philosophical Papers 1909–13*. London: Routledge, 1992.

CP8   *The Collected Papers of Bertrand Russell*, Vol. 8: *The Philosophy of Logical Atomism and Other Essays 1914–19*. London: George Allen & Unwin, 1986.

CP9   *The Collected Papers of Bertrand Russell*, Vol. 9: *Essays on Language, Mind and Matter 1919–26*. London: Routledge, 1994 (reprint of Unwin Hyman edition of 1988).

EA   *Essays in Analysis*, ed. Douglas Lackey. London: Allen & Unwin, 1973.

LK   *Logic and Knowledge*, ed. Robert C. Marsh. London: George Allen & Unwin, 1956.

ML   *Mysticism and Logic*. London: George Allen & Unwin, 1963 (originally published 1917).

PE   *Philosophical Essays*. London: George Allen & Unwin, 1966 (originally published with somewhat different contents and different pagination 1910).

1
The Stereotypical Picture of the Russell/Bradley Dispute

'I don't care who writes a nation's laws – or crafts its advanced treaties – if I can write its economics textbooks.'
—attributed to Paul Samuelson, Nobel prizewinning economist, by Sylvia Nasar, *New York Times*, 14 March 1995, p. D1

The protagonists

This book is a study of two philosophers in dispute. The protagonists are significant. In the blue corner, so to speak, we have F.H. Bradley (1846–1924), politically conservative, in his time the most famous and admired of the British Idealists, whose recognition included the honorary degree LL.D. of the University of Glasgow (1883), an invitation (politely declined) to become a member of the British Academy at its foundation in 1902, election to membership of the Royal Danish Academy (1921), of the *Accademia dei Lincei* and the *Reale Istituto Lombardo* of Milan (1922) and to an Honorary Fellowship of the British Academy (1923), and appointment by King George V to the Order of Merit – the first philosopher to be singled out for what was then a recently established but always very rare honour (1924).[1]

In the red corner, we have Bertrand Russell (1872–1970), politically radical, the principal founder of what came to be known as analytical philosophy, elected Fellow of the Royal Society in 1908 (a singular honour for a philosopher), likewise appointed to the Order of Merit and to an Honorary Fellowship of the British Academy in 1949, awarded the Nobel Prize for Literature in 1950.

1

This public recognition, in both cases, indicates that, in ways which we shall identify, both philosophers are of their different but overlapping times. Those times are, roughly speaking, the Victorian and what is perhaps best called the post-Victorian respectively. At the death of Queen Victoria, on 22 January 1901, Bradley's best-known and most influential books had already been in print for some years, whereas Russell's first great philosophical book, *The Principles of Mathematics*, was still in draft and his most famous philosophical essays were, though not many years away, as yet unwritten.

Interesting points of contrast and comparison do not stop there, for the two philosophers display, and sometimes represent, other contrasts, clashes and rivalries. Bradley, educated at Oxford in the classics, was self-confessedly incompetent in science and mathematics. His entire professional life was spent, reclusively, in Oxford,[2] a university with a reputation for training civil servants. His inspiration in philosophy was largely German, which perhaps encouraged him in developing a literary style that is florid, abstract and obscure, and he was contemptuous of much of the English-language tradition. The metaphysical stance for which he is best-known is his combination of monism – reality is one, there are no real separate things – and absolute idealism – reality is idea, or consists of experience, though not the experience of any one individual, for division of experiencer from experience is forbidden by monism. Russell, educated in mathematics at Cambridge, a university now with a reputation for breeding spies, became not merely a public figure but a political activist jailed more than once for anti-war activities. Writing with a literary style of unsurpassed crispness, he was recognizably in the philosophical tradition which Bradley rejected, and became a trenchant critic of the Idealists' heroes, Kant and Hegel. His metaphysical stance, at the time we are considering, was pluralist, that is non-monist, and resolutely anti-idealist.

At the time at which I am typing this sentence, approximately a century after the events and writings which I shall consider, Bradley is largely unknown to the wider reading public (who are more likely to have heard of his brother, the Shakespearean critic A.C. Bradley) and, when not forgotten altogether, mostly ignored by professional academic philosophers, while his influence on the content and style of philosophy is hardly to be discerned. It is almost a truism that the situation is quite other with Russell. Among the questions I consider in this book is how this came about, and how far this difference in their reputations is justified.

Locating the dispute

The dispute with which we are concerned began in 1900 with a broadside in Russell's book *A Critical Exposition of the Philosophy of Leibniz*, and finished in 1924 with Bradley's death. But this judgment is already controversial.

Some may have general doubts. Can the beginning of any historical process ever really be so precisely dated? And even if it can, would we admit the same of its ending?

Others may have doubts about the dating of this process in particular. Given that Bradley's last contributions to the dispute did not appear in print until his *Collected Essays* was published in 1935, and were comprehensively ignored by the other side, perhaps we should say it finished then. Given that it was G.E. Moore who on Russell's own account turned him away from idealism in 1898 and then announced his own defection with the publication of his epoch-making essay 'The Nature of Judgment' in 1899, perhaps we should say that it began then, and, moreover, should not think of it through expressions such as 'Russell/Bradley'. At least, one might say, we should add the name of Moore to the identification of Bradley's opposition. But if we do, then, given that Bradley made no formal response to Moore's influential paper 'External and Internal Relations' (Moore 1919), maybe we should say that the dispute concluded in 1919. But then, perhaps too we should include, say, the Russell-influenced A.J. Ayer, for whom Bradley was clearly still significant – perhaps even dangerous – enough a figure in the 1930s to be a named target of critical remarks in *Language, Truth and Logic*; and still significant enough in the 1950s for him to commission Richard Wollheim to produce the well-known commentary in the 'Pelican Philosophy' series. So one might argue for a much longer period than I began with.

Reasonable doubt does not stop there. Just as Russell was accompanied by Moore in criticizing Bradley, Bradley was not alone in defending some variant of the monistic idealism that was their wider target. Perhaps then we should think of the dispute in wider terms, such as 'the decline of British Idealism'.[3] But this judgment will further affect the issue of dating. For idealism persisted in Scotland far longer than it did in England.[4] And, perhaps, it should materially affect the breadth of the treatment of the matter, since the highly idiosyncratic Bradley is untypical of the monistic idealists in general.

I shall sidestep these potential controversies. No doubt the Russell/Bradley dispute is part of an historical shift that incorporates a wider range of times and people than my earlier remark represents. But there is sense in thinking of the matters in terms of my dating. For the fact is that the crucial public events, and the closing private episode of Bradley's uncompleted essay on relations, are covered by that period. And I shall not let it distort my account by refusing to consider works which fall outside its limits – indeed, assessment of the historical impact of the dispute will require this. Likewise there is sense in thinking of the matter in terms of 'British Idealism'. For the fact is that Russell – however unfairly, either to Bradley or to monistic idealism – took Bradley to be representative of the movement as a whole, and others since have implicitly accepted that judgment. Likewise, Bradley thought of Russell as his principal opponent and paid careful attention to his views (whereas he thought Moore was philosophically negligible). There was something very personal about this struggle for philosophical supremacy.

In short, we can think of the Russell/Bradley dispute as the philosophical and historical core of the wider historical shift in English-language philosophy away from, *inter alia*, monism and idealism and towards pluralism and realism.[5] And although there might be reasonable disagreement over these matters of identity and chronology, there can be none over the judgment that the dispute was of the first importance for the way in which philosophy has developed in the English-speaking world since. Focusing upon this core, and disentangling its structure, will assist in the attainment of a more distanced and judicious perspective on this wider shift than we currently possess.

The stereotypical picture outlined

> 'This unfavourable picture, though not devoid of a faint resemblance, betrays, by its dark colouring and distorted features, the pencil of an enemy.'
> (Gibbon, *The Decline and Fall of the Roman Empire*, Chapter XV)

In this brief section I shall sketch a picture of the Russell/Bradley dispute. To a large extent – although some of its elements arise from other sources – this is the picture one would get if relying on Russell and Moore for a sense of what was what at issue and of the rival views. This picture – or at least the most significant of its components – became entrenched in English-language philosophy, and still persists except amongst a small number of historically-minded specialists aware of recent developments in the re-examination of British Idealism. It is a depiction of Bradley as holding various views from which Russell or Moore generally dissented: that is, we are presented with a set of (sometimes implicit) contrasts. One should not expect all the elements of the picture to be mutually consistent; nor are they likely all to be present in the conception of any one present-day individual person; further, they are not of equal significance or equally entrenched. Nevertheless, I challenge non-specialist readers to deny that, where they have any impression of these matters at all – and if they have no such impression of such significant and comparatively recent events, this too would be a matter relevant to the argument of this book – it is by and large constituted by a number of these elements. They include at least the following (I have made the contrasts explicit):

1 Bradley, unlike Russell, was not a logician.
2 Bradley, unlike Russell, was a metaphysician in some pejorative sense of the term.
3 Bradley, unlike Russell and Moore, was a Hegelian.
4 Bradley held a coherence theory of truth; Russell held a correspondence theory.
5 Bradley, unlike Russell, confined human knowledge to a subjective prison.
6 Bradley, unlike Russell, was preoccupied with the 'higher', disdaining mere science.
7 Bradley's metaphysical monism was erected upon the basis of elementary confusions; these included confusing predication and identity (unlike Russell), and again, entailment and material implication (unlike Moore).
8 Bradley, unlike Russell and Moore, rejected relations (for example, *greater than*).
9 Bradley's rejection of relations stems from his assumption that the only possible propositional form is subject–predicate.
10 Bradley's attempted *reductio* of relations illegitimately assumes them to be some kind of object, while Russell sees that they are not.
11 Bradley, unlike Russell and Moore, held what is often called the Doctrine of Internal Relations, that is, he rejected external relations and thought that all relations are internal.
12 Bradley's Doctrine of Internal Relations consisted in maintaining, what Russell denied, that relations are reducible to properties.
13 Bradley's Doctrine of Internal Relations consisted in maintaining, what Moore denied, that no relations hold contingently.

14 Bradley's Doctrine of Internal Relations was held as an axiom or dogma, that is, unlike the competing views of Russell and Moore, it was unargued.
15 Bradley's monism and idealism rest on his Doctrine of Internal Relations.
16 Bradley's monistic idealism led him to reject, unlike Russell and Moore, the common sense view of the world as containing numerous everyday objects, indeed as containing *objects* at all.
17 Bradley, unlike Moore, simply *failed to see* obvious facts.
18 On most if not all of the above counts, Bradley was in the wrong and his opponents in the right.

Although I have presented this list, as far as possible, as a set of discrete elements, it is obvious that its items are often not independent. Many of them, for instance, concern the arguments over relations and their connection with the choice between pluralism and monism. For this reason, it will not be possible to discuss these components in detail by taking each individually and in turn, discussing it in isolation. However, by the end of this book, the reader will find that the picture that the list presents has been, gradually, but substantially, redrawn; and this time from life. In the process, it will be shown that some other comfortable assumptions about the recent past will have to be abandoned too.

The sources and pervasiveness of the stereotype

This section is for those who are so far unconvinced; those who need no further persuasion may move directly to the next (p. 18). Here I give more detail concerning each of the above components; where I believe that it forms part of the modern stereotype, I cite evidence that it does. Much of this evidence consists in its presence in popular works, works of reference and textbooks. These are, of course, what most people rely on outside their areas of specialization. And in many cases they reveal what their authors take to be non-controversial.

Although, as I said, it is not possible to discuss systematically these components in isolation from each other, it yet remains possible, by and large, to treat them as individuals when merely identifying their sources and displaying their pervasiveness.

1 Logic   The removal of Bradley from the ranks of recognized logicians is a minor consequence of a much larger historical change, namely, the rise of formal logic. This removal is usually accomplished by simple omission. One might well expect such omission from the general run of logic texts, which after all are not historically oriented and whose writers would have no more reason for referring to Bradley than to, say, Peter of Spain. Far more significant is the example of William and Martha Kneale's great historical work *The Development of Logic*. This book, as its title suggests, is written under the dominance of the idea of progress. Kant is discussed only grudgingly; Bradley, Bosanquet and Hegel are not even mentioned. Anyone who knows merely the titles of some of their books should wonder why they are ignored. A large part of the answer is, of course, that it is the development of formal reasoning with which the Kneales are concerned. The fact that Bradley was a principled critic of the formal tradition is sufficient to exclude him from consideration. One does not need to agree with his criticisms to be able to appreciate the point.

Along with this change in the conception of how to make advances in logic goes a change in the conception of its subject matter. Compare, for instance, on the one hand, a sample of books from the idealist tradition, such as Bosanquet's *Logic* and *The Essentials of Logic*, Lotze's *Logic* and Bradley's *The Principles of Logic* with, on the other, twentieth-century books like Mark Sainsbury's *Logical Forms*, Susan Haack's *Philosophy of Logics*, Wilfred Hodges' *Logic*, Quine's *Mathematical Logic*, Richard Jeffrey's *Formal Logic: its Scope and Limits*, and Stephen Read's *Thinking about Logic*. Each member of the former group has an enormous number of pages devoted explicitly to inference. But only the last of the latter appears to give the subject any prominence, remarking on its opening page that 'the central topic of the philosophy of logic is inference'; and even that impression is immediately undone when the sentence continues, 'that is, logical consequence, or what follows correctly from what', and inference proper is thereafter ignored.[6]

2 Metaphysics Another part of the answer to the question why Bradley is no longer considered a logician is that from the nineteen-thirties onwards he has been thought of as primarily a metaphysician. It might be considered a misfortune to have been a prominent metaphysician just as the impact of logical positivism began to be felt in English-language philosophy. Certainly, for generations of students, Bradley has been known as the person who said, with self-evident absurdity, that 'the Absolute enters into, but is itself incapable of, evolution and progress', a remark supposedly 'taken at random from *Appearance and Reality*' (though certainly taken out of context) and which 'is not even in principle verifiable', hence being 'an utterance which has no literal significance even for [Bradley] himself' (Ayer 1936, p. 36). There could hardly be a better justification for ignoring him. Russell, on the other hand, is presented throughout this most-read of books as a logician, a philosopher of language and a philosopher of mathematics; the idea that such a paragon might also have been, simultaneously, a metaphysician, is suppressed. While the word 'metaphysics' is not, at the time at which I write, the expression of condemnation which the logical positivists tried to make it, in Bradley's case the mud has stuck. We shall see whether or not Ayer's implied contrast between Bradley and Russell, which has subtly and unconsciously shaped the thinking of his successors, can be sustained.

3 Hegel   It is a commonplace in philosophy to describe Bradley as a Hegelian;[7] sometimes it is added that Russell and Moore were persistently anti-Hegelians. To say the latter is, of course, to neglect the fact that these most famous critics of Hegel and idealism had themselves been adherents of idealism until a comparatively sudden conversion away from it to the views for which they have since been famous. That fact, always fairly well-known, eventually itself became a matter of interest, and Russell's idealist period has been thoroughly documented (Griffin 1991) while Moore's has been sketched (Baldwin 1990, ch. 1 §1). Bradley, though, rejected this characterization of himself as Hegelian:

> For Hegel himself, assuredly I think him a great philosopher; but I never could have called myself an Hegelian, partly because I can not say that I have mastered his system, and partly because I could not accept what seems his main principle, or at least part of that principle.
>
> (1883, Preface p. x)

Despite this, both Russell, who frequently mentions Bradley, and Moore, who mentions him comparatively infrequently, treat him as a follower of Hegel. Although a good example occurs in *Our Knowledge of the External World* (Russell 1914b, pp. 47–9), the evidence for this claim about Russell is best found not in isolated passages but in the general tenor of the relevant comments. Several other examples will appear in other contexts below.

Given that Russell's influence on subsequent philosophers is unarguable, it suffices here to identify him as a principal source of the idea that Bradley is a Hegelian. In this book I am content merely to remark this fact, and explore some of its consequences: I shall not try to deal in any detail with the question of just how far Russell is accurate in this respect.[8]

4 Truth   There is perhaps no more commonly repeated contrast between Bradley and Russell than the presentation of their differences over the notion of truth. Bradley is almost unanimously displayed as a coherence theorist, frequently alongside the suggestion that Russell was a correspondence theorist. As far as I can tell, the major source is once again Russell himself.

Russell's adherence to the correspondence theory was announced in his famous essay 'On the Nature of Truth and Falsehood' (Russell 1910: *CP6* p. 123; *PE* p. 158). It is proclaimed, too, in one of his best-known books, *The Problems of Philosophy*, where in Chapter XII he espouses correspondence as the definition of truth (Russell 1912, p. 128). Russell seems also to be the originator of the idea that Bradley held a coherence theory of truth. With the contempt for niceties that accompanied the contempt he seems always to have displayed (perhaps merely for controversial purposes) for the views of 'Hegelians' after he defected from their ranks, he is often content to ignore individual variations of view and to generalize to those he takes to be members of a group on the basis of the arguments of one individual.[9] This seems to have been what happened in an early linking of Bradley with the coherence theory (Russell 1907, especially pp. 136 and 140). In his attack on what he called the Monistic Theory of Truth, as expressed in Joachim's 1906 book *The Nature of Truth*, Russell makes clear that he identifies this monistic theory with the coherence theory (as Joachim himself seemed prepared to do), and gives his standard objections to that theory. A few pages later he claims that the monistic theory of truth is equivalent to the axiom of internal relations (which he frequently attributes to Bradley over a number of years), and goes on to refer constantly to Bradley in illustrative footnotes. Russell chose to reproduce in full Part II of this paper (the part which contains nearly all the references to Bradley) in his widely read *My Philosophical Development*; further, in an early footnote in Part I, he explicitly asserts that he chooses Joachim's book for discussion because it is typical: 'the best recent statement of certain views which I wish to discuss'. In fact it is impossible to read this piece without getting the impression that Russell takes Joachim to be speaking for Bradley (something Joachim himself denied he was doing), and that Bradley is his real target.

However, whether or not it was Russell who was originally responsible for the association of Bradley with the coherence theory is a causal/historical question. The philosophically significant point is that it became standard in the literature provided for students of philosophy. Pick up almost any text book in English which deals with theories of truth, and you will find a section on the coherence theory, with Bradley's name attached to it; pick up almost any philosophical work of reference, and you will find Bradley paired with the coherence theory.[10] More specialized articles and books repeat the pattern.[11] That recent work on Bradley has begun to question this association, while recent work on truth has not, shows that this element of the stereotype is still firmly rooted in the common philosophical consciousness; for philosophers with an interest in Bradley are comparatively few, while those with an interest in truth, or at least the concept of it, are many.

5 Idealism's subjective prison   This is an element of the picture which is less entrenched in the stereotype than many in this list. Nevertheless, readers of Russell's popular *My Philosophical Development* will hardly have missed his complaint that the influence of idealism led him, early in his career, to 'shut [himself] up in a subjective prison' (Russell 1959, p. 62). He makes a rather similar charge concerning the view that judgments – as they were then termed – consist of ideas (Russell 1911: *CP6* p. 155; *ML* p. 160). The break with idealism is thus an escape into a public and independent reality. We shall see in a subsequent chapter the effect this attempt to escape the 'prison' had on his own views concerning judgment, and whether or not the attempt was successful.

6 The disdain of science   Again, perhaps, this is not a well-entrenched component of the stereotype. Still, as we have seen, the contrast between Bradley and Russell over the status of mathematics and science is emblematic of a range of associated contrasts. 'Hegelians', Russell thought, 'condemn the sort of things dealt with by mathematics and physics' (Russell 1959, p. 62), while his own views are intended to vindicate them. Elsewhere he gibes that the primary function of philosophy at Oxford was to 'give the place a moral tone'. While it would be absurd to deny that the great English-language philosophers of the twentieth century were primarily associated with Cambridge, and that it has indeed been characteristic of post-Russellian philosophy to take science seriously, it remains to be seen whether this simple contrast will bear examination.

Although, as I have just said, these two views, that idealism confines us to a subjective prison and disdains science, are less entrenched in the modern stereotype, there is nevertheless reason for mentioning them here. This will become clear in the last chapter of this book, when we consider the reasons for idealism's displacement.

7 Elementary confusions It is common to hold that Bradley's monism rests on his Doctrine of Internal Relations. Russell, for instance, maintained that 'the axiom of internal relations is equivalent to the assumption of ontological monism' (Russell 1907, *PE* p. 142), and reproduced the passage containing this assertion in *My Philosophical Development* (Russell 1959, p. 57).

Of this doctrine of internality, Moore, in his famous and influential essay 'External and Internal Relations', alleged that it in turn rested upon a confusion of entailment and material implication: 'the dogma of internal relations has been held only because', he says, '[it] has been falsely thought' that '$p \supset (q$ entails $r)$' follows from 'p entails $(q \supset r)$' (Moore 1919, p. 97).

Russell, on the other hand, thought the Hegelian (and Bradleian) conception of identity-in-difference rested on the 'stupid and trivial confusion' of the 'is' of predication – as in 'Socrates is mortal' – with the 'is' of identity – as in 'Socrates is the philosopher who drank the hemlock'. 'This', Russell continues, 'is an example of how, for want of care at the start, vast and imposing systems of philosophy are built upon stupid and trivial confusions, which, but for the almost incredible fact that they are unintentional, one would be tempted to characterize as puns' (Russell 1914, pp. 48–9n; cf. also Russell 1918: *CP8* p. 215n; *LK* p. 245n). He had, admittedly, claimed earlier that 'the whole conception of "identity-in-difference" is incompatible with the doctrine of internal relations', but only as part of a two-pronged argument in which he says that 'without this conception, monism can give no account of the world' (Russell 1907: *PE* p. 146; 1959, p. 60). The idea that Bradley is victim to this confusion took root in standard works of reference and introductory texts even of a sympathetically expository kind.[12]

8 The rejection of relations That Bradley 'rejected' relations while Russell did not is a deeply entrenched view of the dispute between them. Of course the view, so expressed, is little more than a slogan and it remains to be seen what it amounts to. Perhaps a natural interpretation is the one which Russell gave it: 'There are no relations and ...

there are not many things, but only one thing' (Russell 1907: *PE* p. 141; 1959 pp. 56–7). But in any case the slogan suggests a way of conceiving of the issue which makes Bradley's side of it implausible from the outset. And versions of the slogan, like 'hostility to relations' and 'attack on relations', pervade the literature: introductory works, works of reference, and scholarly works alike. I shall give just a few examples, to illustrate each of these categories. W.J. Mander's *An Introduction to Bradley's Metaphysics*, for example, mentions Bradley's 'arguments against relations' (Mander 1994, p. 84), showing that even authors sympathetic to Bradley are not immune to this most Russellian way of presenting the matter. The entry on Bradley in Lacey 1976 depicts him as thinking that relations are 'illusory'. Nicholas Griffin writes unhesitatingly of Bradley's 'rejection of relations' (Griffin 1991, p. 183), and Fred Wilson, contrasting Moore with Bradley, says of the former that he 'accepts relations' (Wilson 1996, p. 31). Traces of this conception survive even in E.J. Lowe's masterly historical sketch of the development of twentieth century metaphysical thinking (Lowe 2006). Such is the conception's influence that I inadvertently allowed it to survive, principally in the section headings, in Chapter 2 of this book, before eventually making a conscious decision to allow those headings to stand, prior to the conception's dismantling. Just as we shall see what Bradley's 'rejection of relations' amounted to, and whether this is indeed a fair description of his views, so shall we see too whether Russell's stance – or stances – on the matter should be characterized in terms of this contrast.

9 Subject–predicate   The claim that the rejection of relations stems from the mistaken assumption that the only possible propositional form is subject–predicate is a constant refrain in Russell's writings. It appeared as early as 1900 in *A Critical Exposition of the Philosophy of Leibniz*, where Bradley's adherence to the notion of the Absolute is in Russell's view sufficient to implicate him in the assumption (Russell 1900, p. 15). It was repeated in 1903 in *The Principles of Mathematics* §212, with the assumption this time explicitly attributed to Bradley. In Russell 1907 (*PE* p. 142) the assumption is presented as the basis of the Doctrine of Internal Relations; again, the remarks were reprinted in *My Philosophical Development* (Russell 1959, p. 57). In the essay 'Logical Atomism', produced for a wide readership, the assumption is said to vitiate 'the whole foundation for the metaphysics' of Leibniz, Spinoza, Hegel and Bradley (Russell 1924, p. 162). Such bold claims as this last were not generally accepted; but it is undeniable that they led to a general conviction that there is some close logical connection between the subject–predicate view, the rejection of relations and the Doctrine of Internal Relations.

10 Treating relations as objects   Bradley's most notorious argument concerning relations occurs in Chapter III of *Appearance and Reality*. It is a kind of Third Man argument, apparently to the effect that if things are really related (for instance, if it is true that an object *A* is adjacent to an object *B*) then the relation itself (here, *being adjacent*) will have to be itself related to *A* and *B*, which will require two further relations of which the same can be said, and so on *ad infinitum*. Even to a novice reader this has an air of hocus pocus about it, one naturally explained by the fact that Bradley is treating the relation as though it were another object on a par with those it relates. If this treatment is what 'rejection of relations' relies on, then Bradley was obviously wrong to reject relations. Serious and careful philosophers have drawn and circulated this conclusion. Broad (1933, p. 85), for instance, after making precisely this point, said, 'Charity bids us avert our eyes from the pitiable spectacle of a great philosopher using an argument which would disgrace a child or a savage.'

Russell warned against this reification of relations: 'The conception of the relation as a third term between the other two sins against the doctrine of types, and must be avoided with the utmost care' (Russell 1924, p. 171). Later, in another work produced for a wide readership, he accused Bradley of just this sin: 'Bradley conceives a relation as something just as substantial as its terms' (Russell 1927, p. 263), and the accusation was thought justified by the philosopher who did most to reintroduce Bradley's thought to philosophers in the second half of the twentieth century, Richard Wollheim (Wollheim 1959, p. 115; 1969, p. 113). The effect of this accusation, or of whatever it is that Bradley did to provoke it, is discernible even in the most sympathetic presentations of Bradley's thought: other examples are Acton (1967, p. 361) and, very strikingly, Blanshard (1984, pp. 215*f*).

11 The doctrine of internal relations   Attribution to Bradley of both the denial that any relations are external and the apparently immediate inference that all are internal is near-universal. Like most of the other components of this list, it was established early. It appears explicitly in a footnote to Russell 1907 (*PE* p. 138) and is a governing assumption in the later part of that article which Russell selected for reproduction in *My Philosophical Development*. It turns up repeatedly thereafter in similarly influential places, such as Russell 1924 (p. 172).

Moore, in his classic article 'External and Internal Relations', claimed to find the doctrine in *Appearance and Reality* (Moore 1919, p. 79). Thereafter it appears as something so obvious that it can just be mentioned in passing (for example, Warnock 1958 p. 10). Wollheim accepted the attribution without hesitation in his *F.H. Bradley* (1959, p. 104; 1969, p. 102), and Grayling (1996, p. 26) too claims to find the doctrine in *Appearance and Reality*. Well-read and sympathetic scholars repeat the story (for example, Findlay 1984, p. 275).

The reference books were inevitably affected. Richard Rorty, when writing about relations for the great and much reprinted *Encyclopedia of Philosophy* (Edwards ed. 1967), just *assumed* Bradley to be an exponent of the doctrine (Rorty 1967, p. 126), while being properly uneasy about what exactly that doctrine is (a matter to which we shall return). And Simon Blackburn, for another instance, in his *Oxford Dictionary of Philosophy*, describes the doctrine as 'a cardinal thesis of absolute idealism'; cross-referencing in this work gives us Bradley as 'the most influential exponent of absolute idealism in Britain' (Blackburn 1994, pp. 325, 2). In the two current most substantial and authoritative reference works, authors merely attribute the doctrine to a general 'idealism', though in the latter case Bradley is mentioned as an exponent: Andrew Irvine, writing in the *Stanford Encyclopedia of Philosophy*, says 'Russell saw that the idealist doctrine of internal relations led to a series of contradictions regarding asymmetrical (and other) relations necessary for mathematics' (Irvine 2004, 'Russell's Work in Analytic Philosophy'); Nicholas Griffin (1998, §2), in the *Routledge Encyclopedia of Philosophy*, makes the same assumption that Russell's view is not merely to be described but implicitly endorsed. (It should be stressed that these are all *very good* articles.)

So far I have deliberately left untouched the question of just what is at issue in the arguments over whether or not all relations are internal. While there has been much tangled debate on this question, two broad interpretations of the doctrine were established during the period of the Russell/Bradley dispute and have survived. They constitute the next two components of the stereotype.

12 Reducibility to properties   The idea that Bradley's doctrine of internal relations consists in the supposition that relations are reducible to properties is principally Russellian in origin. In *The Principles of Mathematics* Russell claims to find in Bradley the view that every relational proposition *aRb* is to be resolved into a proposition in which the relation figures as a property of the whole *ab* considered as a single individual (Russell 1903, §§212, 215). By the time we get to his attack on Joachim's views on truth, this claim has modulated into an interpretation of the 'axiom of internal relations' (Russell 1907: *PE* p. 142; 1959, p. 57). As we have seen with other components, Russell's interpretation seeps into the standard literature. Thus Wollheim (1959, p. 119; 1969, p. 117), for instance, allows it in his discussion of asymmetrical relations. But one is most likely to come across it as a background assumption in discussions of related matters such as the identity of indiscernibles.

13 The denial of contingency   The view that Bradley's doctrine of the internality of all relations is – or at least entails – that no relation holds contingently seems to have originated with Moore (1919, p. 103), whose painstaking development of the consequences is rightly regarded as a classic of analytic philosophy. This too has found a ready home in the reference books. For example, Rorty judged it worthy of substantial discussion (Rorty 1967, pp. 126–7); Lacey (1976, p. 185) constructed his entire dictionary entry around it; Blackburn accepted the Moorean characterization without demur, describing the doctrine as 'a kind of essentialism' (Blackburn 1994, p. 325).

14 Axioms and dogmas   We have already seen (in item 7 of this list) that Russell and Moore in influential writings respectively refer to the doctrine of internal relations as being held by Bradley as an 'axiom' or 'dogma', presumably in implied contrast with the reasoned denials of his critics. Such terminology conveys the impression that, unlike its denial, the doctrine was asserted without argument, or at least that it continued to be maintained in the teeth either of direct refutation or of exposure of bad argument, perhaps because of confusion. While the terminology is not a central element of the stereotype – as far as I can see it has not, for example, invaded the reference books – it has nevertheless made an impression. Ayer, for example, clearly follows Moore when he says, 'There is no question, then, but that the dogma of internal relations is false. What is of interest is how it has come to be held' (Ayer 1971, p. 156). Consider too, for instance, this remark, which is itself presented without support: 'As Moore and Russell never refrained from pointing out, the doctrine of relations defended by the idealists was taken for granted' (Wilson 1996, p. 30). And the terminology may have a subliminal background effect. Readers not exceptionally alert may thus have been primed to assess the outcome of the dispute in favour of the Moore/Russell side, or to make assumptions concerning where the burden of proof lies. We shall see, later on, some examples of attempts to place the burden of proof in these matters; and how far they are justified.

15 Monism, idealism and the doctrine of internal relations   Both Bradley's monism and his idealism were attributed to his doctrine of internal relations; in the former case the doctrine figures sometimes as a basis, sometimes as an equivalence. These attributions again appeared early. Russell claimed that 'the axiom of internal relations is incompatible with all complexity. For this axiom leads, as we saw, to a rigid monism' (Russell 1907: *PE* p. 145; 1959, p. 60). Such claims have resonated down the years. Wilson, for instance, in a sympathetic treatment of Moore's essay 'The Refutation of Idealism' (Moore 1903), says that Moore 'proposes to show that idealism is false by showing the falsity of the central implication of the idealist account of relations' (Wilson 1996, p. 31).

16 Monism, idealism and common sense   The relationship between metaphysics and common sense has never been easy. But the idea that Bradley's metaphysics is at a peculiar disadvantage was again established by Russell and Moore.

The former, for instance, suggests that monism is in conflict with the common sense assumption that the world contains many things, saying (on the opening page of what is perhaps, by philosophy students at least, one of his most-read works):

> The logic which I shall advocate is atomistic, as opposed to the monistic logic of the people who more or less follow Hegel. When I say that my logic is atomistic, I mean that I share the common-sense belief that there are many separate things; I do not regard the apparent multiplicity of the world as consisting merely in phases and unreal divisions of a single indivisible Reality.
>
> (Russell 1918: *CP8* p. 160; *LK* p. 178)

And of course Russell's rival view comes out well in this comparison.

Moore, meanwhile, suggests that Bradley's idealism is inconsistent with the common sense view that the world contains everyday material objects at all, and ingeniously shifts the burden of proof (as anticipated in item 14 above):

The question requiring to be asked about material things is thus not: What reason have we for supposing that anything exists *corresponding* to our sensations? but: What reason have we for supposing that material things do *not* exist, since *their* existence has precisely the same evidence as that of our sensations?

(Moore 1903, p. 44)

This idea that the burden of proof lies with the metaphysician who wishes to overturn the truths of common sense reappears in 'External and Internal Relations' (Moore 1919, p. 88), and is of course much more thoroughly and convincingly developed in the most famous and influential of Moore's later essays, particularly 'A Defence of Common Sense' and 'Proof of an External World' (Moore 1925 and 1939). More likely to have been forgotten is the fact that Russell made the same claim but with science taking the place of common sense (Russell 1924, p. 175). Its persisting effect can be illustrated by noting its recurrence, unquestioned, in the thought of one of the most dispassionate and open-minded commentators on these matters (Baldwin 1990, p. 35).

17 Blindness   'I am suggesting', says Moore in 'The Refutation of Idealism' (1903, p. 32), that the Idealist maintains that object and subject are necessarily connected, mainly because he fails to see that they are *distinct*, that they are *two*, at all.' Some things are just 'quite obvious' or 'evident' (Moore 1919, pp. 88, 102). In the later of these two papers, Moore is inclined to attribute the blindness of those who disagree with him to a state of confusion; the idea that philosophical error is to be diagnosed rather than refuted has gripped many minds since (for example, Geach: see Lewis 1991, p. 299), though it is more likely to be attributed to Wittgenstein than to Moore.

18 Right and wrong   Perhaps the best proof of the claim that it has become generally accepted that on most if not all of the above counts, Bradley was in the wrong and his opponents in the right is the fact that over the course of the twentieth century, idealistic monism almost disappeared from view. In the end, it was no longer even argued against. One example will suffice to illustrate the phenomenon. It concerns one of the 'elementary confusions' identified in item 7 above:

Whether or not this fallacy played the role in [idealists'] thought which Moore thought it did is less important, from a historical point of view, than the influence exercised by Moore's diagnosis. Philosophers in general tended to agree with Moore that the absolute idealists had been guilty of this confusion, and his essay was a turning point in discussion of the topic.

(Rorty 1967, p. 127)

This is exactly right.

If any further proof is needed, consider this. The quotation just given comes from Rorty's very long – it must be about 8,000 words – article 'Relations, Internal and External' in the eight-volume *Encyclopedia of Philosophy* (Edwards ed. 1967). Thirty years later, in the ten-volume (and, in terms of words, approximately 30 per cent longer) *Routledge Encyclopedia of Philosophy* (Craig ed. 1998), this topic rates not even an index entry.

Displacing the stereotype

One way of displacing the stereotype would be to provide a systematic exposition of Bradley's work. But this would be preaching to the converted: no one not already convinced of something of the case I am going to present would be likely to read it; and this is not the readership I wish to address. In any case, such expositions are already available: a recent example, which implicitly attacks element 1 of the stereotype, does an excellent job of showing, in compelling detail, in what sense Bradley was a logician, and what his contributions were.[13] Likewise, there are splendid and well-known accounts of Russell's views in the period of my study; I have not the temerity to try to replace or even supplement them.

I am not, then, going to attempt a systematic account of Bradley's logic and metaphysics, let alone of Russell's; in both cases, it would be either too short to be useful (or even intelligible) or so long that the book would become unreadable, and moreover would lose its focus, that being the two philosophers in interaction. Such a focus is not common in philosophical writing;[14] and it may provoke the reader, who is likely to come to a book with different expectations. What I shall do is alternate the long perspective with microscopic examinations of (sometimes neglected) aspects of their views as these affect their interaction. These aspects, selected for both their dialectical and historical importance, can be identified in advance from the Contents pages.

This study of the two philosophers in interaction will, I hope, increase our understanding of some central events in this formative period for analytic philosophy, and lead to the dismantling of the picture presented in the previous section. I am not going to argue that it is mistaken in every respect; rather, that it is frequently mistaken, sometimes exaggerated, sometimes over-simplified, sometimes anachronistic. This project will strike some as mere philosophical archaeology. But I think – as of course I would – that our implicit acceptance of a distorted version of philosophy's recent past has serious consequences. One is that we misunderstand our own history, and thereby misunderstand ourselves and the nature of what we are about. Another is that we are deprived of one of the opportunities to connect what we do in philosophy with what some of the philosophers of the past have done; we may, as a result, fall under the impression that only *we*, and those obviously like us, are really doing philosophy, at least as it ought to be done. This consequence has a mirror version, that of projecting our current concerns back into the past; it is aptly summarized by Gideon Makin:

> [W]e are in danger of unconsciously investing the situation with our own philosophical concerns and interests, letting them take the place of what can only be unravelled by the careful examination of the texts.
>
> (Makin 2000, p. 2)

This should give pause for thought even to those who view the history of philosophy as an utterly different study from that of philosophy itself, for it brings out one of the most unfortunate of these consequences: that we may in our ignorance or incomprehension overlook some interesting ideas which cannot be found in the modern philosophical canon. Such people may enjoy a joke Quine is said to have made, that there are two sorts of people interested in philosophy, those interested in philosophy and those interested in the history of philosophy. Not only are they likely to miss some interesting things, however, but as Alasdair MacIntyre pointed out, the counter-joke is this: 'The people interested in philosophy now are doomed to become those whom only those interested in the history of philosophy are going to be interested in in a hundred years' time.'[15]

The final consequence to which I wish to draw attention can be identified by considering that the exposure of illusion which I undertake in this book is meant to be *exemplary*. There are lessons here.

Perhaps it is inevitable that philosophers who have fresh ideas and want to make their mark should not waste their time on scholarly refutations of those whose time has passed, but should instead rely on quick and easy stigmatization, while those who wish not to be seen as yesterday's men will hasten in pursuit of the new. If that is true, however, then the same processes are at work now, and we are caught up in some process of self-delusion comparable to that I sketch here. That does not conform to the rhetorical vision of philosophy to which most of us subscribe.

2
Finding a Way into Bradley's Metaphysics

'I made little of [my father's philosophy books], but I remember in particular Bradley's *Appearance and Reality*. The work bewildered me; there were hardly any words I did not know, and the sentences were simply constructed, but I could not tell what it all meant. However, I formed the general impression that the author was a wicked man who worshipped a false God called the Absolute . . . My adult views of Bradley are not so very different. Reading a few pages of *Appearance and Reality* now makes me feel as if I had drunk several pints of beer . . .'

Peter Geach, 'A Philosophical Autobiography', in Lewis (1991), pp. 2–3

Preliminary sketch

This section is intended for those readers largely unfamiliar with Bradley's work, so that those to whom this description does not apply may move immediately to the one following.

The most characteristic features of Bradley's metaphysics arise from his arguing that our everyday conceptions of the world (as well as those more refined ones common among his philosophical predecessors) contain hidden contradictions which appear, fatally, when we try to think out their consequences. In particular, Bradley rejected on these grounds the view that reality can be understood as consisting of many objects existing independently both of each other (pluralism) and of experience of them (realism). Consistently, his own view combined monism (reality is one; there are no real separate things) with absolute idealism (reality consists solely of idea or experience). Such absolute or objective idealism stands in contrast to Berkeley's so-called

21

subjective idealism, for monism excludes Berkeley's separation of the mind from its ideas: in Bradley's view, the experience which is the fabric of the world is not owned.

Some of the roots of Bradley's metaphysical monism can be found in his *Principles of Logic* (1883). For centuries, books on logic had treated the subject of judgment: the standard view was that judgments are formed by somehow conjoining ideas. An example is the Port-Royal *Logic*'s Aristotelian contention that judgments are 'necessarily composed of three elements – the subject-idea, the attribute, and the joining of these two ideas' (Arnauld and Nicole 1662: Part II, Ch. 3).[1] Bradley, in contrast, stated flatly that 'It is not true that every judgment has two ideas. We may say on the contrary that all have but one' (1883, p. 11). He alleged further that those who think judgments to consist of separable ideas fail to identify the sense of 'idea' in which ideas are important to logic: ideas in this sense are not separate and datable psychological events but abstract universals.[2] Once ideas are properly understood, Bradley suggests, they can no longer even plausibly be thought of as individual and mutually independent entities which can be put together to create a judgment: the order of dependence is the opposite, ideas being abstractions from complete judgments. We shall see in Chapter 3 below that here, albeit in his archaic vocabulary of ideas, Bradley identifies in advance the difficulties which Russell was later to face in trying to reconcile the unity of the proposition with what he thought to be the mutual independence of its constituents.

After completing *The Principles of Logic*, Bradley turned his attention to giving a full account of the metaphysics which was implicit in the earlier work. The result was *Appearance and Reality* (1893). This is divided into two books. The first, 'Appearance', is brief, and its aim destructive, arguing that 'the ideas by which we try to understand the universe' all bring us ultimately to contradictions when we try to think out their implications. Some of these ideas belong especially to philosophy, such as the view that only the primary qualities are real; others, for instance the notions of cause, motion, self, space, thing and time, are deployed in everyday life. The second book, 'Reality', is long; its aim is to provide a positive account of the Absolute – the ultimate, unconditioned reality as it is in itself, not distorted by projection through the conceptual mechanisms of thought.

The everyday, and also philosophical, view, that reality consists of a multiplicity of related objects, Bradley holds to be a result of the separations imposed by thought; in fact 'the Absolute is not many; there are no independent reals.' (This and all quotations from here on in this section are from *Appearance and Reality*, Chapter XIV.) Reality is one – but one what? Experience, he says, in a wide sense of the term: 'Feeling, thought and volition (any groups under which we class psychological phenomena) are all the material of existence, and there is no other material, actual or even possible.'

So 'the Absolute is one system, and ... its contents are nothing but sentient experience. It will hence be a single and all-inclusive experience, which embraces every partial diversity in concord. For it cannot be less than appearance, and hence no feeling or thought, of any kind, can fall outside its limits.' But how can we understand this diversity to be possible, when we cannot legitimately deploy the notions of discrete objects or terms, and relations among them? Bradley's answer is that we cannot understand this in detail, but can get some grasp on what he means by considering a pre-conceptual state of immediate experience in which there are differences but no separations, a state from which our familiar, cognitive, adult human consciousness arises by imposing conceptual distinctions upon the differences. Reality is like this primitive state, but not exactly like, for it transcends thought rather than falls short of it, and everything, even conceptual thought itself, is included in one comprehensive and harmonious whole. Appearances thus contribute to Reality in a fashion analogous to the ways in which segments of a painting contribute to the whole work of art: detached from their background, they would lose their significance and might in isolation even be ugly; in context, they can themselves be beautiful and make an essential contribution to the beauty and integrity of the whole. Such limited comparisons are all the help we can get in understanding the Absolute and its relation to its appearances: Bradley rejects as impossible the demand for detailed explanations of how phenomena like error and evil belong to the Absolute, instead trying to shift the burden of proof to critics who express confidence in their incompatibility. His general answer is that anything that exists, even the worst of evils, is somehow real: the Absolute must comprehend both evil and good. But, just as (he thinks) truth admits of degrees, a judgment being less true the further it is from comprehending the whole of reality, so reality itself admits of degrees, a phenomenon being the less real the more it is just a fragmentary aspect of the whole. The Absolute is in such a way further from evil than from good, but is itself neither, transcending them both as it transcends even religion – it is in a sense a Supreme Being, but not a personal God.

The foundations of Bradley's thought

It is possible to be presented with an accurate, indeed detailed and systematic, outline of the work of a major metaphysical philosopher
which fails to convey the faintest idea why anyone might actually hold
the seemingly bizarre views displayed, even if it is otherwise clearly
written. This is true of commentaries as well as of the original work.[3]
A fortiori, a snapshot view of Bradley's metaphysics such as that provided in the previous section, although I did my best with it, is likely
to leave a reader similarly baffled. In the remainder of this chapter
I want to try to make this metaphysics at least plausible in the sense
that one can begin to understand, at least in outline, how someone
might come to believe some of the apparently incredible things for
which Bradley is notorious.

But reading Bradley from the other side of the twentieth century can
be a frustrating chore: there is something alien about his writings, and
historically more remote philosophers may appear far closer in spirit,
style and intelligibility. The sources of this impression of the alien are
manifold. Among other things they include: Bradley's forgotten terminology; his casual scholarship combined with unmentioned (and
now unread) influences, both positive and negative;[4] an instinct for
obscurity in expression nurtured by a florid prose style replete with
metaphor; a relentless eschewing of illustrative examples; a determination, particularly in his earlier works, to develop his views gradually
across hundreds of pages which is hard to distinguish from a real
incapacity for tight organization of his subject matter, sitting irritat-
ingly alongside later presentations of argument so laconic as to defy
exposition, as is well described by Donald Baxter:

> Additionally Bradley's text obscures his meaning because the prob-
> lem is not clearly stated, the connections between parts of his argu-
> ment are not explicit, the historical background is taken for granted,
> and many assumptions are left unstated. Yet Bradley writes as if the
> problem were so painfully clear that it is almost too tedious to
> rehearse. Perhaps it was, but now it isn't.
>
> (Baxter 1996, p. 4)

Faced with such material, anyone whose task is to consider the great
changes which came about in English-language philosophy at the
beginning of the twentieth century turns with relief to the crisp and
clear writings of his great opponent, Bertrand Russell. It is not surprising that few have wished to turn back.

Part of the burden of this book will be to show that this contrast (and several others besides) between the two philosophers is misconceived: both Bradley's obscurity and Russell's clarity are to a significant extent superficial.[5] The task is not, however, easily accomplished: one needs to follow both sides of a dispute that is at once tangled, drawn-out and riddled with misconceptions sometimes doubly confusing by being inadvertently adopted by the misunderstood as well as the misunderstander. And this involves a grasp, which must be at once both sympathetic and critical, of apparently diametrically opposed philosophical views in metaphysics and the philosophy of logic and of language. But in order fully to understand any metaphysician it is necessary to determine the order of priority amongst his various doctrines; and it is natural then to look for those which are fundamental to the rest, fundamental in the sense of providing some insight into how the others could have come to have been accepted. (Russell, as we have seen, thought Bradley's doctrines to rest on a view about the nature of the proposition; and there is something in this, though not what Russell thought there was.) This is a matter on which, as we just observed, even the metaphysician concerned may be unforthcoming, so that exposition may be controversial. And in Bradley's case the difficulty is compounded by the fact that he appears to warn us off:

I will however begin by noticing some misunderstandings as to the method employed in ultimate inquiry by writers like myself. There is an idea that we start, consciously or unconsciously, with certain axioms, and from these reason downwards. This idea to my mind is baseless. The method actually followed may be called in the main the procedure used by Hegel, that of a direct ideal experiment made on reality. What is assumed is that I have to satisfy my theoretical want, or, in other words, that I resolve to think. And it is assumed that, if my thought is satisfied with itself, I have, with this, truth and reality. But as to what will satisfy I have of course no knowledge in advance. My object is to get before me what will content a certain felt need, but the way and the means are to be discovered only by trial and rejection. The method clearly is experimental.

> (1911b, *ETR* p. 311; cf. also *loc. cit.* p. 312, 1893,
> *AR* pp. 127–8, and 1897, *AR* p. 509)[6]

In view of this we need to tread very carefully in seeking the foundations of Bradley's thought. While the quotation itself contains clues, these clues are themselves puzzling. What are we to understand by 'certain felt need' and 'ideal experiment'?

Intellectual satisfaction

In a passage (1897, *AR* pp. 491–2) comparable to the one above, Bradley speaks of 'satisfying the intellect' and the context makes clear that this is the 'certain felt need'. But what is it to satisfy the intellect?

What satisfies the intellect is truth (1906, *ETR* p. 1; 1911b, *ETR* p. 311), and such satisfaction is the practical criterion of truth; that is, the function of the notion of intellectual satisfaction is to enable us to determine when we have arrived at truth. The criterion is not intended to be a touchstone which applies to any statement or inference taken in isolation (1922, *PL* pp. 619–20), but, because of the nature of what does satisfy the intellect, is operative only when a statement or inference is considered in relation to others. Satisfaction is not just feeling pleased about things (1906, *ETR* p. 242; 1924, *CE* p. 671):[7] it is satisfaction of the *intellect*, and that is arrived at only in a quite definite way, for the intellect demands unity (1897, *AR* p. 511). What kind of unity? It is the ideal self-development or self-completion of an object (1897, *AR* p. 507; 1922, *PL* p. 598), the object being an ideal content taken as real (1922, *PL* p. 598). This is not exactly lucid: but the vocabulary does not need to be fully understood yet to be recognized as that in which Bradley gives his final account of inference (1922, *PL* p. 598), and where there is genuine inference there is also implication (1922, *PL* p. 600).

The point is now starting to emerge: although because, as we shall see, Bradley was a critic of formalization in logic, one must think of his notion of implication as wider than a modern logician would allow, it is nevertheless clear that he is clear that he has arrived at truth only if his propositions express implications, that is, necessary connections (1893, *AR* p. 349; 1897, pp. 501, 509 and 511; 1922, *PL* p. 600).[8] It is not, then, truth in the everyday sense – in which we distinguish, for example, between 'The Earth is roughly spherical' and 'The Earth is flat' – which satisfies the intellect, but truth in some philosophically charged sense. Nevertheless, our practice of intellectual enquiry does reflect Bradley's suggestion. A typical empirical explanation of some particular phenomenon works by conferring on it a kind of necessity, one relative to the truth of a general proposition under which the phenomenon is subsumed. If an explanation of the truth of the general proposition is then sought, a natural response is to render it in turn relatively non-contingent by subsuming it under a higher-order proposition – and so on until we come to rest at the limits of our empirical knowledge on some law which is not similarly explicable. But, and this is Bradley's point, when we reach this position and 'conjoin aliens inexplicably' (1897, *AR* p. 502) we are still not satisfied, but rather struggle to find a way of rendering intelligible our presently fundamental laws by finding something more embracing yet. Our intellect is genuinely not content to rest in mere contingency, as is illustrated by, for instance, the ontological argument, and some recent efforts in cosmology.

All this is of course familiar, and it is no accident that the Covering Law Model of explanation flourished in a period when the prevailing tradition, of logical atomism and logical empiricism, acknowledged the fundamentally contingent in its metaphysics; for the function of that model within that tradition is to pander to the Bradleian demand for intellectual satisfaction – which the tradition by its nature cannot meet – by giving, in the way just described, the appearance of necessity within an overall framework of utter contingency. But the provision of this appearance, while admittedly seeming quite plausibly to reflect the reality of scientific practice, fails to do more than pander to the demand; for the intellectual satisfaction it affords is partial and temporary, merely disguising the ultimate and perpetual frustration posed by the ineradicable contingency. (And here we see one of the grounds for Bradley's hostility to science as a basis of metaphysics.) However, the goal postulated by the Covering Law Model, of a coherent system of logically related propositions as comprehensive as possible, clearly corresponds to Bradley's idea of perfect truth (1909b, *ETR* p. 203; 1909c, *ETR* p. 223), even if it is in the end unsatisfactory because flawed with contingency at the highest level of explanation. And what Bradley says here can in principle be detached from his contentious views about truth,[9] and recognized as in essence fairly simple and plausible despite the difficulty of his language, for we can see it as offering something perhaps more satisfying to the intellect than truth (at least as we have learned to think of that notion under more recent influences), namely, explanation and understanding.

Ideal experiment

Now that we have some grasp of what satisfaction of the intellect consists in, let us have a look at the other fundamental feature of Bradley's philosophy, the notion of *ideal experiment*. Bradley says very little in a general way about what an ideal experiment is, and does not give a formal explanation of the notion at all.[10] But despite his recorded opinion that to give illustrations is dangerous (1911b, *ETR* p. 339n) he does give some examples. The examples are nearly all in the chapter of *The Principles of Logic* entitled 'Fresh Specimens of Inference' (pp. 394–430); they include various species of reasoning and are summed up later:

> Inference is an experiment, an ideal experiment which gains fresh truth.
>
> *(1883, PL* p. 492)

However, the fresh truth cannot be a truth concerning a different subject-matter.

> Inference is an experiment performed on a *datum*, which *datum* appropriates the result of the experiment.
>
> (1883, *PL* p. 479; cf. also 1883, *PL* p. 431)

This may tempt one to suppose that the notions of *inference* and *ideal experiment* are equivalent; but to say this without qualification would be misleading. For Bradley also calls supposal an ideal experiment (1883, *PL* p. 86) and in the above quotations he always says '*an* experiment', as though there are others.

Nevertheless this tempting supposition is at bottom correct. For supposal is, Bradley says, 'thinking for a particular end' (1883, *PL* p. 85), 'with a view to see what the consequence is' (1883, *PL* p. 86), and is thus not to be detached from inference. And when Bradley comes, under the influence of Bosanquet, to his later, more considered account of inference as 'the ideal self-developement [*sic*] of an object' (1922, *PL* p. 597), this object being 'an ideal content before us, taken to be real' (1922, *PL* p. 598), that is, an affirmed judgment, he stressed the fact that inference cannot lead you to a completely different subject, neglecting the reference to experiment in his original account. And what I think this means is that by 'inference' Bradley is talking, as many logicians do, of valid inference only, and that if we take the general form of inference as 'A, therefore B', ideal experiments are simply thoughts of this form, some of which are valid – that is, genuine inferences, corresponding to implications and preserving truth (1922, *PL* pp. 423 n. 3 and 598) – and some of which are not.[11] And the mysterious talk of 'ideal self-development of an object' is just a way of putting a point related to Hume's claim that there are no logical relations between distinct existences. For Bradley, this point arises against the background of a question no longer asked by logicians: What must the world be like for inference to be valid?[12] No wonder that, in the final paragraph of the Preface to the first edition, he confesses to an inability to exclude metaphysics from his logic book. (Bradley is not alone: Russell's metaphysics during this period is in part governed by the same question.)

Leaving metaphysics on one side for the moment, we find Bradley maintaining what, despite the difficulty of the surface language, is something rather simple and uncontroversial. Why then is the language difficult? Why describe the inference as 'ideal experiment'?

'Ideal' is fairly easily explained. Ideas belong to thought: 'the idea in judgment is the universal meaning', says Bradley (1883, *PL* p. 10; cf. also 1897, *AR* p. 526), and an ideal experiment is an experiment concerning connections between universals (1883, *PL* p. 441) which could, unlike a physical experiment, be accomplished solely in thought, though a physical version may be employed (1922, *PL* p. 423, n. 3). Roughly, it is a process in which we posit premises and then see what appears to follow.[13]

But why also 'experiment'? I think the answer here is that for Bradley the outcomes even of deduction may not only surprise the reasoner, but are in some sense or senses not guaranteed (1883, *PL* pp. 259, 266–71, and 530). If this sounds absurd, remember the difficulty which Wittgenstein had in making people understand just such a point[14] (and compare the similar problem concerning the non-relational character of experience, in the following section). What Bradley means here is perhaps several things at once for which he gives some variety of reasons, but a reasonably clear summary comes in this passage:

> The idea of a complete body of models of reasoning, to be followed as patterns and faithfully reproduced to make and guarantee the individual inference, I set down as a superstition. No such code of rules and examples could, as we have seen, warrant its own infallible application; and, in the second place, no collection of models could conceivably be complete, and so anticipate and prescribe beforehand the special essence of every inference.
>
> (1922, *PL* p. 618)

It is striking to find Bradley anticipating the later Wittgenstein's emphasis on the distinction between a rule and its application.[15] Both men, too, were interested in reasoning as a human activity, despite the anti-psychologism which Bradley learned from Frege's teacher Lotze and Wittgenstein from Frege himself. In Bradley's case, however, his 'anti-psychologism' was not as thoroughgoing as his proclamations suggest, and his interest in the activity of reasoning extends to the point of thinking it proper to investigate its psychological accompaniments; this, as he later recognized, introduces confusion into some early parts of the first edition of *The Principles of Logic* (unlike Wittgenstein's tentative but unconfused explorations of the matter in Section xi of the so-called Part Two of *Philosophical Investigations*).

Consistent with the views expressed in the previous quotation is Bradley's refusal to put the 'laws' of logic on to an exalted plane:

> A principle will neither demonstrate its applications nor can it be demonstrated by them. The principle is demonstrated when we see it in, and as the function of, an individual act.
>
> (1883, *PL* p. 531)

> The degree in which the various types [of inference and judgment] each succeed and fail in reaching their common end [of contributing to the width and coherence of the body of our knowledge], gives to each of them its respective place and its rank in the whole body.
>
> (1922, *PL* p. 620)

And here we see Bradley taking up a position very similar to that associated with Quine.

Now, however, we come to a difficulty. As we have seen, for Bradley reasoning is ideal experiment. But in several places he appears to contrast ideal experiment with reasoning. For example, in maintaining against Russell that one cannot think without inconsistency of a relation on its own and devoid of terms, Bradley says, 'This is, however, not so much a matter for argument and discussion as for actual experiment' (1914, *ETR* p. 303; cf. also 1911a, *ETR* p. 289). In the famous proof of idealism (1893, *AR* pp. 127–8) he gives not a deduction but a series of instructions to the reader as to the conducting of an ideal experiment, an experiment whose results in his own case he reports with the apparent expectation that the reader will produce the same ones, and in a clear reference back to this proof he says (1911b, p. 316n):

> We have here a matter for observation and experiment and not for long trains of reasoning . . . [I]f Prof. Perry wishes to get an idea as to the view which he is anxious to refute, why should he not suppose (for a moment) that on my side there is no argument at all, and that on his side there is an inference by way of vicious abstraction?

What can be made of this? I think the appearance of inconsistency can be resolved, though Bradley himself seems not to notice the tension in his thought here. In the places where he draws the contrast with experiment, he refers to argument, not to inference, and typically to argument from some axiom he is supposed to hold (for example: 1911a *ETR* p. 289; 1910a, *ETR* p. 259; 1911b, *ETR* p. 311), while in the quotation he speaks similarly, making the added reference to 'long trains of reasoning'.

What he seems to have in mind is a Cartesian contrast between, on the one hand, those inferences which one can grasp with, as it were, one movement of the mind, and on the other, those inferences which proceed step by step to a distant conclusion and which cannot just be seen to be valid; but he also seems at the same time to be thinking of the contrast between conditionals, whose antecedents are of course not separately asserted, and arguments, which have a categorical first premiss, particularly arguments with premisses of a very general and all-embracing kind. We may be seeing as well the influence of one of the orthodoxies of his time, introspectionism in psychology.[16]

But now, we may ask, if this is all that the difference between argument and ideal experiment amounts to, if they both belong, roughly speaking, to the sphere of logic, why make such a fuss about the difference? Normal arguments must begin from a premiss which within the context of the argument is taken for granted. But Bradley's experiments are meant to be free of presupposition, to be made directly on reality (*PL,* p. 563; 1911b, p. 311), and moreover on reality as experienced and not as served up, already sliced, in sentences.

Despite this difference, however, I think that his ideal experiments are meant to reveal what later philosophers were inclined to call logical or conceptual truths; and, furthermore, truths which are either what has been called self-evident or are self-evidently directly underpinned by something itself self-evident.[17] This would explain why he says (1911a, *ETR* p. 289) that he cannot see how to argue about these matters, and does not argue downwards to the truths he wishes to maintain. We must not forget, too, that for him logic, while not reducible to psychology, works through ideas, which always possess a psychical aspect (1922, *PL* p. 38 n. 8) and are thus to be studied through introspection rather than through the linguistic expression which is subsequently (1883, *PL* p. 32) grafted on to them. Philosophy written in a non-linguistic climate can be about the same things as that written in a linguistic climate (though they may not be, as we shall see when we come to consider Russell's views on propositions and judgments); but the products of the former can often be understood from the perspective of the latter only by a translation into the more familiar idiom. Again, this may not always be possible, and may be misleading even when it is possible. But one must start somewhere: so here are some examples to demonstrate my claim that Bradley's ideal experiments were meant to reveal self-evident conceptual truths.

First, Bradley says that by experimenting he cannot find that any relation survives the total removal of its terms (1914a, *ETR* p. 295). Put in an older idiom not alien to Bradley (for he is an heir to a long tradition in philosophy beginning with Aristotle) but still familiar to most modern readers, this is the claim that relations are not substances, that is, not complete or individual (1883, *PL* pp. 71 and 187; 1893, *AR*, p. 9; 1897, *AR* p. 509; 1909c, *ETR* p. 227n; 1911a, *ETR* pp. 289–90).[18] And the notions of substance and completeness give us a clue to how the point could be expressed as one in the philosophy of language: without a special context, producing a relational expression like '... is a compatriot of ...' is not a complete linguistic act. The expression is not an assertion, nor is it a referring expression introducing some object of which we can go on to predicate something. The parallels with points made by philosophers of language are obvious.

Secondly, he says 'In actual experience we can never find a thing by itself; it is obvious that some context will always be present there' (1883, *PL* p. 563). This looks like a psychological, but again is a logical, point. If, for example, we interpret 'experience' as 'perception', then picking something out logically involves a background against which it is picked out. If we generalize 'experience', in the manner typical of nineteenth-century idealism, to include all psychical activity,[19] then we get instead the logical claim on which Bradley's idealism is partly founded and which is outlined in the next paragraph.

Thirdly, in the course of his proof of idealism, Bradley, after instructing the reader to try the experiment of thinking of something in the absence of all perception and feeling, says in a passage reminiscent of Berkeley's so-called 'Master Argument':

> When the experiment is made strictly, I can myself conceive of nothing else than the experienced. Anything, in no sense felt or perceived, becomes to me quite unmeaning . . . I cannot try to think of it without realizing either that I am not thinking at all, or that I am thinking of it against my will as being experienced . . . The fact that falls elsewhere seems, in my mind, to be a mere word and a failure, or else an attempt at self-contradiction.[20]

> (1893, *AR* p. 128)

Here again the ideal experiment is designed to reveal a logical point. Bradley invites us to try to conceive of an unexperienced object. This seems straightforward enough, until we remember that for idealists, 'experience' and 'feeling' cover all forms of psychical activity, and the instruction thus comes to 'Conceive of something unconceived'. And this description of what we are to do is plausibly regarded as either 'a mere word' or an instruction to attempt something self-contradictory or self-defeating.[21]

Fourthly, he claims that the non-contingency of the fact that a term is not diverse from itself is revealed by ideal experiment, saying that the contrary supposition 'either is meaningless or self-destructive' (1911a, *ETR* p. 290).

It seems clear from these four examples that ideal experiment is, as Bradley conceives it, a method of uncovering what we might call relatively self-evident conceptual or necessary truths, even though he might himself resist this description of it. With these examples behind us we can now afford to let in others which may seem less apparently self-evident to us by reminding ourselves that they may have appeared rather differently to Bradley: the impossibility of purely external relations as revealed by ideal experiment (1911a, *ETR* p. 290), for one – which is clearly to Bradley an obvious impossibility – and, for another, the impossibility of reflexive relations through the revelation by experiment that relations imply diversity (1911a, *ETR* p. 289).

The sceptical principle, mark I

Our result so far, then, is this. In his own view, at least, Bradley's metaphysics rests on no assumption. Instead, it is the product of an as far as possible presuppositionless enquiry into the nature of reality, pursued by ideal experiment and with the goal of satisfying the intellect. The intellect, it turns out, is satisfied only by a system of necessarily connected propositions which is as comprehensive as possible. (Those who think that Bradley held a coherence theory of truth, and that all such theories are wrong, may substitute 'truths' for 'propositions' here if they wish to retain some sympathetic insight into Bradley's thought.) And ideal experiments are conditional postulations revealing what are standardly recognized as necessary truths, that is, on Bradley's view, propositions which are high up in the system.

It may be suggested here that this is already to prejudge the issue of the nature of reality in favour of some sort of monism; but although this charge turns out to have something in it, it is, when stated baldly, unjust. For as we saw, even metaphysics of contingency like logical empiricism pay lip-service to this conception of intellectual satisfaction; and Bradley is so far prepared to admit the bare possibility of an ultimate contingency and atomism as to feel obliged to argue against it (1897, *AR* pp. 500–11). What convinced him initially that one would not have to admit it was the fact that experience, as we shall see, did not present him with terms, qualities, and relations in the manner in which thought (or language) is obliged to represent that experience.

So Bradley's philosophy begins from immediate experience, from 'feeling' as he often terms it. Immediate experience is not to be assumed to be captured in the ways that we describe it. This quasi-Cartesian starting point seems to him to need no justification: it is all one has to work with. (I say '*quasi*-Cartesian' to emphasize the reliance on experience while drawing back from the egocentric presuppositions and tendentious intellectual apparatus of Descartes's own first philosophy.) Furthermore, no kind of experience, such as perception, is to be assumed without argument to be privileged over others. This theme runs throughout his writing.

I have said that 'in his own view' Bradley's metaphysics – or, more accurately, the method which produces it – is assumptionless. We shall find that this requires qualification. However, I think it only fair to him to take him seriously and to find out how far we can get in deriving and understanding the main features of his metaphysics on this slender basis. Bradley starts, then, by taking experience as it comes, allowing himself to perform ideal experiments on it, and retaining those results which satisfy the intellect. And the first thing he notices about experience is that it is non-relational (1909c, *ETR* pp. 230–1). He does not mean that it is simple, and lacking variety (1897, *AR* p. 508; 1911b, *ETR* p. 311). What he means is hard to explain, in just the way that his suggestion that deduction does not in a sense guarantee its outcome is hard to explain. This is because he is making that typical philosopher's move of rejecting a philosophical picture of ordinary facts, and this always leads to misunderstanding, for one is inclined to think that he is denying those ordinary facts instead. Part of that picture is the assumption that language mirrors reality.[22] When we take an experience of an object – a green leaf, say, to use his example (1924, *CE* pp. 633 and 656) – experience has both a unity and a diversity which are not and cannot be adequately reflected in the language we use to describe the experience, language which necessarily deploys the tools of terms, quality, and relation (cf. 1897, *AR* p. 512;

1924, *CE* p. 630). For with that language we must say things like 'Here is a leaf', which both splits the object from its background and fails to reflect its diversity, or 'The leaf is green', which again abstracts certain features of the actual experience leaving others unmentioned and furthermore splits up these features in a way in which they are not split in reality. While such sentences attempt to restore the original unity (they are, as Bradley shows himself to be well-aware, not merely lists of their constituent words), they necessarily fail. Of course we cannot say clearly what it would be for them to succeed, for success in this matter is, as Bradley with his talk of perfect truth requiring thought's suicide recognizes, inconceivable; and therein lies the urge to misunderstand him, to take him as denying the obvious truth that in some sense the experience is relational since it contains diversity.

It may look as though Bradley is, right at this early stage, making assumptions, for to us, who see as it were almost through the eyes of our language, it can seem just perverse to deny that experience reveals to us objects in relation. But this is precisely the point: the way we think of experience is affected by our language. (Although Bradley would want the point put the other way round, with the blame falling on thought rather than on language.) And Bradley's 'great problem' is the relation of thought to reality (1897, *AR* p. 492). So he cannot, as so many philosophers have done, take for granted that the categories of thought are automatically reflected in reality. And if it is said that he cannot take for granted that they are not, and his appeal to the evidence of experience is rejected, then it must be pointed out that his metaphysical views do not rest just on this observation of experience's non-relational character.

They do not rest on this alone, because his subsequent arguments about predication and relations are meant, *inter alia*, to show that any attempt to prove the apparent non-relationality of experience misleading and to analyse it relationally is doomed to failure. What the observation does is, when combined with his determination not to make assumptions, to license the weak form of what may be called his sceptical principle. I say 'the weak form' because there are three distinct forms discernible in his work and although he appears not to distinguish them himself the weak form is the only one which might be regarded as independently plausible and to which – given that he is trying to proceed without making assumptions – he is so far entitled. The principle is stated in various places but perhaps the closest approximations to the weak form are these:

For, if the qualities impart themselves never except under conditions, how in the end are we to say what they are when unconditioned?

(1893, *AR* p. 11)

And you cannot ever get your product standing apart from its
process. Will you say, the process is not essential? But that is a conclusion to be proved, and it is monstrous to assume it . . . And, if we
have no further information, I can find no excuse for setting up the
result as being fact without the process.

(1893, *AR* p. 23)

Each of these is a more particular version of the general principle
which is at work in both cases and which I take to be formulable as
follows:

> *One is not entitled to **assume** of something which is always experienced
> in combination with something else, that it is capable of existing uncom-
> bined.*

This version of Bradley's sceptical principle, although I have characterized it as weak, does quite a lot of work in his philosophy, for it
licenses one form of his long-standing hostility towards *abstraction*.
Bradley employs this form quite explicitly against Mill's Method of
Difference (1883, *PL* pp. 560–2), and argues that while abstraction is
legitimate in certain contexts and for certain limited and practical purposes, it takes the performance of an ideal experiment to prove this
legitimacy in each case. Thus, ideal experiment shows that for the purposes of arithmetic one may treat an integer as a whole consisting of
separable parts, since the sums involved do work in practice, despite
the fact that numbers form an internally related system, a fact that
cannot be forgotten when we come to give a philosophical account of
number rather than merely do arithmetic. But the work that the principle in this form does, which is of immediate interest to us, is to open
the door to both monism and idealism, because it places the burden of
argument on those wishing to oppose these doctrines. However, before
monism and idealism can be actually proved, the weak form must be
replaced by stronger ones. In order to see what licenses this replacement, we must first proceed to an apparently independent matter:
Bradley's attack on predication and on the correlative idea that we can
understand reality as consisting of things which have qualities.

The attack on predication[23]

What underpins this attack is Bradley's demand for satisfaction of the intellect, that is, for a necessary connection between different things if their coexistence is to be understood (1911b, *ETR* pp. 314–15). This is not just a refusal to accept bare contingency as 'our ignorance set up as reality' (1897, *AR* p. 517); it is the result of a claim to find such contingency self-contradictory, both in general (1893, *AR* pp. 345–9) and in the case of predication (1897, *AR* pp. 500–11). Let us look at what he says concerning the case of predication. Suppose we have a billiard ball. It is both white and round. These properties are, in the object, in some way unified (in the sense that we are not dealing with two things, one of them white and the other round), and at the same time in some way held apart (they are not the same property). Now according to Bradley, we are forced by the need for intellectual satisfaction to find a necessary connection between the ball's whiteness and its roundness, and this leads into attempting to identify the two properties with each other, to attribute them as it were to the same feature of the ball. (Again, this is hard to understand because it is an identification whose intelligibility Bradley rejects. One could compare Wittgenstein on the subject of private designation.)

Why does the need for intellectual satisfaction force us to try to identify the two different properties? This happens, he thinks, in the following way. In ordinary predication ('the ball is white and round') the link between them is presented as bare co-presence. Recognizing that this is inadequate since it does not do justice to their unity, while lacking knowledge of the true explanation of this unity (an explanation which will also show how they are not only linked but also kept apart), the intellect falls back – so he says – on the only remaining logical connection which can guarantee the unity, namely identity:

> It is idle from the outside to say to thought, 'Well, unite but do not identify.' How can thought unite except so far as in itself it has a mode of union? To unite without an internal ground of connexion and distinction is to strive to bring together barely in the same point, and that is self-contradiction.
>
> (1897, *AR* p. 505)

It is this kind of reasoning which led Russell to accuse Bradley of the 'stupid and trivial' confusion of predication with identity. Whatever one thinks of the reasoning (not much, probably), the charge is quite unfair.[24] The distinction between the 'is' of predication and that of identity was not then as obvious as it now seems,[25] so that it was natural for Bradley to consider identity as the sole alternative to what I have called 'bare co-presence' in attempting to find an intelligible account of the linking of diverse attributes in the one object. Indeed, identity was not generally thought of as the strong relation, involving indiscernibility, that it is assumed to be today, so that the Hegelian idea of identity-in-difference was neither especially Hegelian nor the puzzling conception that we now find it.[26] A conception of predication as identity can be found, for example, in Hobbes, and on his views it makes sense: if there are no (abstract) universals, and all words are names of whatever object they apply to, then the sentence 'Socrates is bald and wise' applies three names, 'Socrates', 'bald' and 'wise', to the one thing, namely, Socrates. Bradley rejects this kind of account.

His point, as briefly and compellingly as I can express it, was that predication is an inadequate device for expressing the connection between a thing and its properties: it seems to link things quite arbitrarily, and such arbitrariness both seems not to do justice to the phenomena and is intolerable to the philosophical understanding. Interpreting the 'is' of English predication as identity removes the arbitrariness, but at the cost of inconsistency. Hence ordinary predication is, while perfectly satisfactory for everyday business, ultimately unintelligible.[27] Even if one suspects that he is asking for the impossible and then complaining when it is not supplied, one can at least begin to see what he is getting at.

A rather clearer argument to the same effect is mounted early in *Appearance and Reality*, one which relies on his view, which we noted earlier (p. 27f), that to be real is to be a substance, an independent thing. On this assumption, if predication is to be faithful to reality, then both logical subject and logical predicate must meet this requirement: both must introduce substances. The subject does not, because a thing is nothing when divorced from a predicated quality (1893, *AR* p. 16) – there is no such thing as an apple devoid of the colour it actually possesses, for instance; so Bradley asks, whether, instead, predication can be treated as expressing a relationship amongst the qualities themselves. And he answers, 'No', for two reasons. First, if the relation between qualities is regarded attributively, so that one quality is really only an attribute of the other, then we merely repeat the original problem of understanding predication (*ibid.* p. 17). Secondly, if we respond to this first reason by suggesting that the relation itself is a reality, then that relation must be capable of existing independently of its related terms. In that case, when it does happen to relate terms in fact, the coming of the terms into relation with the independently existing relation requires an explanation, which promptly generates an infinite regress of explanatory relations. Thus only an identity-statement stands a chance of not immediately and automatically falsifying reality by its very form.[28]

The very same point holds where we attempt, not to attribute two different, 'compatible' predicates to a single subject, but to attribute one to a designated subject. But in Bradley's mind the two cases probably come to the same thing, for he has argued (1883, *PL* Bk I Ch. II) that all designation proceeds through universals and that even the most apparently recalcitrantly singular, designatory proposition like 'Napoleon was fond of Josephine' must be understood as combining predicates.

Bradley sums up his view thus:

> A thing cannot without an internal distinction be two different things, and differences cannot belong to the same thing in the same point unless in that point there is diversity. The appearance of such a union may be fact, but is for thought a contradiction.
>
> (1897, *AR* p. 501)

He does not mean, as we would, that this, being a contradiction, is impossible, 'for the intellect can always accept the conjunction not as bare but as a connexion, the bond of which is at present unknown . . . [and] can accept the inconsistent if taken as subject to conditions' (1897, *AR* p. 503). He means that experienced facts cannot be understood; for the conditions can never all be filled in.

The attack on external relations

We have now seen how the demand for satisfaction of the intellect, interpreted as the demand for connections of implication between diverse but related things, leads directly to the rejection of predication as unintelligible except subject to unknown conditions. Bradley's next move, the attack on external relations, has the same foundation.

That any external relations are impossible is revealed by ideal experiment (1911a, *ETR* pp. 290–1; 1914a, *ETR* p. 295); and the tendency to believe the opposite is the result of ignoring the sceptical principle in its weak form. How is the impossibility revealed? To see this, we must first bring out what, in Bradley's view, an external relation is:

What should we mean . . . by a relation asserted as simply and barely external? We have here, I presume, to abstract so as to take terms and relations, all and each, as something which in and by itself is real independently.[29] And we must, if so, assume that their coming or being together in fact, and as somehow actually in one, is due in no way to the particular characters of either the relations or the terms . . . [T]he fact is somehow there, but in itself it remains irrational as admitting no question as to its 'how' or 'why'. Or, if you insist on a reason, that would have to be sought neither in the terms nor the relation, but in a third element once more independently real and neither affecting, nor again affected by, either the relation or the terms.

(1924, *CE* p. 642)

With this understanding of the nature of externality we find by ideal experiment that a diversity of independent but limited 'reals' is self-contradictory:

Relational experience must hence in its very essence be called self-contradictory. Contradiction everywhere is the attempt to take what is plural and diverse as being one and the same, and to take it so (we must add) simply or apart from any 'how'. And we have seen that without both diversity and unity the relational experience is lost, while to combine these two aspects it has left to it no possible 'how' or way, except one which seems either certainly less or certainly more than what is relational.

(1924, *CE* p. 635; cf. 1893, *AR* p. 126)

The point here is the same as that concerning predication, merely substituting the unity of a relational fact for that of an object as what requires explanation. And once it is seen that externality makes explanation impossible, requiring an intolerable contingency between the related elements (1897, *AR* pp. 514 and 517), the complaint is the same: that the attempt to remove the contingency and truly understand the unity results in self-contradiction.[30]

The sceptical principle, marks II and III

At this stage, Bradley has sufficient to license the two stronger versions of his sceptical principle. The intermediate version is this:

*No argument can **prove** of something which is always experienced in combination with something else, that it is capable of existing uncombined.*

And the strong:

*It is **meaningless** to suppose of something which is always experienced in combination with something else, that it is capable of existing uncombined.*

But he does not manage to keep these clearly distinguished from each other, nor from the weak version which, at a prior stage of the development of his system, was the only one to which he was then entitled. Accordingly, we find the accounts of all the versions run together, and a tendency to move from the intermediate, what we might call an agnostic, version of the principle, to the strongest or atheist version in the same breath. So, for instance, in one place he starts with the intermediate version and moves directly to the strong:

If a thing is known to have a quality only under a certain condition, there is no process of reasoning from this which will justify the conclusion that the thing, if unconditioned, is yet the same. This seems quite certain; and, to go further, if we have no other source of information, if the quality in question is non-existent for us except in one relation, then for us to assert its reality away from that relation is more than unwarranted. It is, to speak plainly, an attempt in the end without meaning.

(1893, *AR* p. 13)

But just prior to this, as we can see by completing a passage quoted earlier only in part, he has already moved straight from the weak to the strong version:

For, if the qualities impart themselves never except under conditions, how in the end are we to say what they are when unconditioned? Having once begun, and having been compelled, to take their appearance into the account, we cannot afterwards strike it out. It being admitted that the qualities come to us always in a relation, and always as appearing, then certainly we know them only as appearances. And the mere supposition that in themselves they may really be what they are, *seems quite meaningless or self-destructive.*

(1893, *AR* p. 11, my emphasis)

Although, as we shall see, his failure to keep these versions of the principle strictly separate is fatal to his reasoning, they are justified in Bradley's view by the attack on external relations. For to suppose something separable from something else with which it always comes combined is to suppose that that relationship of combination is external, one which can be broken with indifference to its terms, as if they were held together by screws rather than by welds. This is because separability without damage implies the independence of the terms, that their being in a given relation is nothing logically to do with their natures. Abstraction, then, can now be seen not merely according to the weak version as a blind, unjustified leap; it is a definite destruction of its subject–matter, which always leads to philosophical (though still not necessarily to practical) error. And furthermore, these stronger versions of the principle provide another basis, alternative to the one outlined earlier (p. 27f), for the claim crucial to the demonstration of idealism: that reality is internally related to experience.

But now we see Bradley reject internal relations as well.

The attack on internal relations

That Bradley *in some sense* rejects internal relations is so clear from his published writings (for example 1909c, *ETR* pp. 238–9; 1924, *CE* pp. 641–6, 665, and 667–8) that it is initially puzzling that he still has a reputation for adhering to the 'Doctrine of Internal Relations', that is, the view that all relations are internal.[31] Given the dates of the material I have just cited, one possibility, which we shall consider in Chapter 6, is that in later life he moved away from an earlier adherence to some doctrine of internal relations. In any case, when it comes, the rejection is sharp and quick. The notion of an internal relation is one which depends on the distinction between internal and external relations. But this distinction is untenable, not because the attack on external relations has shown that all actual examples fall on one side of it, but because it depends in turn on the distinction between a term's original or intrinsic nature and the nature as qualified by the fresh external relation into which it has entered. But this means that the term must have two respects, and the original argument against predication showed that the attribution of two different qualities to a single thing leads to contradiction.

Curiously, Bradley does not consider the objection that if there are no external relations then the problem of relating their consequent relational qualities to the intrinsic qualities of the object just does not arise. Perhaps this is because the reply would be so obvious: that the problem of relating to each other different intrinsic relational qualities will pose precisely the same difficulty, one which as we have seen Bradley regarded as ineliminable.

Again, as is usual with the notions he rejects as inadequate for philosophical understanding, Bradley allows the external/internal distinction a limited value, for it corresponds to our useful distinction between accident and essence. But the place at which we draw this distinction is one determined by convenience and not by reason, and every relation is, he says, both internal and external; a philosophy which draws a hard distinction here is bound to go wrong. There are no absolutely essential natures.

At this point we see how Bradley's metaphysics reaches inexpressibility. What he rejects is tolerably clear; and in general terms we can go on to see what he embraces. But the detail will necessarily elude us. For the consequence of the demand for necessary connections between diverse things has been to deprive us of the means for expressing those connections, since this task requires predication and expressions for internal relations. Thus the intellect alone is incapable of achieving what would meet its own requirements; and Bradley was forced to resort to metaphor whenever it came to setting out what reality is like. But he himself saw this uninviting metaphysical conclusion coming, and well in advance: 'this ideal may itself be a thing beyond the compass of intellect, an attempt to think something to which thought is not equal, and which logic in part refuses to justify' (1883, *PL* pp. 489–90; cf. 1897, *AR* p. 508).

Nevertheless, the outlines of some of Bradley's most famous and characteristic doctrines should now be becoming apparent; and indeed his monism is only one step away. For, given that relativity necessarily infects everything it touches with contradiction, and that we can admit as real only what is not contradictory, it follows straight away that what is real must be, in one sense of the several that the word possesses, a substance. This move is described succinctly by Bradley himself:

From this I conclude that what is real must be self-contained and self-subsistent and not qualified from the outside. For an external qualification is a mere conjunction, and that, we have seen, is for the intellect an attempt of diversities simply to identify themselves, and such an attempt is what we mean by self-contradiction.

(1897, *AR* p. 509)

This doctrine appeared in his thought as early as 1883 (*PL*, pp. 188–9); but there, for once sticking to his stated aim of refraining from metaphysics in the attempt to confine himself to logic, he did not continue the argument to its inevitable conclusion.

To monism and idealism

The move to monism is now immediate, for a plurality of such substances with no relation between them is ruled out by their very diversity being itself a relation (1893, *AR* p. 25); while a plurality of internally related substances is logically impossible since their internal relations would undermine the independence that makes them substances (1893, *AR* pp. 124–5; 1922, *PL* pp. 696–7); and a plurality of genuinely independent substances would imply their being externally related and that is already proved self-contradictory (*AR*, pp. 125–6):[32]

> And, since diversities exist, they must therefore somehow be true and real; and since, to be understood and to be true and real, they must be united, hence they must be true and real in such a way that from *A* or *B* the intellect can pass to its further qualification without an external determination of either. But this means that *A* and *B* are united, each from its own nature, in a whole which is the nature of both alike. And hence it follows that in the end there is nothing real but a whole of this kind.
>
> (1897, *AR* p. 510)

And the very next sentence makes it clear that 'a whole' does not mean 'one amongst others'.

We have, then, reached the monism for which Bradley is famous: 'The universe is one in this sense that its differences exist harmoniously within one whole, beyond which there is nothing' (1893, *AR* p. 127). But this whole has the nature of its constituents (1897, *AR* p. 510), for their properties are not completely lost when we abandon predication and relations (1893, *AR* p. 114); and as a constituent of every (partial) whole is experience, Bradley concludes, following the ideal experiment described earlier (p. 27*f*), that reality as a whole is experiential:

> But to be utterly indivisible from feeling or perception, to be an integral element in a whole which is experienced, this surely is itself to be experience.
>
> (1893, *AR* p. 129)

So, finally, if rather obscurely, and via Bradley's version of monism, we have reached idealism;[33] not of course subjective idealism, for as Bradley sees (*ibid.*, p. 128) this would involve a relation between experience and its possessor, but absolute idealism, in which finite possessors of experience are regarded as mere appearance along with everything else familiar to us.

One might find my presentation of Bradley's derivation of idealism a bit quick. But Bradley himself is not much less summary. Commentators on this derivation (for example Wollheim 1959, pp. 201–3, 1969 pp. 197–200; Cresswell 1977, p. 183; Mander 1994 ch. 6; Montague 1964, pp. 158–62) have frequently attempted to recast Bradley's loose and discursive presentation into a more or less complex argument. This seems to me a mistake. In fact, the three pages (1893, *AR* pp. 127–9) Bradley devotes to the matter are stunningly insouciant, and while someone may yet eventually manage to read them in some way which reveals a carefully constructed argument, it is difficult to think of them as anything more than a casual gesture at establishing his point. This casualness has various sources. The most respectable is that Bradley is more inclined to rest his case on a 'best explanation' argument: by the end of *Appearance and Reality* the reader will have found that idealism 'is the one view which will harmonize all facts' (*ibid.*, p. 129). But another is that he was writing in a climate so damp with idealism that an earnest attempt at proof would have seemed as superfluous as trying to convince someone of the reality of water while they were being washed away in a flood.[34] No wonder that an 'ideal experiment' enables him to say at the outset that the truth of idealism 'seems evident at once' (*ibid.*, p. 127). We might also conjecture a third: the deleterious effect on philosophical writing of not having to teach the subject.

We have now seen how the principal tenets of his metaphysics are derived from the narrow basis of the performance of ideal experiments on reality as experienced with the goal of achieving satisfaction of the intellect. Perhaps this basis, and what is derived from it, is not always as crisply delineated by Bradley as one would wish. But precisification can be falsification: rather than sort out in detail the theoretically separable strands of his thought, I have tried here to understand *Bradley*, and thereby provide a perspective from which the details of the derivation can be evaluated without distortion. If we are to understand him, we should take seriously his claim to have started virtually from nothing in deriving his notorious conclusions.

Contingency, sufficient reason, and circularity

There is an obvious objection to that last claim, which should be considered before closing this chapter: that he is assuming what he needs to prove, that ultimate contingency is not a given fact about the world. If he is, his views rest, after all, on an assumption not merely grand but with insufficient independent plausibility, the Principle of Sufficient Reason. This was Russell's allegation,[35] and followers of Bradley have been content to acknowledge the Principle as 'the real and sole basis' of their claims,[36] even if Russell's own version of it was too idiosyncratic for them.

Bradley faced this objection from the side of ultimate contingency quite explicitly:

> To me such a doctrine is quite erroneous. For these ultimates
> (*a*) cannot make the world intelligible, and again (*b*) they are not
> given, and (*c*) in themselves they are self-contradictory, and not
> truth but appearance.
>
> (1897, *AR* p. 502)

What he seems both to need and to want to show is that the Principle of Sufficient Reason is not an assumption, nor even a methodological postulate, but something unavoidable. Would his three points above, if established, prove this? Point (*a*) is not going to worry an advocate of ultimate contingency like the Wittgenstein of the *Tractatus*, for he would probably himself be happy to deny that the world is intelligible in Bradley's sense of the word. So Bradley's defence must rest on the remaining two points.[37] I shall take (*c*) first.

The proof that things conjoined by bare contingency are self-contradictory, as we have seen (pp. 37–40), rests on the claim that in seeking to provide an account of the conjunction satisfactory to itself, the intellect, failing an account of the link between the things that is one of implications, seeks to identify the things with each other, which is self-contradictory. But this contradiction is derived purely from a claimed intellectual dissatisfaction with a bare, contingent, external conjunction; and this dissatisfaction itself can be rationalized only in terms of the conviction that the world cannot exhibit such conjunctions. Thus this defence of the Principle of Sufficient Reason rests upon that principle itself, and hence is useless.

One could try to respond to this charge of uselessness by arguing that conjunctions, as I said earlier (p. 33*f*), belong, for Bradley, essentially to the way language or thought presents things as being and not to the way they actually come in experience, and that, linked as things are in a manner which language cannot adequately represent, conjunctions cannot be treated merely as having links of the kind which language *can* represent. While this response may yet leave it open to an opponent of Bradley to insist that the links are nevertheless possibly contingent, it does seem to point to the fact that the real cornerstone of Bradley's objection is (*b*), the claim that ultimate contingencies are simply not given in experience; and so, presumably, there is no need to suppose, without proof, that they exist.

Let us assume, then, with Bradley, that in some sense this is true: in the sense that experience is a manifold, presenting diversity in unity of a kind to which linguistic representation cannot do justice. Now, employing the weak version of Bradley's sceptical principle, the only version he is entitled to, *prior to* accepting the very arguments (concerning predication and relations) which the advocate of contingency is challenging, we do not have sufficient to justify his claim that ultimate contingencies will not be unearthed, in science or philosophy, in attempting to account for the content of experience. For the justification of this claim, the stronger versions are needed – and indeed in considering (*b*) Bradley refers disparagingly to the abstraction that 'discovering' such ultimate contingency would require and which those versions prohibit – but what in turn justifies those versions is, as was just said, the very set of arguments which the believer in contingency is attacking.

So with the only justified – that is, virtually assumptionless – form of the sceptical principle, then, Bradley cannot rule out the possibility of the ultimate contingency of the way things are. And I think he half-sees this, as his hesitancy (1897, *AR* p. 503) on the subject suggests. In this way, then, Bradley eventually pays the price for, as we saw, failing to distinguish clearly the three versions of the sceptical principle which plays such a determining role in the production of his metaphysics.

There is, however, another passage (1906, *ETR* pp. 15–17) which could be interpreted as an attempt on Bradley's part to argue that we must, to think at all, reject the idea that ultimate contingency is possible. Philosophy demands, and in the end rests on, faith, he says: philosophical activity lacks sense unless it is assumed that its goal is attainable. He is talking of truth, but he has an ideal of completeness in mind, as we shall discover:

> Hence the only scepticism in philosophy which is rational must confine itself to the denial that truth so far and actually has been

reached. What is ordinarily called philosophical scepticism is on the other hand an uncritical and suicidal dogmatism.

(1906, *ETR* p. 17)

Perhaps, then, the Principle of Sufficient Reason is for him not so much a grand assumption on which his other views are based, as a rationalization of that restless spirit of enquiry which is the hallmark of all intellectual endeavour and which reaches its quintessence in metaphysics. Or it could be, perhaps, not a general and *a priori* demand of a metaphysic that it make the world intelligible in a special sense, but a summing-up of a series of individual judgments about particular intelligibilities and unintelligibilities.[38] Treating Bradley's use of the Principle in this way appears to offer a way of justifying his claim to have a metaphysics based solely on a method itself devoid of presupposition. But a price has to be paid for this, and the price is that he and a metaphysician of contingency now have nothing to say to each other in deciding upon the status of a putative example of ultimate contingency. As so often in metaphysics, the achievement of security against one's opponents leaves them equally invulnerable: this is, in effect, a reappearance of the circularity in argument which we were seeking, on Bradley's behalf, to avoid. But then it was, after all, Bradley himself who wrote the second as well as the first part of this famous sentence (1893, *AR* Preface p. x), 'Metaphysics is the finding of bad reasons for what we believe upon instinct, but to find these reasons is no less an instinct.' Subsequent philosophers, including Bradley's most effective critics, have been more optimistic about the possibility of finding good, even decisive, reasons in metaphysics.

3
Judgment

> 'When we say A judges that, etc., then we have to mention a
> whole proposition which A judges. It will not do either to
> mention only its constituents, or its constituents and form but
> not in the proper order.'
>
> —Wittgenstein (1913b), p. 96

Introduction

In the last chapter we found, and explored, a way into Bradley's
thought. The assumption on which undertaking that exploration was
based was that the probable reader would be either unfamiliar with
Bradley or likely to subscribe, in whole or in part, to some version of
the stereotypical picture of the Russell/Bradley contrast sketched in
Chapter 1 and which forms the focus of this book. The aim was to
ensure that consideration of the confrontation between them could
proceed from a familiarity with Bradley's views, not uncritical, but sufficiently sympathetic to open the possibility of considering, on an
informed basis, whether that picture is more caricature than portrait.

This chapter will be very different. First, it will focus principally upon
Russell. Secondly, I shall take for granted that understanding his
thought does not require a similar effort of imaginative sympathy as
understanding Bradley's. For the twentieth century belonged to Russell;
and his degree of intellectual remoteness is accordingly much less than
Bradley's. (Any reader unprepared to take my word for it should just
compare *The Problems of Philosophy*, still a good introduction to Russell's
thinking at the time it was written, with any of Bradley's books.)
Thirdly and in consequence, my main purpose will not be to provide
the kind of sketch-map for Russell as I did for Bradley. Such a bold

undertaking would, in any case, be more like trying to map a river whose course is constantly changing than the comparatively stable topography which Bradley represents. Instead, it will be to identify a little-recognized problem in the theories of judgment which Russell developed in the years 1903 to 1918, to examine its causes and effects, and to trace its connection with the tangle of arguments and allegations which constituted the Russell/Bradley dispute. The theory of judgment does not figure directly in the standard picture of that dispute. Nevertheless, it is central to gaining a better understanding than that picture provides: Bradley and Russell had rival accounts of the nature of judgment, accounts which are responsible for their more notorious rivalries (indeed, Bradley's reaction to the first of Russell's theories produced, directly, some of the best-known of the differences between them); and what might be termed Russell's chain reaction to his own first theory, while it has obscured the nature of those differences, also casts fresh light on those concerning the notion of truth.

It is of course a truism that a constant problem in understanding past intellectual disagreements is the loss of the notions, or the vocabulary, or both, in which those disagreements were characterized; and that problem arises here. The very title of this chapter is one that is rooted in the past, and even a sophisticated philosopher of the early twenty-first century recognizably working in the same area as Russell and Bradley is unlikely to think of himself as having a theory of judgment. And there is probably no single expression with which such a person could adequately capture what the writers of the early twentieth century had a theory *of*. Perhaps the best word in current philosophical usage is 'proposition'. But another good candidate is 'belief', in the sense of believing rather than of what is believed. Which of these is more appropriate is partly a matter of the nature of the theory, as we shall see. But perhaps the best way to think of a theory of judgment is as a theory of both beliefs and propositions: of what it is to judge, that is, to believe, that something is true, and of what it is that is judged true. For those who had a theory of judgment, as for those who currently work in the semantics of belief, these matters inevitably go together, and are sometimes confused.

An initial contrast between Bradley and Russell on judgment

In *The Principles of Logic* Bradley announces with great confidence a view of judgment which, however, over the course of the book, and especially in the transition from its first to its second edition, is eventually superseded by a final account. For our purposes, it does not matter what are the details of the transition and the eventual differences. What is important here is what is common to both versions. First, Bradley held that judgments are 'ideal', being constituted of idea, that is, of meaning in the sense of something belonging to thought and possessing intentionality. Secondly, although commentators stress correctly that Bradley, like Frege, was against psychologism in logic (see, for example, Bradley 1883, *PL* p. 7), his anti-psychologism did not take the form of assigning thoughts to a 'third realm', and it remains true that he held that judgments are in some sense psychological: despite admitting much later that he had initially overestimated the role of imagery in judgment, he still maintained that judgment belongs to thought and that 'every idea . . . has an aspect of psychical event' (Bradley 1922, p. 38n). Further, he thought that judgments were not stitched together from a gaggle of individual meanings: on the contrary, the unified judgment is the real entity, and the individual meanings are derived from it:

> We take an ideal content, a complex totality of qualities and relations, and we then introduce divisions and distinctions, and we call these products separate ideas with relations between them. And this is quite unobjectionable. But what is objectionable is our then proceeding to deny that the whole before our mind is a single idea; and it involves a serious error in principle. The relations between the ideas are themselves ideal. They are not the psychical relations of mental facts. They do not exist between the symbols, but hold in the symbolized. They are part of the meaning and not of the existence. And the whole in which they subsist is ideal, and so one idea.
>
> (Bradley 1883, p. 11)

(The otherwise mysterious reference to 'qualities and relations' in this passage can be decoded through his remark on the next page that, 'In this ideal content there are groups and joinings of qualities and relations, such as answer to nouns and verbs and prepositions.') In other words, it is as though he thought of a judgment as like a continuous piece of wood; the numerous adjacent small cubes into which it can in principle be decomposed are not things from which it has been assembled, although one can for some limited purposes (for example, calculating its volume or mass) treat it as if it were a collection of such fragments. He subscribed, that is, to a version of what subsequent philosophers have called meaning-holism; and this he never retracted. The matter with which he is dealing is one raised also by Frege, who famously argues that

> . . . not all the parts of a thought can be complete; at least one must be 'unsaturated', or predicative; otherwise they would not hold together.
>
> (Frege 1892, p. 54)

Roughly speaking, Frege's idea is that the two words expressing the thought that Raleigh smoked introduce two things of very different sorts, namely the object Raleigh, which is complete or saturated, and a concept whose unsaturated nature is revealed by the fact that the proper expression for it is not 'smoked' but '. . . smoked', that is, something needing completion. Frege's own view is thus less extreme than Bradley's, since he held that some parts of thoughts are saturated; if he had expressed himself in Fregean terminology, Bradley would have said that all the constituents of judgments are unsaturated, the word 'Raleigh' no more introducing an independently real object than does '. . . smoked'.

Russell, on the other hand, considered the constituents of judgments to be entities in their own right: not aspects of a prior whole, but real parts. Each of the three words expressing the judgment that Goebbels admired Hitler serves to introduce a separate element of reality with equal ontological status, namely, the man Goebbels, the relation of admiration (a universal), and the man Hitler. For Russell, a judgment is not like a single piece of wood, whose individual pieces are notional rather than real; rather, it is like a model assembled from pieces existing in their own right, all of which are in Frege's terms 'saturated'. His best-known view of this sort was often just called without qualification 'Russell's theory of judgment' (for example, Geach 1957, p. 45). It is better termed – and now usually is – the multiple relation theory of judgment, since it had a very different, and historically very important, predecessor. But even this fuller title conceals significant and revealing complications and variants. For this reason, I shall refer to Russell's theories of judgment by the dates of their appearance, from 1903 to 1918.

As I said at the outset, my main purpose in this chapter is to examine a little-recognized problem in the theories of judgment which Russell developed in those years. It is a problem which, sometimes in a rather subterranean fashion, was partly responsible for the rapid succession of those theories. I shall argue that both Bradley and Wittgenstein were fully alive to it, and that while for Russell the problem was in principle unsolvable, the other two philosophers could handle it in related, though different, ways. I shall not be trying to argue that either Bradley or Wittgenstein had a correct theory of judgment, nor even that their theories did not face other serious difficulties. I shall be trying to argue that their views differ materially from Russell's in this respect: they don't fall at this particular early hurdle, that is, they have at least a way of dealing with this problem which is not, to the unbiased eye, obviously hopeless at the outset. On Bradley's holistic view, the problem is prevented from arising at all. Within Wittgenstein's atomism, the problem is dissolved. But both philosophers dispose of it by rejecting a key Russellian assumption concerning relations. For the moment, however, it will be enough to see how the problem arises, to trace the common thread among Russell's various unsuccessful attempts to solve it, and to see how it – and the contrasting views of Bradley and Wittgenstein – is connected with the long-running arguments over relations. These connections will surface at various points in later chapters too.

Russell's 1903 binary relation theory of judgment

The principal purpose of *The Principles of Mathematics* is revealed in its title. Although it was subsequently overshadowed by *Principia Mathematica* so that it was often neglected until comparatively recently, its merits were not overlooked by Karl Popper, who assessed it thus:

> The achievement of the book is without parallel. Russell rediscovered Frege's logic and theory of numbers, and he laid the foundation of arithmetic and analysis. He gave the first clear and simple definition of real numbers on this basis (an improvement on Cantor, Dedekind and Peano). And he not only gave a theory of geometry but a new approach to mechanics . . . He had been the first to give a satisfactory theory of irrational numbers, a problem which had agitated mankind for 2,400 years. And he had given a really brilliant solution of the ancient problem of motion.
>
> (Magee 1971, pp. 143–5)

It was perhaps the understandable focus on these kinds of issues that made some of the treatment of more purely philosophical matters rather hasty. For example, Russell's account of judgment in that book is the merest sketch. Judgment is a single primitive binary relation between two entities, a judging mind and a proposition. But the sketch is pregnant with consequences. A proposition does not consist of words; 'it contains the entities indicated by words' (Russell 1903, §51; all subsequent references in this section will be to this work unless otherwise stated). These Russell called 'terms', and they include, for example, men, chimaeras, numbers and relations (§47). This gives Russell a very striking account of the nature of propositions: they are not linguistic, and their constituents include quite everyday objects. From now on, I shall call this *the doctrine of real propositional constituents*. The motivation for Russell's adopting this unusual view comes out most dramatically in his correspondence with Frege. Frege, arguing that 'the word "true" is not a predicate like "green"', had said in a letter of November 1904, 'Truth is not a component part of a thought, just as Mont Blanc with its snowfields is not itself a component part of the thought that Mont Blanc is more than 4000 metres high.' Russell ignored the point about truth and took up the example to attack Frege's sense/meaning distinction, saying,

> I believe that in spite of all its snowfields Mont Blanc itself is a component part of what is actually asserted in the proposition [*Satz*] 'Mont Blanc is more than 4000 metres high'. We do not assert the thought [*Gedanke*], for this is a private psychological matter: we assert the object of the thought, and this is, to my mind, a certain complex (an objective proposition, one might say) in which Mont Blanc is itself a component part. If we do not admit this, then we get the conclusion that we know nothing at all about Mont Blanc [itself].
>   (Russell wrote this in German. The final word was left out of the standard English translation, Russell 1904b)[1]

Ignore the cross-purposes about thoughts. The crucial claim in this passage is the last one. It is one of those Russellian ideas which appear explicitly only infrequently, but are nevertheless a constant presence, shaping the direction of the reasoning. The idea helps explain the occurrence of some of the odder features in the early sections of *The Principles of Mathematics*. And – given that Russell's primary interest was in propositions rather than the Alps – it makes it unmistakably clear that the motivation behind his unusual account of the nature of the proposition is epistemological. No doubt he was imposing a subjectivist and idealist interpretation on Frege which Frege himself would surely have rejected. Still, justified or not, his worry seems to be that if our propositions consist of senses rather than of the actual things we are talking about, then there will be an impenetrable barrier to knowledge of those things.

We can discern the same train of thought at work several years later:

> But in this view [that 'judgments consist of ideas'] ideas become a veil between us and outside things – we never really, in knowledge, attain to the things we are supposed to be knowing about, but only to the ideas of those things.
>
> (Russell 1911, *CP6* p. 155)[2]

Russell's reaction, evident as early as 1903, is to insist that the very objects about which we speak actually compose our thoughts. And the existence of a proposition does not depend on anyone's formulating it – they are all out there waiting for us.

'Every term', he says, '. . . is a logical subject . . . possessed of all the properties commonly assigned to substances' (§47). This idea that everything is at bottom an object, and of the same sort, is, Russell thinks, unavoidable: the attempt to deny it leads to self-contradiction (§49). His explanation of the contradiction is unclear, but it looks to be a version of Frege's notorious problem concerning the concept *horse* (Frege 1892, p. 45), namely that if one regards the proposition as composed of both saturated and unsaturated elements (in Frege's vocabulary, of objects and concepts), then it is impossible to talk about the unsaturated ones, for as soon as one puts the unsaturated, predicative, element into subject position in order to say something about it, then it becomes something else, something saturated. Thus the concept *horse*, as it occurs in, say, 'The concept *horse* is unsaturated', is not a concept but an object (whereas it is a concept as it occurs in, say, 'Phar Lap was a famous horse'). This not only makes it impossible to talk about concepts, but certainly looks inconsistent. Had Russell used Fregean terminology, then, as we just observed, he would have held the constituents of propositions to be, all of them, saturated.

Why did Russell think that propositions, as well as being composed of entities, are themselves entities? Because he held that they were unities (§54), and he subscribed to the principle *ens et unum convertuntur* (§47; the commitment is repeated in a 1910 letter to Bradley quoted in *CP6* p. 350). What makes a proposition a unity? His answer is that its constituents are related by the proposition's verb: 'the true logical verb in a proposition may be always regarded as asserting a relation' (§53).[3] That is, in 1903 Russell openly commits himself to the view that every proposition asserts the holding of a relation. (That this is so, and that Bradley took great pains in reading and commenting on *The Principles of Mathematics*, are facts which must be borne in mind in keeping track of the Russell/Bradley dispute.) Moreover, the verb, Russell says, 'when used as a verb, embodies the unity of the proposition' (§54).[4]

What, then, is the unity of the proposition? It is what distinguishes a proposition from a list of its constituents, so that unlike a mere list it 'holds together' and says something.[5] It is clear that, for example, the sentence 'Desdemona loves Cassio' has a unity which the string of words, 'Desdemona', 'loves' and 'Cassio', does not. The former, unlike the latter, expresses a proposition. For Russell, this is a given. But this seemingly undeniable unity, when combined with Russell's principle that 'Every constituent of every proposition must, on pain of self-contradiction, be capable of being made a logical subject' (§52), generates a particularly vicious version of the problem of unity, one which makes the question of how unity is achieved apparently unanswerable. On pain of contradiction, the verb must itself be a term, something capable of appearing as a logical subject; in Frege's parlance, as we saw, saturated. But it must be a very unusual kind of term, for it must simultaneously be the source of the proposition's unity, relating all its constituents while itself being one of the related items (that is, unsaturated too). That is, the verb is unlike other terms in that it has, he says, a 'twofold nature . . . as actual verb and verbal noun, [which] may be expressed . . . as the difference between a relation in itself and a relation actually relating' (§54). Yet as soon as we make the verb a logical subject, we are forced to identify it as 'a relation in itself' rather than as 'a relation actually relating', destroying the unity of the original proposition in which it was the source of that unity. He illustrates the point like this (§54):

> Consider, for example, the proposition '*A* differs from *B*.' The constituents of this proposition, if we analyze it, appear to be only *A*, difference, *B*. Yet these constituents, thus placed side by side, do not reconstitute the proposition. The difference which occurs in the proposition actually relates *A* and *B*, whereas the difference after analysis is a notion which has no connection with *A* and *B* . . . A proposition, in fact, is essentially a unity, and when analysis has destroyed the unity, no enumeration of constituents will restore the proposition. The verb, when used as a verb, embodies the unity of

the proposition, and is thus distinguishable from the verb considered as a term, though I do not know how to give a clear account of the precise nature of the distinction.

Russell's problem, then, is that while he cannot deny propositional unity, he can find no account of the proposition which can do justice to it. Perhaps anxious to get on with mathematical matters, he left the matter unresolved. Opinions differ over how serious his problem is.[6] But a related difficulty is certainly serious: whether true or false, a proposition is a unity, hence an entity. In fact it is a complex entity whose constituents are the things it is about, which makes it hard to see how it can differ from what in Russell's later vocabulary would be called a fact.[7] The difficulty, in thin disguise, is just the perennial conundrum: how is false judgment possible? But the source of the difficulty is new: it is the combination of Russell's attachment both to the unity of the proposition and to the idea that propositional constituents are the things the proposition is about. This makes it hard for him to give a sensible account of truth, and the correspondence theory, despite the stereotype, is noticeably absent from *The Principles of Mathematics*. Rather, he says merely that truth is an unanalysable property: true propositions just have it, false ones just lack it (§52). I shall follow Ernest Sosa (1993) in calling this view 'primitivism'. The world, then, contains both objective falsehoods and objective truths: 'objective', here, meaning that they are entities in no sense mind-dependent.

Bradley missed this second, related, difficulty. But he did not miss the one Russell announced, concerning what are in effect inconsistent demands of relations, as we can see in this extract from his critique of *The Principles of Mathematics*:

> Mr. Russell's main position has remained to myself incomprehensible. On the one side I am led to think that he defends a strict pluralism, for which nothing is admissible beyond simple terms and external relations. On the other side Mr. Russell seems to assert emphatically, and to use throughout, ideas which such a pluralism surely must repudiate. He throughout stands upon unities which are complex and which cannot be analysed into terms and relations. These two positions to my mind are irreconcilable, since the second, as I understand it, contradicts the first flatly. If there are such unities, and, still more, if such unities are fundamental, then pluralism surely is in principle abandoned as false.
>
> (Bradley 1910b, p. 281)

And Bradley thought this difficulty was indeed serious. So serious, in fact, that, whereas Russell after some prevarication put it on one side so that he could get on with more important things, for Bradley the unity of the proposition formed the basis of an overwhelming objection by *reductio* to the idea that a relation could be thought of in Russell's way, as another constituent of propositions and capable of appearing as logical subject. (The passage also shows Bradley asserting that the unity threatens pluralism in general. As we shall see in Chapter 6, this is an exaggeration.) This idea, in Bradley's rather than Russell's language, is the idea that relations are real; we noted in the previous chapter (p. 26f) that it is the focus of much of his critical attention right up to his death in 1924.[8] We shall see in Chapter 6 (p. 155f) that, as Bradley understood externality, any relation that is independently real is *ipso facto* external. Thus in Bradley's mind Russell's attachment to the idea that any relation is a logical constituent of a proposition which could in principle appear as subject term commits him to the view that all relations are external, an extreme doctrine which sometimes (and otherwise inexplicably, since no one ever openly avows it, appears as the focus of a Bradleian attack). The idea that relations are real is central to Russell's conception of logic at this period, so that, as Graham Stevens (2003) has shown, Bradley's allegation that Russell cannot account for the unity of the proposition threatens that conception and its attendant programme of logical analysis. It is this idea which enables Russell to maintain the doctine of the unrestricted variable, that is, the claim that any entity whatsoever may be a value of a free variable. And this claim in turn is meant to underpin the universality of logic as the sole science whose subject matter is everything. We shall examine the question of the reality of relations in Chapter 6. But in this chapter, and again in the next, we shall pursue the second and less prominent difficulty, since it has an important, though indirect, connection with the stereotype and casts fresh light upon the Russell side of it.

The origins of the multiple relation theory of judgment

When Russell announced his conversion to his new multiple relation theory of judgment (Russell 1910), he did so against the background of its 1903 predecessor (though he does not mention *The Principles of Mathematics* and appears to attribute the earlier theory, rightly or wrongly, to Meinong). But the 1903 theory's commitment to the existence of objective falsehoods, which had been clear to him all along, is now presented as his principal reason for rejecting it. He now finds it impossible to believe in the existence of these objective falsehoods, and can no longer bring himself to maintain that although Charles I died on the scaffold, and Bishop Stubbs died in suitably respectable fashion, nevertheless the world contains such things as *that Charles I died in his bed* and *that Bishop Stubbs was hanged for murder*. And he holds this incredibility of objective falsehoods to provide sufficient reason for not believing in the existence of their counterparts in the case of truths.

Interestingly enough, he contemplates the possibility of an asymmetric theory in which true propositions are complex objects but false ones are not. But he immediately rejects this; not on the grounds that false propositions would disintegrate altogether, but rather because there would then be an intrinsic difference between true and false propositions which would be visible on inspection. This, he says, is obviously impossible: and indeed it is obvious that we cannot in general tell truths from falsehoods by sheer inspection. But Russell forgets the radical nature of the 1903 theory here, and helps himself to the common sense which it appears to preclude, for on that theory he is not entitled to the obviousness of the impossibility: the constituents of judgments are real things, and actually related in the way the judgment claims. Hence inspecting the proposition cannot be distinguished from inspecting the world, and inspecting the world is just how we should go about distinguishing truths from falsehoods. (This looks like an instance of a common phenomenon, observable in both philosophy and psychology: helping oneself to the data and treating them as part of the theory so that the theory can gain a spurious plausibility by its being surreptitiously self-authenticating. The usual source of this error is the employment of the same expression, for example, 'proposition' or 'mental image' to designate both *explanandum* and *explanans*. More recent philosophers can also plead the malign influence of the idea that theories should be closed under implication.) Lacking the possibility of a retreat to his primitivist theory of truth (which of course he is now arguing against), and only dubiously entitled to the idea that propositions may be inspected introspectively or by the study of sentences (only dubiously, because he holds their constituents to be real things, not representatives of them, and because by 1910 he has moved some distance from his 1903 idea that logic is usually reflected in English grammar[9]), Russell has got himself into a position where it might reasonably be said that only if false propositions were not there to be found would the difference between them and the true ones be visible on inspection. And only if one thought this an introspectively determinable matter should one find it cause for alarm. These considerations suggest that Russell should have considered the possibility of there being false sentences without false propositions (in his 1903 sense of 'proposition'). His (largely post-1903) idea that logical form may not be reflected in surface grammar – a matter to which we shall return – is suggestive of this possibility. But his insistence on a univocal account of meaning closes it off, for it clearly requires some distinction like Frege's within the realm of meaning that can account for the intelligibility of falsehoods. Russell's other commitments, then, are pushing him relentlessly into conflict with the unity of the proposition which at the same time he finds undeniable. What he seeks is a theory which will do enough justice to that unity to save the appearances while allowing him to avoid the need to admit objective falsehoods.

With the multiple relation theory, Russell abandons the binary relation which, in the 1903 theory, holds between one object, a mind, and one other, a proposition. In its place, he puts a set, a multiplicity, of relations between the mind, on the one hand, and what in the earlier theory he would have called the constituents of the proposition, taken severally. In the new theory, there are no propositions, at least none in the extreme realist sense of 1903. (In some of his writing over the period of his holding the multiple relation theory, Russell occasionally refers to propositions, but it is usually clear in context that he is now thinking of these as linguistic entities, as sentences of a certain sort.) It follows that there is no propositional unity. Russell attempts to do justice to his pre-theoretical recognition of unity by holding that all needed unity is provided by the mind in the act of judging.

However, there is more to the introduction of the multiple relation theory than meets the eye.[10] We have just seen that his official introduction of the multiple relation theory in 1910 offers it to us as a solution of some puzzles about truth and falsehood, and there is no indication of any connection with wider concerns. But one thing we should never forget when reading Russell's early twentieth-century work is the discovery of the paradox which threatened to bring down the entire logicist project, and his obsessive concern for a resolution of it. His attempts at resolution, as we all know, involved various forms of the theory of types. In 1908 he published the first version of the ramified theory (Russell 1908). This postulated two hierarchies, one of types and one of orders. At one point he remarks that 'Functions of various orders may be obtained from propositions of various orders by the method of *substitution'* (p. 77). This is an allusion to his substitutional theory of classes and relations, on which he had worked for the preceding two or three years, but which did not come to general notice until the 1970s. Now this theory requires an ontology of propositions on which the substitutions are performed. If one thinks of propositions as linguistic entities, the idea of dividing them into orders is not especially disturbing. But, as we have seen, Russell had an extreme realist account of the nature of propositions. And this was combined with something else we have remarked: that, unlike Frege's, his ontology was fundamentally simple – at bottom, everything is a *term* and can figure as a logical subject in propositions without restriction. Now he is disturbing this simplicity, dividing non-linguistic entities into fundamentally different kinds which somehow constrain how they can be put together and thereby what it makes sense to say, and moreover creating actual infinities of these kinds. Driven solely by the need to avoid the paradoxes, Russell looked like committing himself to what Nicholas Griffin called 'the most baroque ontology ever devised by the philosophical imagination' (Griffin 1985, p. 217).

But it was not long before he seemed to have found a way out. The multiple relation theory of judgment offered a way of doing without propositions as entities, and the hierarchy of orders needed by the ramified theory of types could be provided by a hierarchy of meanings of the words 'true' and 'false'. Section III of Chapter II of the Introduction to the 1910 first edition of *Principia Mathematica* is headed 'Definition and Systematic Ambiguity of Truth and Falsehood'. In it Russell claims that 'the words "true" and "false" have many different meanings, according to the kind of proposition to which they are applied'. This is 'not difficult to see', he says, and demonstrates this by explaining the distinction between the simple cases of first truth and second truth, where second truth is, roughly speaking, truth about first truth. He goes on to apply the idea to truth-functions, effectively giving a recursive definition of truth in terms of the correspondence relation between atomic judgments and facts. The whole is then briefly, but crucially, embedded in the multiple relation theory of judgment, so that propositions-as-entities are abandoned, without the loss of the hierarchy needed to exclude the paradoxes. He retains his extreme realism about propositional constituents, but now they are constituents of propositional acts. The multiple relation theory had become vital to Russell's endeavour to preserve the logicist programme from the effect of the paradoxes.

The 1910 version[11]

Russell's rejection of his 1903 theory of judgment has two notable consequences. One is that its associated primitivist theory of truth is likewise rejected in favour of a correspondence theory in which a fact, to which a true judgment corresponds, is supposed to be something quite different from that judgment itself. The other is that he no longer treats judgment as a binary relation between the judging mind and a single entity, the proposition, but rather as 'a multiple relation of the mind to the various other terms with which the judgment is concerned' (Russell 1910: *CP6*, p. 122; *PE*, p. 155). Propositions, in the 1903 sense, have disappeared from the scene altogether. These consequences are significant: they introduce an element of psychologism into Russell's previously resolutely anti-psychologistic views. For example, in the 1903 theory, the psychological act of judging could be said to have a truth-value only derivatively, with the primary truth-bearer being the object of this act, the proposition. In the multiple relation theory, in contrast, the act itself is the primary truth-bearer. This, as we shall see, turns out to have consequences for Russell's logic.

The full account of the 1910 theory, together with its version of the correspondence theory of truth, can be summarized as follows (using some of Russell's own words). When we judge that, say, A loves B, we have not a two-place relation between the mind and the whole proposition as a unit but a multiple relation between the mind and the individual constituents of the proposition, so that there is 'before the mind', separately, the person A, the person B, and the relation of loving. The judgment is true when there is a corresponding complex object, A's loving B, and false when there is not. We may notice here that the idea that all the constituents of a proposition are saturated, that is, independent and substantial, thus survives the replacement of the 1903 theory, and indeed is essential to the 1910 theory in a way that it is not to its predecessor. For whereas the binary relation theory required only the reality of the unified proposition (it was other considerations, that is, an awareness of the Fregean problem with unsaturated constituents which imposed on Russell the view that these constituents had to be as substantial as the proposition they composed), the multiple relation theory requires in its own right the reality of the constituents as independent objects of acquaintance. The 1910 version of the theory has, too, a further feature: Russell stipulates that these constituents must be before the mind in such a way that the relation is not present 'abstractly' but 'as proceeding from A to B'.

Thus in the 1910 theory the existence in the world of objective falsehoods is – apparently – avoided by sacrificing propositions: the unity
of the proposition is consequently sacrificed too in favour of the unity
of what one might call the propositional act which brings together in
thought things which may not be so related in the world.[12] In other
words, the unity is imposed by the mind. But these sacrifices are
illusory.

To see this, consider the exposition of the theory. If all it means is
merely that we can think that *A* loves *B*, and that it is really *A* and *B*
and loving and not some representational substitutes that we are
thinking about, then of course it is true; but then this is what the
theory is supposed to be explaining. If, however, it is meant to be an
account of how we can think that *A* loves *B*, it collapses judgment and
judged fact. Let me explain what I mean.

On Russell's 1903 view of the constituents of propositions, the difficulty about judgment was that the unity of the proposition requires
that either the world contain peculiar entities – so-called 'objective
falsehoods' – such as *that Charles I died in his bed*, or false judgment is
impossible. The 1903 theory opts for the first horn of this dilemma.
Russell held it to be a virtue of the 1910 theory, which retained this
realistic view of constituents but as constituents of propositional acts
rather than of the 1903 propositions, that it avoids both: 'We therefore
escape the necessity of admitting objective falsehoods, or of admitting
that in judging falsely we have nothing before the mind' (*ibid*.: *CP6*
p. 120; *PE* p. 153); and, reinforcing the latter point, 'the possibility of
false judgments is fully allowed for' (*ibid*.: *CP6* p. 122; *PE* p. 155).
I think it is fair to say that although critics from Wittgenstein onwards
have rejected the theory, this last claim has been allowed to stand: the
impression has been that if the theory worked, it would account for
false judgment. But is this impression correct? And, if not, why not?

In expounding the 1910 theory, Russell recognizes one of the shortcomings of the 1903 theory to which we have already drawn attention:
that it could give no account of how relations, which figure in all
propositions, manage to combine the roles of being propositional constituents and of being the sources of propositional unity. He tries to
overcome this problem in the 1910 theory by insisting that there is no
propositional unity: one of the inconsistent roles disappears in favour
of the unity of the propositional act, a unity provided by the different
relation of judging, leaving the other to be filled without difficulty.
But then he remembers that he must also account for the 'sense' or
'direction' of non-symmetrical relational judgments, that is, of the

distinction between '*A* loves *B*' and '*B* loves *A*', two different unities with the same terms. ('Sense' is Russell's own choice of expression. I shall generally use the more natural 'direction'.) He tries to manage this by his already-noted specification that 'the relation must not be abstractly before the mind, but must be before it as proceeding from *A* to *B* rather than from *B* to *A*' (*ibid.*: *CP6* p. 123; *PE* p. 158). This is clearly a repetition of the requirement that, after all, the relation must be more than just another constituent, though so far it looks as if we have no more than a re-statement of the problem masquerading as a solution of it. And in this explanation of what 'not being abstractly before the mind' means, a commitment to the propositional unity he has been denying re-emerges in a compound with his solution to the problem of accounting for the direction of a non-symmetrical relation.[13] It is at least clear that both present genuine requirements: unity is needed for the relation to provide a judgment, as opposed to a mere list, so that we can distinguish the mind's mere simultaneous acquaintance with *A* and love and *B* on the one hand from, on the other, any judgment at all involving these; direction is needed for the relation to distinguish the judgment that *A* loves *B* from the judgment that *B* loves *A*. It is unsurprising that Russell did not consistently keep the two requirements separate: anything that enables the direction requirement to be met would normally enable the meeting of the unity requirement as well. (Though not the other way about, as Russell realized in 1913.) It is also unsurprising that the 1910 theory should get into trouble. It effectively separates unity from direction, attributing the former to the propositional act, unified by the relating relation of judgment, and the latter to the judged material, the order of whose constituents is determined by the sense of the related relation; but then it explains direction in a way which involves unity. The two requirements must indeed be simultaneously satisfied, but without being confused with one another.

Can the confusion be sorted out? Because of this compounding of two different (albeit connected) problems, there are two ways in which we might interpret the theory's requirement that the relation not be present 'abstractly'. We might think (and some of Russell's own words might encourage us in this) that it should be understood as meaning merely that the relation's direction must figure in the judgment. This would allow us to express the different directions involved in non-symmetrical (and asymmetrical) relations, so that the theory can distinguish the judgment that *A* loves *B* from the judgment that *B* loves *A*. But if this is all that is meant, the 1910 theory remains vulnerable to one of Bradley's criticisms of *The Principles of Mathematics*, that it lacks the resources to account for the unity of the proposition: all we get is two ordered lists, *A*, love, and *B*, on the one hand, and *B*, love, and *A* on the other, plus the idea that these orderings are somehow significant. (This significance cannot consist in the different orderings' being themselves further constituents, because this would generate a vicious infinite regress of propositional constituents.) Even if we respond to this by saying that the theory shows propositional unity to be unnecessary, with the unity of the propositional act being a perfectly adequate substitute, there is still no account of the unity of the act: the theory cannot account for the distinction between an ordered list and a judgment except by attributing the ability to form both and distinguish them from each other to an otherwise mysterious power of the mind.

In the face of this objection, we might take the requirement that the relation not be present 'abstractly' to mean, not that the relation's direction must figure in the judgment, but that the relation is to really relate *A* and *B* and thus supply unity to the proposition judged, a unity additional to that of the propositional act. On this interpretation, the actual objects are before the mind in their actual relation, with that relation actually relating them. This, one supposes (as Russell himself seems to have supposed), would have to include the direction as well for there to be unity: that is, the imposition of unity automatically imposes direction. (Unity without direction would result in the creation of a logical monster: a unified proposition – with Russellian constituents, not some mere symbolic construct – that remained ambiguous between '*A* loves *B*' and '*B* loves *A*'. But Russellian propositions, unlike sentences of natural languages, cannot be ambiguous.) Yet if that is so, the combination involved in the judging cannot after all differ from the actual fact which is being judged to obtain.

Perhaps all this means is merely that, when the judgment is true, judgment and judged fact coalesce, the former absorbing the latter as a proper part. The point may be illustrated by the use of a 'map' of the complex corresponding to a sample binary judgment made by a mind or subject *S* (see Figure 3.1).

The justification of using this diagrammatic representation to depict Russell's view is that it is derived from the one which, as we shall see, he himself used to illustrate the application of his 1913 version of the multiple relation theory (and helps to bring out vividly both the differences and similarities of the two versions). The map represents the mind's relationships of acquaintance with the three constituents of the

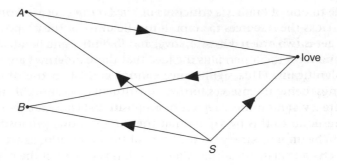

Figure 3.1

judgment that *A* loves *B* by means of the three arrows leading from *S* to the other nodes of the diagram. It represents the direction of the judgment (which cannot be captured by the three arrows just mentioned) by means of two further arrows, which lead from *A* to love to *B*. It is immediately apparent from the map that the larger fact of the judgment illegitimately includes the judged fact '*A* loves *B*' as an existing unity (look at the lines, which are essential for the map to incorporate the expression of unity, and at the arrows, which are essential for it to express direction too) and cannot be formally distinguished, within the resources of the 1910 theory, from a case where the larger fact, in Russell's view, really does include the smaller as a proper part, as when *S* perceives *A*'s loving B.[14]

It might not yet be clear that this consequence is damaging: what is wrong with the idea that the combination involved in the judging cannot differ from the actual fact which is being judged to obtain? Isn't this just what Russell wanted? But in fact the results are catastrophic. There are two versions of the catastrophe, depending on our starting point.

We might begin from the position that a false proposition can be erroneously judged to be true. This has the consequence that the old dilemma reappears but with a different outcome: where the 1903 theory required the existence of objective falsehoods, the 1910 theory makes, despite Russell's claims to the contrary, false judgment impossible. Not, though, because it makes false judgments disintegrate, but because any coherent judgment at all will make itself true in the act of formulation. The theory seems committed to attributing a kind of psychokinetic power to the mind, in that simply by judging, rightly or wrongly, that *A* loves *B* I bring *A* and *B* into the relation of love. If I fail to do this, then I fail to achieve the unified proposition without which there can be no judgment. So false judgment is impossible, because any judging creates the fact that makes the judgment true. (Indeed, the difficulty is still more fundamental than this. Mere formulation of a proposition suffices to pose the problem: propositional unity is required for understanding just as it is for judgment, as Russell realized in 1913. Thus even formulating a proposition, let alone judging it true, will create the fact which makes it true.)

The other possible starting point is the recognition that psychokinesis is impossible, that we cannot – of course – bring objects into a non-mental relation with each other merely by taking thought. But this, in combination with the 1910 theory of judgment, restricts our judgmental capacity to the passive recognition of truths; again, false judgment turns out to be impossible, though for a different reason: that false judgments resist formulation.

Russell clearly would not have owned to attributing psychokinetic powers to the mind; yet in 1910 he thought the mind to have the capacity to bring objects into a non-mental relation with each other in the propositional act, in such a way as to meet the requirement of the unity of the proposition. But this had to be accomplished without the creation of the judged fact. It is as if he was committed not only to a psychokinetic power, but one counterbalanced by what one might call a psychoinertial power. For the mind, in judging that, say, *A* loves *B*, is supposed to be able to bring the real things *A* and *B* and love, not just mental or linguistic proxies, into the appropriate relation without actually making *A* love *B*. These powers are not only magical but mutually inconsistent.

The 1912 version

It is not always noticed that the theory of judgment presented in *The Problems of Philosophy* (1912) is different from the 1910 theory. The 1912 theory is only a modification of its predecessor, but the modification is significant. It arose in response to criticisms, related to those I made in the previous section, which Russell received from G.F. Stout. Russell wrote in reply:

> As regards the sense of R in judging aRb, you make a point, which had already occurred to me, but is met by a slight re-wording of the account of sense in judgement, & this re-wording is in any case necessary to my theory. There must never, so I now perceive, be any

relation having sense in a complex except the relating relation of that complex; hence in the act of judging, the sense must be confined to the judging, & must not appear in the R. But, judging being a multiple relation, its sense is not merely twofold like that of a dual relation, & the judging alone may arrange our terms in the order 'Mind, a, R, b' as opposed to 'Mind, b, R, a'. This has the same effect as if R had a sense in the judgment, & gives all one wants without being obnoxious to your objections.

(Original MS; rewritten by Stout in his 1911, p. 350)[15]

Russell refers to the change as 'a slight re-wording', but it is clear that it is far more. In the 1910 theory, Russell had tried (but, as we saw, failed) to separate unity and direction ('sense'), transferring the former from the judged relation (that is, the relation belonging to what was judged) to the propositional act but leaving the latter where it was. But he soon noticed the difficulties this attempt created: how could a relation have direction without relating and thereby imposing unity? And he dealt with it in the 1912 multiple relation theory by re-uniting direction and unity, transferring direction also to the propositional act so that 'sense' belonged to the relation of judging rather than to the judged relation. The sole relating relation, in the 1912 theory, is that of judging.

Russell's satisfaction with the 1912 theory did not last long, as we shall see. But was it an improvement on the 1910 theory? And, in particular, did it meet the difficulties we have identified here?

The theory works like this. When I judge that *A* loves *B*, the relation love appears purely as a relation in itself – a related relation, one might say, that is, an independent or saturated item — not as a relating one. What then makes this into a judgment? Suppose my mind leaps from *A* to love to *B*, or groups them in that order: this is not a judgment that *A* loves *B*. It will not be a judgment unless love is allowed to appear as a relating, or unsaturated, relation itself.[16] And once that is allowed, all the old difficulties of the 1910 theory re-emerge. The sole alternative to allowing the appearance of love as a relating relation is to specify that the relation *judgment* is special: in this context, it is the sole relation which combines its *relata* into a judgment, rather than a mere collection, even an ordered collection. No doubt this is correct. But it is an idea which we criticized in the previous section as appealing to 'an otherwise mysterious power of the mind', with the relation of judgment taking the place of the mind. In other words, it is not a theory of judgment at all: it merely imposes a new jargon on the expression of what we knew already. Geach, and earlier, Ramsey, may have seen this for themselves.[17] Though Ramsey was talking about the 1910 version, his verdict still applies here:

> We are driven, therefore, to Mr Russell's conclusion that a judgment has not one object but many, to which the mental factor is multiply related; but to leave it at that, as he did, cannot be regarded as satisfactory . . . Similarly, a theory of descriptions which contented itself with observing that 'The King of France is wise' could be regarded as asserting a possibly complex multiple relation between kingship, France, and wisdom, would be miserably inferior to Mr Russell's theory, which explains exactly what relation it is.
>
> (Ramsey 1927, p. 142)

The 1913 version

Russell's post-1910 unease over the idea that his theory of judgment has a problem keeping judgment distinct from judged fact surfaces again in the 1913 *Theory of Knowledge*, albeit in a different though related version. There are a couple of things to sort out before I can display this version clearly. I begin by noting that his response to the problem is to try a further modification: his revised theory is that judgment requires (while the corresponding fact does not) an ingredient additional to the mind and the constituents of the judgment, a logical form.[18] However, Russell's attempt at a 'proof that we must understand the "form" before we can understand the proposition' (Russell 1913, p. 116) is introduced with a complication arising from a confusing presentation of the matter, a complication we must first set on one side. He begins the proof by referring to the 1912 theory thus:

> I held formerly that the objects alone sufficed [for understanding the proposition], and that the 'sense' of the relation of understanding would put them in the right order; this, however, no longer seems to me to be the case.

What does he mean by this talk of getting the objects 'in the right order'? From his own words it would seem that he is talking about getting objects into the right places with respect to non-symmetrical relations like *loves*, for this was the difficulty concerning direction which he had previously talked of with the expression 'sense'. But in fact Russell has already ruled this out himself: on page 112 he has said,

Thus if our analysis has been correct, the proposition '*A* precedes *B*', which seemed fairly simple, is really complicated owing to difficulties concerned with 'sense'. These difficulties are not an essential part of the difficulty of discovering what is meant by 'understanding a proposition'. We shall do well, therefore, to take examples which do not introduce 'sense'.

Peter Hylton, after noticing this potential muddle, rightly observes about his actual practice (Hylton 1990, pp. 344–5):

> Russell treats the order of constituents as a separate problem, one that is not solved by the notion of form. He also makes it clear that form is required for all judgements, including subject–predicate judgements and those involving symmetrical relations.

The example which Russell chooses to consider in his proof is accordingly one which does not involve 'sense': it is the symmetrical relation of similarity, and the problem he illustrates with it is that of uniting objects in thought, that is, in what we have called the propositional act. In fact, despite Russell's beginning the proof with talk of 'order', the problem actually uppermost in his mind is, as we shall see in a moment, that of unity.

So let us put on one side as a mere distraction the problem of direction, and concentrate on the problem of unity. Russell's main proof of the necessity of form runs like this (Russell 1913, p. 116; there is another on page 99):

> Suppose we wish to understand '*A* and *B* are similar'. It is essential that our thought should, as is said, 'unite' or 'synthesize' the two terms and the relation; but we cannot *actually* 'unite' them, since either *A* and *B* are similar, in which case they are already united, or they are dissimilar, in which case no amount of thinking can force them to become united. The process of 'uniting' which we *can* effect in thought is the process of bringing them into relation with the general form of dual complexes. The form being 'something and something have a certain relation', our understanding of the proposition might be expressed in the words 'something, namely *A*, and something, namely *B*, have a certain relation, namely similarity' . . . In an actual complex, the general form is not presupposed; but when we are concerned with a proposition which may be false, and where, therefore, the actual complex is not given, we have only, as

it were, the 'idea' or 'suggestion' of the terms being united in such a complex; and this, evidently, requires that the general form of the merely supposed complex should be given.

The difficulty for an account of judgments which holds actual objects to be their constituents, as Russell sees it, is that either the objects and relation are already united (in actual fact, whether judged to be the case or not), or they are not. In the latter case, nothing can be done in the way of uniting them in judgment; and in the former, nothing remains to be done. This is just another way of recognizing the problem with the 1910 theory's requirement that the unifying relation be present not merely 'abstractly'. And his solution is that judgment differs from fact in that its unification proceeds via the inclusion of a logical form: in the case of his chosen example, the general form of dual complexes is what is supposed to enable the mind to provide that sort of unity which makes possible the understanding of '*A* and *B* are similar', without delivering the kind that creates the corresponding fact too. Hylton appears to accept this (Hylton 1990, p. 346):

> How can we give a meaning to 'unite in thought' which keeps this notion clearly distinct from uniting in reality? Russell's answer is that the judgement represents the constituents as combined in the right way not by so combining them but by including 'the way they are to be combined' as a further entity. And the mode of combination of all these entities (including the form) clearly need not be (and in fact cannot be) the same as that of the fact corresponding to the judgement, so we are in no danger of having to identify uniting in thought with bringing about the corresponding fact.

And later Russell gives a 'map' of the five-term complex involved in the understanding of his exemplary proposition '*S* judges that *A* is similar to *B*',[19] where the form of the particular proposition understood is symbolized by '$R(x,y)$' (see Figure 3.2).

This map functions in the same way as before, except that no direction is included (since the relation is symmetrical) and the form is added as an extra object of acquaintance. It is different from a map of the proposition '*A* is similar to *B*', in which neither *S* nor the form of dual complexes would figure. Does this difference solve the problem?

That question amounts to: can the 1913 introduction of the form into the apparatus of the 1910 version of the theory do the job demanded of it? This job is, in effect, to enable the mind to do what it

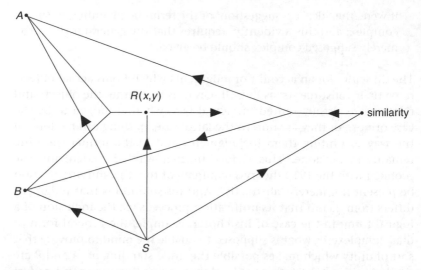

Figure 3.2

was meant (but failed) to achieve on its own in the earlier theory: unify the judgment without creating the judged fact. But any impression that the 1913 version can provide what is needed is an illusion, as can be seen from the map: only its relative complexity disguises the fact that *A is similar to B* still appears in it as a unified whole, now attached to the form as well as to the judging mind; though the addition of this second extra object, the form, can help matters no more than did the original addition of the mind.

Furthermore, this second extra 'object' turns out, on Russell's own admission, not to be a mere form, but an actual proposition, 'Something has some relation to something', and thus an entity which merely re-poses the difficulties over unity in its own case which it is brought in to solve in the case of the original proposition. Russell sees this objection (Russell 1913, p. 130) and attempts to answer it by alleging that in this special case the proposition is both simple, and thus presumably a guaranteed unit, and *also* a fact, and alleging further that by introspection one finds understanding it to be just acquaintance with it. But this desperate response which, as even Russell acknowledges, bristles with difficulties, is to be valued more for its curiosity than its credibility.

I shall just mention two other problems with Russell's multiple-relation accounts of judgment which were long neglected in the literature: first, it is hard to see how to extend the account, in any version, to general propositions; secondly, the logic of *Principia Mathematica* requires an infinite number of propositions whose existence cannot wait upon the contingent inclinations of human minds to formulate them, that is, to perform the appropriate propositional acts. I say little about them here because the neglect has recently been remedied.[20] But the second carries an extra twist. The need for an infinite number of propositions, which because it invokes a finite mind the multiple relation theory cannot supply (that is, not because it eschews propositions in the 1903 sense, nor because it allows the replacement of the infinite hierarchy of orders with a hierarchy of meanings of 'true' and 'false'), is particularly awkward for Russell, given that, as we have seen, the multiple relation theory is vital for the avoidance of paradox. And there is yet more difficulty with the 1913 version. For example, one might ask, why should only the judgment and not the fact require in addition to the objects this 'way they are to be combined' as an ingredient? This is a serious question, because on Russell's theory of forms, as Hylton points out (1990, p. 345), 'the logical form which figures in the judgement is the form of the corresponding fact'. But it is a question to which the theory has no answer.

The 1918 non-theory

It was, of course, Wittgenstein's criticism, and not these difficulties, which as a matter of historical fact was the occasion of Russell's abandoning the 1913 version. But it is clear that an inchoate awareness of the difficulties had made Russell already uneasy about it and so vulnerable on the subject, as is demonstrated by his immediate collapse in the face of a criticism which he admitted at the time he could not understand (and over whose nature there is still disagreement).[21] For some time, though, he seems to have lived in the hope that the multiple relation approach to judgment might just need some sort of philosophical epicycle to deal with that criticism, as his 1917 description of the 1910 version as 'somewhat unduly simple' testifies.[22] In this he reveals an approach to philosophy, exemplified earlier by the 1913 attempt to salvage the multiple relation theory, which is very characteristic of him (and just as uncharacteristic of Wittgenstein even as they worked together), namely that he will find some sort of technical fix to solve the problem.[23] But in the discussion of belief (as he is now consistently calling judgment) in the 1918 lectures 'The Philosophy of Logical Atomism', although he is still describing the 1910 (or 1912) version as being 'a little unduly simple', he is clearly close to despairing of it, and makes no attempt at offering a solution of its problems.[24]

There are two problems with belief identified in these lectures. (All quotations in this section come from two pages of Russell 1918: *CP8*, pp. 198–9; *LK*, pp. 225–6.) One is the objection to the *Principles of Mathematics* account of propositions which inspired the 1910 version in the first place. The 1910/1912 theory, as we saw, attempted to deal with it by sacrificing the unity of the proposition in favour of the unity of the propositional act. Despite his describing this theory as just 'a little unduly simple', Russell's treatment of the second problem shows that by this stage, under Wittgenstein's influence, he has come to appreciate that it is of a difficulty that no mere addition of an epicycle could hope to overcome. The admission of the second problem is an implicit concession to Bradley (that it was such a concession is made explicit only in their private correspondence, never in print): that in giving an account of belief (or judgment; or, more fundamentally, understanding), the subordinate verb (that is, the one other than 'believe') has to occur as a verb – whereas in the 1912 version Russell treated it as a term like any other. And yet despite its occurring as a verb, it cannot *really* relate, for otherwise there would be no false judgment. In what is doubtless a conscious harking back to the unfinished *Theory of Knowledge*, Russell makes the point in terms of the impossibility of achieving what he had attempted in 1913, that is, of making a map in space which is 'logically of the same form as belief', and says of the 1912 theory that it made the error of 'putting the subordinate verb [i.e. relation] on a level with its terms as an object term in the belief', showing us another failed map to illustrate the point (see Figure 3.3).

'[I]n the symbol', he says, 'you have this relationship relating these two things and in the fact it doesn't really relate them.' (Not, incidentally, because we are dealing with fictional objects, but because Russell

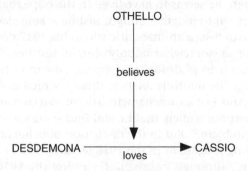

Figure 3.3

is here assuming for pedagogic purposes that it is true that Othello is mistaken in believing that Desdemona loves Cassio.) This is quite right. But what he has said just previously shows that he is not in fact much closer to full clarity about the nature of the problem:

> I mean that when *A* believes that *B* loves *C*, you have to have a verb in the place where 'loves' occurs. You cannot put a substantive in its place. Therefore it is clear that the subordinate verb (i.e. the verb other than believing) is functioning as a verb, and seems to be relating two terms, but as a matter of fact does not when a judgment happens to be false.

In other words, the problem is still perceived as one of false judgment. Although Russell hovers on the verge of recognition, he does not seem quite to see, what even a revised map with 'CASSIO' and 'OTHELLO' interchanged would reveal, that it concerns true judgment as well; for, just as was clear from these maps' 1913 predecessor, one cannot specify what is believed, truly or falsely, without invoking the very propositions whose existence he has denied.[25] He says that the verb 'as a matter of fact does not [relate two terms] when a judgement happens to be false'. The conversational implicature here is that when a judgment happens to be true, it does so relate. This all seems innocent enough: the difficulty is that it is inconsistent with the correspondence theory of truth, for he still thinks of the judgment as distinguished from the fact only by the addition of the mind as an extra ingredient – there is nothing for the fact to correspond with other than itself, and even the way in which he describes the problem, let alone canvasses solutions, means that judgment is always going to include the fact judged.

What is clear to Russell is that he has nothing better to offer in response to these difficulties; and at this point he leaves them unresolved.

Subsequent developments

For there to arise a theory of judgment which stood a chance of being workable within the framework of doctrine which characterized logical atomism, at least one of two historically crucial steps had to be taken.

Russell took one of them when in 1919 he eventually made what had previously seemed to him an unthinkable concession to idealism, abandoning the doctrine of real propositional constituents and replacing real objects with their symbols as constituents of propositions.[26]

This of course allows for a proposition to be unified without automatic creation of its truth-making fact. But Russell's change of heart on this point was preliminary to his moving away from logical atomism altogether in the direction of neutral monism. And while it provides for the unity of the proposition, on its own it still has no account of this unity, no answer to the question of what differentiates a proposition from a list.

To find both steps taken within the atomist framework, one has to look at the *Tractatus Logico-Philosophicus*. There the constituents of propositions are not the Objects which compose the facts which make up the world, but representations of those Objects, their Names, which go proxy for them in propositions. (I capitalize the crucial words as a reminder that Wittgenstein's objects and names are far from being ordinary ones.) This as we have just seen provides the possibility of having the unity of the proposition without each judgment's self-fulfillingly creating the judged fact, and a proposition could now be regarded as a mental or linguistic entity. That is the first step, the one shared with Russell. The second step, which Wittgenstein took alone (though followed shortly by Ramsey, who took special notice of this feature of the *Tractatus*[27]) was the more important idea that propositions are able to represent facts because the propositional signs are themselves facts: this allowed the proposition the unity required for saying something without the addition of an explicitly represented relation which is to bind the proposition's constituents together while at the same time being one of those constituents itself. Indeed, the unifying relation *cannot* be explicitly represented; it is shown, but cannot be named. It was that attempted addition, characteristic of Russell's realistic thinking about propositional constituents, which had been the primary source of such problems as the creation of Bradleian infinite regresses, and the need to make the implausible distinction between the relation as it is in itself and the relation as relating. Neither the relation which unifies the proposition, nor anything that could be called its Name, is itself a constituent of that proposition; and that relation is not necessarily the one which would unify the corresponding fact if there happened to be one. And only Names, not Objects, are unified within the proposition; the possibility of the unification of the Names shows the possibility of a corresponding unification of the Objects.

As Ramsey also noticed (*loc. cit.*), Wittgenstein's idea not only enables an account of the unity of the proposition, but also allows the solution to the problem of representing a non-symmetrical relation's direction ('sense'). It was obviously a desirable feature of a solution to one of these problems that it should also provide a solution to the other without blurring the distinction between them.

In this way, Wittgenstein was able to acknowledge the unity of the proposition by eliminating the idea of the relating relation's (or some symbol thereof) being itself a constituent of the proposition, without this elimination's appearing to be, as Russell had feared, the beginning of the slippery slope to monism.

These are some of the historical roots or at least anticipations of two of the more widely canvassed recent approaches to the study of what we now prefer to call 'belief'. Some of these evolved from the taking of what I called 'the first step'. As Russell's thinking developed through what we can call his 1919 theory of judgment (Russell 1919b), this step was combined with a tendency to behaviourism; and it gave rise to two initially competing ideas. One of these two ideas, that of an internal symbolism, can be developed into, for example, Fodor's methodological solipsism and the hypothesis of a language of thought. The other idea, reflecting the influence of behaviourism, produced the suggestion that a belief can be explicated as a causal function from desire to action. This latter line of development goes through Ramsey; a recent manifestation is 'success semantics' (Whyte 1990).

The crucial development which made all this possible was (to revert to Bradley's language) Wittgenstein's recognition of the unreality of relations. We shall see in Chapter 6 the interesting effect this recognition had on Russell; for it came from someone whose opinion, unlike Bradley's, he had committed himself to respecting.

4
Truth

'He said, "Where have you been?"
And I said, "I have been out." This is called a white lie.
A white lie is not a lie at all. It is where you tell the truth but
you do not tell all of the truth. This means that everything
you say is a white lie because when someone says for example,
"What do you want to do today?" you say, "I want to do
painting with Mrs Peters," but you don't say "I want to have
my lunch and I want to go to the toilet and I want to go home
after school and I want to play with Toby and I want to have
my supper and I want to play on my computer and I want to
go to bed."'

Mark Haddon, *The Curious Incident of the Dog in the
Night-Time*. London: Jonathan Cape, 2003, p. 62

Introduction

In Chapter 2 we saw that there is a circularity buried in Bradley's
attempts to argue for the major tenets of his monism. This, of course,
does not show that his monism is wrong: merely that it is unproven.
And I doubt whether Bradley himself would have been much perturbed
by this demonstration. After all, he himself denied that his metaphysics was erected on foundations, so that the status of his own arguments would be questionable even in his own eyes. (We shall see in a
later chapter that he is inclined to think that what is persuasive about
his metaphysics has nothing to do with anything approaching demon-
strative proof.) And to what set of metaphysical views is there not
some serious objection? Further, surely 'not proven' is a much less

serious charge than, say, 'inconsistent'? What is more important than this about the content of that chapter is that we can begin to see from it that Bradley seems not to be easily identifiable with the comically bizarre figure in the history of English-language philosophy that, as we saw in Chapter 1, was sketched in the writings of Russell, Moore and the logical positivists and became standard through generations of textbooks.

In Chapter 3 we observed (as had Bradley) Russell's passing embarrassment at the inconsistency of his view of relations as themselvesconstituents of propositions with the unifying role he attributed to them in recognition of the fact of propositional unity. And, further, we traced the course of Russell's struggles to avoid the dismaying consequences of the combination of his doctrine of real propositional constituents with the requirement of propositional unity, consequences which even his attempt to satisfy the requirement with the unity of the propositional act of judging rather than of the proposition judged did not enable him to avoid. In subsequent chapters it will be shown that these problems over the nature of the proposition developed into what became the best-known of the points of contention between the two philosophers. But they also have implications for the topic of truth.

In this chapter, it will be established conclusively that what we saw in Chapter 1 is a central, long-standing and firmly established element of the stereotype, the coherence/correspondence contrast between Bradley and Russell, is fundamentally flawed: even at best grossly misleading, at worst plain wrong.

Bradley and the coherence theory of truth

It is one of philosophy's myths that Bradley held a coherence theory of truth, and one against which there is conclusive contrary evidence. Some of this evidence is merely negative, though this on its own should be enough: there is no published work of his in which a coherence theory of truth is ever expressed; and neither have I found it in those of his papers which remained unpublished in the time that the myth became established. The belief that Bradley had a coherence theory of truth is simply false. And I want to make clear the status of this assertion. It is not a matter of interpretation of some texts over which people might reasonably differ. There is simply no argument about it. All one needs to do is to read the relevant pages without preconceptions. Yet the belief that he did have such a theory – indeed, that it is characteristic of his philosophy, and he a characteristic exponent of the theory – is, as we saw in Chapter 1, one of the most widely propagated elements of the stereotype we are considering.

Many of the writings I cited in the relevant section of that chapter are widely used student texts and reference works, and are thus particularly influential. Some of these texts are recent, and will presumably continue to be influential. Some of the writings are ostensibly works of scholarship, whose authors should have known better. There are some notable exceptions, but until very recently these just gave some other mistaken account.[1] And the standard mistaken account can still be found even in very recent reference works. But let us be quite clear: although we shall see how Bradley could have come to be thought of as a coherence theorist, and different theories of truth are sometimes answers to different questions, the coherence theory of truth in common understanding is that the nature of truth consists in (some sort of) coherence between representational entities rather than in correspondence between the representation and the represented. This is a view that, contrary to the common myth, Bradley never held.

It follows that Russell's usual objection to Bradley's views on truth is an *ignoratio elenchi*. This is the one that Ralph Walker (1989) called the 'Bishop Stubbs objection', after Russell's chosen example of that highly respectable nineteenth-century cleric. The objection is that we may invent some patently false proposition like 'Bishop Stubbs was hanged for murder' and then construct indefinite numbers of coherent sets of propositions into which this false proposition will fit, and hence by the coherence theory will count as true, but the genuinely true one that he died in his bed will not. Accordingly, Russell concludes, Bradley's coherence theory is not merely false but obviously and absurdly so. Walker (1989, pp. 3–4) says that the Bishop Stubbs objection, in Russell's original form, 'misses the point, because it is not being suggested that truth consists in cohering with any arbitrary set of propositions ... Instead coherence theorists maintain that truth consists in coherence with a set of beliefs, and some specific set of beliefs at that.' He goes on to argue, however, that this defence only postpones the issue, since it gives rise to a vicious circularity, an objection which will 'hold ... against any pure form of the coherence theory of truth' (*ibid.* p. 103). But whatever the merits of these arguments against the coherence theory,[2] both are irrelevant to Bradley's views.

Bradley on coherence and correspondence

At first glance, there seems to be nothing about coherence in the first edition of *The Principles of Logic*; in fact, even the rather thorough index which Bradley compiled for the second edition contains no trace of the word. If, however, we look instead for related Bradleian vocabulary, we do find a reference which tells us that 'system' is the 'criterion' of truth. Although Bradley's explanation of the former term is both obscure and metaphysically loaded, it is introduced by a rather clearer allusion to 'gaining all the facts and ... getting them consistent'.[3] In other writings he refers to these two aspects of the criterion as 'all-inclusiveness' and 'harmoniousness'. In any case, this gives us a clue to what he will say later about coherence when, following Stout, he replaces his own vocabulary of 'all-inclusiveness' and 'harmoniousness' with 'coherence' and 'comprehensiveness' respectively but still regards the two conditions as aspects of the single principle of system (1909c, *ETR* p. 223).[4] The burden of the following passage, from a paper attacking the view of Russell and Stout that judgments about our immediate experience are infallible, is typical of these later remarks:

> Prof. Stout denies, I understand, that coherence will work as a test of truth in the case of facts due to sensible perception and memory. Mr. Russell again has taken the same line ... What I maintain is that in the case of facts of perception and memory the test which we do apply, and which we must apply, is that of system. I contend that this test works satisfactorily, and that no other test will work. And I argue in consequence that there are no judgements of sense which are in principle infallible.
>
> (Bradley 1909b, *ETR* p. 202)

In this passage, Bradley omits mention of the comprehensiveness condition for the test of truth, and in consequence I shall allow myself too the brevity of referring merely to coherence. This is not to suggest that the comprehensiveness condition is unimportant (unlike reference solely to coherence by Bradley's contemporary critics, which is usually a sign that comprehensiveness has been ignored): on the contrary, it provides his way of circumventing the 'Bishop Stubbs' objection, that is, the suggestion that coherence is an inadequate account of truth because it allows as true various incompatible sets of propositions, some of which will contain propositions that are patently false. Bradley holds that only one such set will be comprehensive: 'as judgments become more coherent and comprehensive ... they become more true' (Allard 2005, p. 204), a process to which, as we shall see later (p. 93*f*), there is only one limit. Coherence, then, understood as including comprehensiveness, is in Bradley's view the test of truth. But this on its own gives no grounds for supposing that, even so understood, he thought it also to be the nature of truth. And it cannot be alleged in defence of those who have propagated the myth that they themselves have done so from within a philosophical standpoint where no distinction is drawn between test and nature. For example, Russell, who as we saw in Chapter 1 was the principal source of the myth, espoused correspondence as the definition of truth in *The Problems of Philosophy* (Russell 1912, p. 128 and index); earlier in the same work (p. 122) he had rejected coherence as the definition – but said, nevertheless, 'we may often use it as a criterion' (p. 140). On the face of it, Bradley's view of coherence – apart from the question of whether it includes comprehensiveness – differs from that of Russell only in virtue of Bradley's asserting that it is the sole test. (Thus some commentators attribute to Bradley a coherence theory of justification.) A theory of the test of truth is certainly a theory about truth; but it is not what those who have attributed the coherence theory to Bradley have usually had in mind.

What, though, is Bradley's view of the nature of truth? As always with Bradley, this kind of question is not straightforward to answer, because in philosophy in general he is inclined to say something like, 'Well, X is perfectly satisfactory for practical purposes, but if we want to be strictly and metaphysically accurate, then we have to recognize that X has to be abandoned in favour of ... [and then comes something very obscure or unlikely].' In order to understand what Bradley's views on truth are, it is essential to remember this and to realize that there is accordingly good reason for misunderstanding him. For in this case our X is *correspondence*, and in consequence there are those who have thought him to be a correspondence theorist. In the first edition of *The Principles of Logic* one can indeed find an inchoate form of correspondence theory, though Bradley rarely uses this term; he called it the 'copy' theory. Here is a characteristic passage:

> A judgment, we assume naturally, says something about some fact or reality. If we asserted or denied about anything else, our judgment would seem to be a frivolous pretence. We not only must say

something, but it must also be about something actual that we say it. For consider; a judgment must be true or false, and its truth or falsehood can not [*sic*] lie in itself. They involve a reference to a something beyond. And this, about which or of which we judge, if it is not fact, what else can it be? ...

There is a natural presumption that truth, to be true, must be true of reality. And this result, that comes as soon as we reflect, will be the goal we shall attain in this chapter.

(Bradley 1883, pp. 41–2)

There is, then, an 'official' correspondence or copy theory of truth in *The Principles of Logic*; it is there because, in Bradley's view, it is one of the presuppositions of logic – and, as his talk of 'natural presumption' suggests, of everyday thinking. Those who have been sufficiently independent-minded to have disentangled themselves from the myth and thought Bradley to have been a correspondence theorist are not mistaken; they merely have not got the full story. Even these remarks just quoted occur near the start of a long and tangled chapter which involves heavy qualification (with more to come when in later chapters Bradley moves on to the topic of inference). In fact the quotation continues immediately:

But we shall reach [this goal] with a struggle, distressed by subtleties, and perhaps in some points disillusioned and shaken.

So even in this early work on logic we can, then, discern ambivalence about correspondence. Both the source of this ambivalence, and his later distancing of himself from the correspondence theory, emerge in one of the notes added to the second edition of *The Principles of Logic* (Bradley 1922, p. 591 n. 1):

The attempt, made at times in this work for the sake of convenience (see on Bk. I. II. §4), to identify reality with the series of facts, and truth with copying – was, I think, misjudged. It arose from my wish to limit the subject, and to avoid metaphysics, since, as is stated in the Preface, I was not prepared there to give a final answer. But the result of this half-hearted attempt was an inconsistency, which in this Chapter is admitted.[5]

The parenthetical reference is to a section in which he says, 'For our present purpose we must answer the question ['What is fact?'] from a level not much above that of common sense.' The inconsistency to which Bradley refers here has two components. One of them is this: in various places in *The Principles of Logic*, culminating with its brief final chapter, he argues against the correspondence theory, presenting for it a string of problems. Although the arguments are too often surrounded with hedging conditionals and florid metaphor, guaranteed to irritate a more straightforward reader, they amount to those marshalled far more clearly and unequivocally in a later essay. We shall examine them later in the chapter (p. 89*f*). Here it is sufficient to summarize his central objection. In effect, it is that the correspondence theory embodies the idea that the way that we think is directly mirrored in reality, and in this the theory presupposes a false metaphysics. It should not be surprising, then, that the second component of the inconsistency is the presence in the same work, *The Principles of Logic*, of his other, preferred, theory of truth, the one which is supposed to be metaphysically accurate. Mostly it lurks there in embryonic form (for example, in the closing chapter already mentioned, particularly pages 589–90).[6] But arriving at an ultimately correct account is, Bradley thinks, the business of metaphysics, whereas the concern of the *Principles* with logic, whose presuppositions may include theories which, however necessary they may be for the practice of argument, he would regard as ultimately indefensible, allows him to work in terms of the correspondence theory. For this reason, the presence in the *Principles* of another theory of truth with which it is inconsistent does not imply the absence of the correspondence theory. The full ambivalence between logic and metaphysics, an ambivalence which pervades the book and affects far more in it than just the question of the nature of truth, appears with great clarity in the following comparatively early remarks:

> An idea is symbolic, and in every symbol we separate what it *means* from that which it stands for. A sign indicates or points to something other than itself; and it does this by conveying, artificially or naturally, those attributes of the thing by which we recognize it. A word, we may say, never quite means what it stands for or stands for what it means. For the qualities of the fact, by which it is recognized and which correspond to the content of the sign, are not the fact itself. Even with abstracts the actual case of the quality is hardly nothing but the quality itself. The ideas and the reality are presumed to be different.

It is perhaps an ideal we secretly cherish, that words should mean what they stand for and stand for what they mean. And in metaphysics we should be forced to consider seriously the claim of this ideal. But for logical purposes it is better to ignore it. It is better to assume that the meaning is other than the fact of which the meaning is true. The fact is an individual or individuals, and the idea itself is an universal.

(Bradley 1883, p. 168)

This ambivalence on Bradley's part should not surprise us, for it is just one facet of a general problem with that book: the problem, that is, of determining how successful Bradley was, or even could be, in his stated aim of keeping metaphysics out of a book on logic, and confining himself to working within what he took to be the presuppositions of a lower science while leaving aside the question of the ultimate justification of those presuppositions. (Cf., for example, Bradley 1883, pp. x–xi, 28, 49 *et passim*.) For 'metaphysics' here we may read, without dangerous inaccuracy, 'his real views'.[7] But what are we to make of a book on logic which claims that it presupposes a false metaphysics? And what are we to make of a metaphysics which claims that theories whose truth is necessary for the practice of reasoning are ultimately indefensible? These are questions which are unavoidable in any assessment of the overall coherence of Bradley's views. On the face of it, of course, the metaphysics has to give way, since its conclusions appear to act as a kind of *reductio ad absurdum*, undercutting the arguments which get us to those very conclusions. One way in which Bradley can attempt to evade this obvious difficulty is by exploiting his doctrine of degrees of truth, which is meant to do justice to the claims of logic, science and common sense while yet denying them ultimate truth. We shall see later whether or not this strategy can be sustained. Russell, at least, thought it was just trying to have your cake and eat it too, and mounted a withering attack on it.[8]

Russell and the correspondence theory of truth

As we saw in Chapter 3, from 1910 onwards Russell proclaimed his adherence to a correspondence theory; and this adherence is a central component of the standard picture of the Russell/Bradley dispute.

However, the attentive reader will already have discerned in the previous chapter that this adherence is not easy for Russell to maintain.

Let us look again at how the correspondence theory emerges in combination with the 1910 theory of judgment.

Russell's aim in 'On the Nature of Truth and Falsehood' (Russell 1910) was to provide a fresh account of truth, for which a new theory of judgment is required. In this essay the new theory is developed against the background of what he claims to be the view of Meinong: that judgments 'have' unitary but complex objectives in virtue of which they are true or false. (I deliberately leave this vague, because the theory as Russell presents it for rejection is utterly incredible.) His grounds, in summary, are that it is impossible to believe in the existence of real objectives where a judgment (or proposition, as he now calls it) is false, and that this provides sufficient reason for not believing in them even where the judgment is true. In consequence, he opts for a correspondence theory of truth, in which a fact, to which a true judgment corresponds, is something quite independent of that judgment itself, and a replacement theory of judgment in which judgment is 'a multiple relation of the mind to the various other terms with which the judgment is concerned' (Russell 1910, *CP6* p. 122). A full account of the theory, together with its version of the correspondence theory of truth, is given in the last couple of pages of the paper. We summarized it in Chapter 3 (p. 62) thus: When we judge that, say, *A* loves *B*, we have 'before the mind' the person *A*, the person *B*, and the relation of loving, in such a way that the relation is not present 'abstractly' but as proceeding from *A* to *B*. The judgment is true when there is a corresponding complex object, *A*'s loving *B*, and false when there is not.

As we saw (pp. 62*ff*), this presentation of the multiple relation theory embroiled Russell in a confusion of the problem of direction (that is, how it is ensured that the 'proceeding' goes from *A* to *B* and not the other way around) with the problem of unity. Because this confusion was sorted out in the last chapter, it may be ignored here. The question now is, can Russell consistently combine the multiple relation theory (in any of its three versions) with a correspondence theory of truth?

The 1910 theory of judgment was meant to circumvent the 1903 theory's creation of objective falsehoods, a creation which had forced Russell into a primitivist theory of truth. But we saw in the discussion of the previous chapter that the prospect of its achieving this circumvention is illusory: the theory makes false judgment impossible. This is because: either, by a kind of psychokinesis, any judgment at all will create the fact which would make it true, that is, its own truth-maker; or, psychokinesis being impossible, judgment will be restricted to the passive recognition of truths. The immediate consequence is that the theory of judgment is after all incompatible with its companion correspondence theory of truth. If we look at *what is judged*, there is not a second object, a truth-bearer, with which the truth-maker can correspond; and if we look at *the judging*, correspondence will fail because the judging fact, including as it does the judging mind (represented by '*S*' in the diagram (p. 66 in the previous chapter), does not correspond to the judged fact but includes it. A correspondence theory of truth could fit Russell's theory only if the mind manipulated symbols of the objects of judgment, not the objects themselves.

As the modification which Russell introduced in announcing the 1912 theory of judgment was intended only to address the problem of direction, it is clear that it will be no better off than its predecessor in fitting the correspondence theory of truth.

Do things improve with the 1913 version, in which a 'form' is added to the judgment to distinguish it from the judged fact? What happens if the answer is no? In that event, according to Russell's own statement (Russell 1913, p. 116), where something is *not* the case it will be impossible to judge that it is the case; and where something is the case, the judged proposition will be indistinguishable from the actual fact. But this will make a correspondence theory of truth impossible, and ensure that we have no account of falsehood at all. As with the 1910 theory interpreted on the assumption that psychokinesis is impossible – an assumption now supposedly rendered unnecessary by the form's doing its job of enabling the unifying of the judgment without the creation of the judged fact – judgment will be restricted to the passive recognition of truths.

This had not been clear to Russell in 1910. It was this kind of unclarity, perhaps, which made him think the 1910 theory compatible with a correspondence theory of truth. In 1913 he recognizes the problem over unity that he had missed in 1910, and distentangles it from the problem of direction with which he was still confusing it in 1912, but he does not see that in his attempt at a solution all that happens is that what we identified previously as an inconsistent combination of magical powers is transferred from the mind alone to the mind with access to logical forms. Nor does he see that his solution still forces him away from the correspondence theory of truth, and for the same reason that there was a problem with the 1910 theory. He seems to imagine that the form's presence in the judgment but absence from the fact allows him to account for the truth of a judgment in terms of a correspondence between two complexes. But, again, if we look at *what is judged*, there is not a second object, a truth-bearer, with which the truth-maker can correspond; and if we look at *the judging*, correspondence will fail because the judging fact, including as it does now the form as well as the judging mind, does not correspond to the judged fact but includes it. Things do not, then, improve with the 1913 version: the doctrine of real propositional constituents appears to be inconsistent with a correspondence theory of truth.

But why did Russell himself not recognize this? It is, after all, not particularly hard to see the problems. One reason is a fact we have already observed: that his theory even in 1910 included the mind itself as a substantial ingredient in the judgment, which precludes the identifying of the judgment and the fact judged and seems thereby to impose correspondence as the account of truth. Another is this: the doctrine of real propositional constituents requires that, if judgment is not to be restricted to the passive recognition of truths, then in judgment the mind puts actual physical objects into actual relations. But the multiple relation theory of judgment was not intended to attribute psychokinetic powers to the mind. How did Russell manage to avoid confronting this unpalatable consequence? The answer is surely that the phrase 'before the mind' has to be interpreted as 'acquaintance', and that Russell's realism was a representative realism in which the objects of acquaintance, that is, the constituents of propositions, are sense-data and their properties and relations; even though he thought of sense-data as physical, these are not the everyday objects of the physical world. But as, after 1913, he gradually abandoned representative realism and moved towards thinking of physical objects as logical constructions out of sense-data, it became increasingly difficult to imagine that the combination of the doctrine of real propositional constituents – now themselves more obviously sense-data – with the multiple relation theory of judgment could allow a correspondence theory of truth. Something had to give.

The ostensible aim of the multiple relation theory of judgment, to allow for the possibility of false propositions, is usually presented, by Russell and commentators, as being achieved by the replacement of a single relation of the judging mind to the proposition by a multiple relation of the mind to the objects of judgment. But, even putting on one side the role of the multiple relation theory in resolving the paradoxes, the matter is more complicated than that. It is vital for the possibility of false judgment that there be some distinction between the physical objects about which some judgment is made and the constituents of the judgment. It was not only his overt deployment of Cartesian scepticism, but also the less obvious combination of the doctrine of real propositional constituents with the multiple relation theory of judgment, which had pushed Russell in *The Problems of Philosophy* away from the extreme realism of his immediate post-idealist metaphysics, towards a representative realism, that is, a theory which makes some concession to idealism. Not a very big concession, given that he thought sense-data not to be mental; but it is a step towards his eventual abandonment, in 1919, of both doctrine and theory in favour of a mentalistic view of the nature of propositional constituents.

The derivation of Bradley's metaphysical theory of truth

As we saw in the last chapter, on the traditional understanding of them which Bradley accepted (with certain heavy qualifications which do not affect the issue here), the truth-bearers are judgments, and these involve ideas. The truth-makers, that is, what make the truth-bearers true or false, he thinks of as facts. Now there is a set of problems clustering around the notion of judgment which Bradley sums up succinctly in a passage near the start of *The Principles of Logic*:

> How then are ideas related to realities? They seemed the same, but they clearly are not so, and their difference threatens to become a discrepancy. A fact is individual, an idea is universal; a fact is substantial, an idea is adjectival; a fact is self-existent, an idea is symbolical. Is it not then manifest that ideas are not joined in the way in which facts are? Nay the essence of an idea, the more it is considered, is seen more and more to diverge from reality. And we are confronted by the conclusion that, so far as anything is true, it is not fact, and, so far as it is fact, it can never be true.
>
> (Bradley 1883, pp. 43–4)[9]

The suggestion is that, because of the inherent limitations of symbolism, it is impossible ever to have a true judgment in the sense that it accurately reflects the reality with which it deals. The correspondence theory, applied to symbolic thought and taken quite literally, commits us to the view that no judgment is ever actually true. These grounds of Bradley's dissatisfaction with the correspondence theory were shared by Frege:

A correspondence, moreover, can only be perfect if the corresponding things coincide and so are just not different things ... It would
only be possible to compare an idea with a thing if the thing were
an idea too. And then, if the first did correspond perfectly with the
second, they would coincide. But this is not at all what people
intend when they define truth as the correspondence of an idea
with something real. For in this case it is essential precisely that the
reality shall be distinct from the idea. But then there can be no complete correspondence, no complete truth. So nothing at all would be
true; for what is only half true is untrue. Truth does not admit of
more and less.

(Frege 1918, p. 3)

Frege's view that truth is not a matter of degree leads him in the end,
via another Bradleian argument, to reject the correspondence theory
entirely. Reaction against the correspondence theory has driven many
philosophers into versions of coherence theories. But neither Bradley
nor Frege is one of these, for they think that all attempts to define
truth in these kinds of ways involve a vicious circle; and in any case
such theories provoke another sort of unease, related to Russell's
'Bishop Stubbs' objection. As McDowell puts it (1994, p. 15):

Such theories express precisely the unnerving idea that the spon-
taneity of conceptual thinking is not subject to rational constraint
from outside. Coherentist rhetoric suggests images of confinement
within the sphere of thinking, as opposed to being in touch with
something outside it.

Suppose one shares this suspicion that the coherence theory of truth
neglects the intuition that truth involves both mind and world rather
than just mind. And suppose too that at the same time one sympa-
thizes with Bradley and Frege and suspects that the correspondence
theory respects the intuition only at the cost of making symbol and
symbolized too different from each other for truth to be possible. Then
the result may be that one starts to wish for a conception of truth
about which neither suspicion can arise: a conception which respects
the existence of both mind and world while not making them mutually alien. Such a yearning can afflict the most hard-headed of philosophers, as we can see in the following passage:

Although ... the correspondence theory comes in as an opponent of
such sceptical or otherwise evasive theories as the coherence theory

and the pragmatist theory, it is itself a sceptical theory of a milder
kind. If the best we could achieve was that our statements should
somehow correspond to what is there, we should still be falling
short of having things just as we state them to be.

(Mackie 1973, p. 57)

What is wished for here seems to be a theory which imposes no gap
between mind and world, thereby doing justice to the idea that when
we think truly, *what we are thinking is what is the case*. Bradley's eventual
metaphysical theory of truth is an attempt at fulfilment of this wish.

This train of thought is behind the most important of a string of
problems which are marshalled in Bradley's consideration of the correspondence theory. They emerge at intervals through the extended and
meandering sprawl which constitutes *The Principles of Logic*; I shall
draw on a more accessibly compressed discussion in 'On Truth and
Copying' (1907). First, judgments about the past and the future cannot
be the result of copying (*ibid.*, *ETR* p. 107; cf. 1883, *PL* p. 47). Second,
the very facts whose copying is supposed to give us truth are themselves 'the imaginary creatures of false theory', whose seemingly independent existence is merely the result of projecting on to the world the
divisions imposed by thought, whereas if thought is to be capable of
truth those divisions must exist independently of thought itself (*ibid.*,
ETR, p. 108; cf. *PL* p. 45). Third, '[d]isjunctive, negative and hypothetical judgements cannot be taken as all false, and yet cannot fairly be
made to conform to our one type of truth', and neither can '[u]niversal
and abstract truths' (*ibid.*, *ETR*, p. 109; cf. *PL*, p. 583).

Bradley then moves on to the pragmatic theory of truth, and suggests a fourth objection: that at bottom, both theories commit the
same error. This error is that of defending the supposition of a 'truth
which is external to knowledge' and a 'knowledge which is external to
reality' (*ibid.*, *ETR* p. 111). The argument that this is an error seems to
turn on the claim that the supposition involves a vicious circularity:
for 'p' to be true, it must be true also that 'p' is a copy of p, or that
believing 'p' is advantageous (and so *ad infinitum*); and for 'p' to be
known to be true, it must also be known that 'p' is a copy of p or that
believing it is advantageous (and so *ad infinitum*).

The first of these objections might be easily dismissed as arising from
a misunderstanding. But Bradley's discussion of the correspondence
theory in 'On Truth and Copying' is infected by a strain of antirealism, which would be expected from one who by this stage is committed to idealism. This helps to explain why he calls it the copy
theory, since he appears to assume that it is a theory of the genesis as

well as of the nature of truth. In his view, truth cannot be verification-transcendent, and on the correspondence theory must be obtained by a process of copying reality. But the correspondence theory is usually associated with metaphysical realism. This objection thus rests on a far wider disagreement; I shall say no more about it.

The second objection also stands or falls with the outcome of major metaphysical issues, and likewise cannot be decided independently. These issues are inextricably entwined with the Russell/Bradley dispute; in subsequent chapters it will be shown who, if either, has the better of the arguments.

The third required the invention of the theory of truth-functions for a plausible answer to be provided. We shall see later on, however, that despite this plausibility Russell still faced problems in finding facts to correspond with certain types of sentences; and arguments over truth-makers continue as I write.

The claim on which the fourth rests is a common allegation against substantial theories of truth like the correspondence theory, and philosophers divide over whether to take it seriously. One who does not take it seriously is Walker (1989, p. 99), who asserts without argument that the correspondence theory's regress is non-vicious.[10] But if we take the notions of correspondence and fact at face value, so that the fact is an independently existing counterpart of the proposition and there must be a further fact for each true proposition about correspondence to correspond to in order to be true, then the regress will be vicious. When one thinks of the elaborate apparatus employed in the *Tractatus Logico-Philosophicus* to avoid such a regress, in particular the distinction between showing and saying, one could reasonably wonder whether the regress can be dismissed without paying a comparable metaphysical price. Frege certainly took the objection seriously, for his just-quoted initial argument against the correspondence theory is followed by the consideration of an obvious response, that all that is required is 'correspondence in a certain respect' (*loc. cit.*), to which (where Bradley would have merely dismissed this talk of 'respects' as vicious abstraction; see the next section) Frege provides just this objection of vicious circularity, which he supposes gives us, when generalized, good reason for holding that the notion of truth is '*sui generis* and indefinable' (Frege 1918, p. 4).

My concern just now is not to decide any of these issues, but to see how Bradley continues, for at this point he announces his metaphysical theory of the nature of truth. Perhaps because it is so strange to the eyes of analytic philosophers, it is still usually overlooked, both as a component in the stereotype, and as a contender among the usual rivals for the post of the correct theory of truth. Nevertheless, Bradley is pretty clear and firm on the subject:

> The division of reality from knowledge and of knowledge from truth must in any form be abandoned. And the only way of exit from the maze is to accept the remaining alternative. Our one hope lies in taking courage to embrace the result that reality is not outside truth. The identity of truth knowledge and reality, whatever difficulty that may bring, must be taken as necessary and fundamental.
>
> (Bradley 1907, *ETR* pp. 112–13)[11]

This view has come to be called the identity theory of truth. But does it even deserve the title of 'theory', let alone to be taken as a serious contender in the same race as, for instance, the correspondence theory? To many eyes it will look self-evidently absurd. Nevertheless, it has respectable antecedents and adherents, and as we have just seen, it can figure as a solution to some serious philosophical problems. At the very least no other theory could be consistent with Bradley's metaphysics. But all this demands further investigation.

The nature of Bradley's metaphysical theory of truth

Is it possible to make the statement of the theory into something more than the slogan 'the identity of truth and reality'?[12] It looks as if, in our terms, Bradley means that truth consists in the identity of some *x* with a reality that makes *x* true; and the identity theory's most general form is that the truth-bearer is identical with the truth-maker. This more conventional formulation still perhaps looks uninviting. But one must remember that it is couched in a dualistic language more suited to the expression of a correspondence theory, ordinary philosophical thought being so saturated with correspondence assumptions.[13] A new philosophical theory is sometimes, of necessity, expressed in language whose application the theory is intended to undermine.

One of the major impediments to understanding the identity theory is that, unless we already subscribe to some recent and sophisticated philosophical ideas about truth, it is natural to think of truth as a relation between two very different things: language, or more generally, representation, and reality. Certainly, the idea that language and reality might be identical is hard to take seriously, whatever some philosophers may have thought.[14] Thus Anthony Manser (1983, p. 133), in an otherwise generally sympathetic account, talked of Bradley's 'attempt to make language and reality coincide'. But Manser's late twentieth-century way of thinking is utterly foreign to Bradley, for whom the question was always one of the relation of *thought*, not of language, to reality (1897, *AR* p. 492). The suggestion that the value of *x* is *thought* is an improvement on Manser's suggestion that it is *language*: the theory itself no longer seems obviously unintelligible. One can, for instance, begin to see how it might appeal to an idealist metaphysician who would regard the truth-maker as experience rather than some physical state of affairs, and the truth-bearer as a thought rather than a linguistic item. Truth-bearer and truth-maker, against this metaphysical background, do not look so hopelessly different that an identity theory becomes an *a priori* impossibility.

As we saw, Bradley's appeal to identity arose out of his claim that the correspondence theory's view of facts as real and mutually independent entities is unsustainable: the impression of their independent existence is the outcome of the illegitimate projection onto the world of the divisions with which thought must work, a projection which creates the illusion that a proposition can be true by corresponding to part of a situation even though it rips that part from its background and separates it up into further parts which are not separate in reality. Take, for example, these statements: 'On my desk there is a piece of paper. This piece is of A4 size. It displays the text I am currently revising.' Each of these statements would, on at least a naïve correspondence theory, appear to be true by corresponding to a fact. But these facts are detached from their unmentioned background (the desk from my office, the paper from its colour), and from each other (the paper from its size and imprinted text). Bradley called this 'vicious abstraction', of a sort which falsifies reality, and his hostility to it ensures that, when his views are consistently carried through, at most one proposition can be true – that which encapsulates reality in its entirety. Bradley's hostility to abstraction is one of the permanent features of his philosophy: as it applies to the topic of truth, the idea is that we do not speak the truth if we say less than the situation we are talking about would justify our saying, just as we do not speak the truth if we say more, or something entirely different. The identity theory of truth is perhaps the culmination in Bradley's work of this idea.[15]

This seeming extravagance, however, enables his identity theory of truth to meet a condition of any theory of truth, that it must make room for falsehood, since he can account for falsehood as a falling short of this vast proposition and hence as an abstraction of part of reality from the whole. The result is his adoption of the idea that there are degrees of truth: that proposition is the least true which is the most distant from the whole of reality. Although the consequence is that all ordinary propositions will turn out to be more or less infected by false-hood, Bradley allows some sort of place for false propositions and the possibility of distinguishing worse from better.

Whatever he himself may have thought, it seems that Bradley's views imply that at most one proposition could be fully true. But even this one putative proposition has so far been conceived as describing reality, and its truth as consisting in correspondence with a reality, even if one not distorted by being mentally cut up into illusory frag-ments, the correspondence theory's mythical facts. As a result, even such a gigantic proposition, for the very reason that it remains a description, would still be infected by falsehood. For it would still have to display reality's connected aspects by means of separate fragments (when we get around to that part of the proposition which deals with what is on my desk the word 'paper' would still have to be separate from the expression 'A4' in a way that its size is not separate from the paper itself);[16] and it would itself both have to be, as an existent, part of reality and yet, as reality's description, separate from it. The only resolution of these difficulties which Bradley could see was that the total proposition, to attain complete truth, would have to cease to be a proposition and *become* the reality it is meant to be *about*. This last claim, so apparently bizarre and off-putting, can, as we have just seen, be made intelligible by presenting it as both the most extreme expres-sion of Bradley's hostility to abstraction and a reaction to the most fundamental of his objections to the correspondence theory, which as we saw is the same as Frege's: that for there to be correspondence rather than identity between proposition and reality, the proposition must differ from reality and in so far as it does differ, to that extent must distort and so falsify it.

But we can now see something of what I called the 'metaphysical price' which his version of the identity theory exacts. The price has several components. One is idealism, a metaphysical position which even on its own is too costly for most philosophers. Another is the doctrine of degrees of truth, whose consequences, to say the least, need working out, but which is needed for the defence of the identity theory itself. A third is the extravagant implications of Bradley's hostility to abstraction. This hostility initially motivates the identity theory, but, when it is allowed to remain unbridled, its implications begin to threaten even the theory itself. For although Bradley himself described

his view of truth in terms of 'identity', so that there is some justification for calling it an identity theory of truth, this title turns out to be
misleading, since the theory, in so far as any theory is left when the
point of inexpressibility is reached (as here), is, as we have just seen,
eliminativist: when truth is attained, propositions disappear and only
reality is left. The justification for talking of eliminativism rather than
of identity is that on this view reality turns out not to have a fact-like
structure expressible in any propositional form at all. Hence Bradley,
despite using the word 'identity' to describe his view, says as well that
'in the proper sense of thought, thought and fact are not the same' and
talked of the attainment of complete truth in terms of thought's
'happy suicide' (1893, *AR* pp. 150, 152).[17] In effect, as the proposition
approaches complete truth, it disappears altogether in favour of reality,
the one ideal limit of the process of increasing coherence and comprehensiveness:

> But if truth and fact are to be one, then in some such way thought
> must reach its consummation. But in that consummation thought
> has certainly been so transformed, that to go on calling it thought
> seems indefensible.

> (1893, *AR* p. 152)

In this way, Bradley does justice to his rejection of the Hegelian
identification of the rational with the real, the rejection which he
expressed with such eloquence in *The Principles of Logic* (1883, pp. 590*f*)
in a passage celebrating the sensuous life, incorporating it into his metaphysics in a way that is almost unintelligible to a logician, or a scientific
materialist, of the present day. Despite his contributions to philosophical logic and the philosophy of language (some of which we have yet to
explore), Bradley thus reveals himself in this respect as a thinker utterly
alien to the temper of the analytical philosophers who were to follow,
for whom philosophy was to become a technical and highly professional discipline which was to lose touch with the educated public at
large.

    Bradley's metaphysical theory of truth, when its consequences are
fully explored, thus turns out to be self-destructive. He, of course, did
not regard this as an objection. But it is likely to seem so to those –
surely the overwhelming majority – unwilling to share his entire metaphysical vision, with the result that the theory appears to be merely an
idiosyncrasy or historical curiosity. But that thought should make us
wonder whether it could be more than this: might an identity theory

of truth in principle be detachable from its surrounding Bradleian doctrine? And, given that he was not working in an intellectual limbo, can
it be found in the thought of others at the time?

The availability of the identity theory of truth

In order to decide whether or not the identity theory of truth is more
than just an idiosyncratic historical curiosity, it will help to ask how it
is related to its characteristically Bradleian surrounds: monism, idealism, and the views that the criterion of truth is coherence and that
truth has degrees. How separable are the components of this bundle?

In fact, the theory and the criterion are more independent than one
might imagine. What motivates the coherence criterion is not the
identity theory *per se* but Bradley's monism.[18] This is made clear by
Bradley's own procedure in an essay from which I have already quoted,
where he defends the coherence criterion of truth (Bradley 1909b).
In that essay Bradley considers the denials of Russell and of Stout 'that
coherence will work as a test of truth in the case of facts due to sensible
perception and to memory'. And he proceeds by connecting the claim
that there are infallible judgments of sensible perception and memory
with the claim that there are independent facts (p. 203), presumably
on the basis that the truth of the latter claim is a necessary condition
of the truth of the former. Rejecting as he does the mutual independence of facts, he rejects the possibility of infallibility of judgment,
arguing that we must not confuse sensory data themselves, raw and
unconceptualized, with judgments based upon those data, and that
any judgment stands to be revised in the light of subsequent experience. Nowhere in this paper is any appeal made to the identity theory
of truth.

In the light of this degree of independence, we can note that it
might, for example, be possible to hold a correspondence theory
together with some form of monism more restricted than Bradley's (in
that there would be an ultimate distinction between truth-bearer and
truth-maker) and a coherence criterion. Alternatively, one could hold
to the identity theory while abandoning monism and the coherence
criterion: thus one could in principle hold that an utterly isolated judgment is true just in case it is identical with the utterly independent fact
whose specification provides the judgment's content. This of course
requires the bringing of truth-bearer and truth-maker into the same
ontological vicinity. Idealism accomplishes this by pushing the latter
towards the former, claiming the truth-maker to be something

variously described as mental, spiritual, or experiential. In principle, however, at least on the face of it, it ought to be possible to accomplish this neighbourliness by pushing from the other direction, claiming the constituents of truth-bearers to be, for instance, the very things that we talk *about*. In this way, a logical atomist might, for example, be able consistently to proclaim adherence to an identity theory. We shall explore this possibility with respect to Russell in the next section.

What about the doctrine of degrees of truth? As we saw, this arises in Bradley's thought in response to the difficulties entailed by his idea that no judgment can ever be absolutely true. If he had taken the Fregean line that 'what is only half true is untrue' then that idea, which of course is itself expressed as a judgment, is self-defeating. The doctrine of degrees of truth offers an immediate avenue of appeal here, since it can be suggested that the claim that no judgment can ever be absolutely true is more true than its denial, and hence rationally to be preferred to its denial. Now the claim that no judgment can be absolutely true has two sources in Bradley. One of them is the views of judgment which we saw him expressing early in *The Principles of Logic*, essentially that judgment is ideal while reality is substantial, and hence that judgment is intrinsically unfitted for capturing reality. The other source is the monism which never appears in full-blooded form in the *Principles*, flowering instead in *Appearance and Reality*. Here the problem with attaining truth is that it involves not only completion of an infinite process, as we have to get the whole truth about Reality into our judgment, but also the eventual self-destructive nature of the process as Bradley conceives it. In theory these differing sources can be separated; and thus one might, in principle, be motivated to adopt the doctrine of the unattainability of truth, and defend it by appeal to the doctrine of degrees of truth, without being burdened by what one might think of as the extravagances of monism; nor need one take on the added burden of defending the coherence criterion.

But although the idea that there are degrees of truth has not been favoured in post-idealist philosophy, it is worth noting that it is not as obviously absurd as is sometimes supposed. One of the sources of the identity theory of truth was, as we saw, the problem of how truth can ever be attained when judgment (language, symbolism) necessarily abstracts from its subject matter. This feature of language has been stressed quite recently:

> A signal (structure, event, state) carries the information that *s* is F in *digital* form if and only if the signal carries no additional information

about s, no information that is not already nested in s's being F. If the signal *does* carry additional information about s, information that is *not* nested in s's being F, then I shall say that the signal carries this information in analog form. When a signal carries the information that s is F in analog form, the signal always carries more specific, more determinate, information about s than that it is F.

(Dretske 1981, p. 137)

Dretske illustrates the point by contrasting someone's saying 'The cup has coffee in it', which carries that information in digital form, with someone's showing a photograph of the same situation, which necessarily conveys more information, for example, concerning the quantity of coffee or the shape of the cup, and carries the information in analogue form. We can see from this that the analogue/digital distinction helps us to grasp what Bradley is after when he claims that judgment abstracts viciously from the concrete whole, falsifies the original, separates in language what is not separate in reality.

It is clear that the problems to which the doctrines of and about truth offered by Bradley are intended to be solutions – particularly the doctrine of the infinite degrees of truth – are problems arising from the digitality of language in a sense close to Dretske's. This digitality, which Bradley stressed and Russell ignored, is essential to all natural languages; notoriously, it gives rise to Sorites paradoxes.[19] Only its removal can obviate any necessity for degrees of truth – to take a simple example, by having a symbol for all the shades of red which, unlike the word 'red' itself, varies systematically to suit every shade. Unless language were to be impossible to learn, the only such symbol suitable to the task would be the colour itself. But this suggestion is tantamount to the identity theory of truth. Thus it is not clear that Bradley would need the doctrine of degrees of truth for a language that met his requirements. But such a language, it seems, would no longer be symbolic in any recognizable sense, and the kind of knowledge which could be captured in it would have to be non-conceptual, immediate and intuitive, the sort that is attributed by Leibniz and Kant to an omniscient creator.

But even if I am wrong about the amount of independence there is among these several Bradleian doctrines, what does seem to emerge without much difficulty is that truth, as he conceived it, can be seen by us as a limit notion, a regulatory ideal of judgment which is no more to be deplored in principle than is, say, the notion of a substance's electrolytic properties at infinite dilution. And it can further be recognized

that someone might hold the identity theory of truth without recognizing or admitting either of the sources of difficulty which led Bradley to
suppose that complete truth was impossible of attainment.[20]

Russell and the identity theory of truth

Perhaps because of its strangeness, the identity theory of truth has
been, as we saw, largely overlooked as an ingredient of Bradley's
thought. This should now make one wonder: given the apparent possibility of detaching this theory from its Bradleian background, might it
have been overlooked in other places as well? In particular, would not
an advocate of the doctrine of real propositional constituents be likely
to hold an identity theory of truth? Now we saw earlier that the theory
of truth which Russell actually held in association with his 1903 theory
of judgment was primitivism. Both directly reflect the influence of
G.E. Moore. It is widely acknowledged that Moore, shortly after his
abandonment of his early idealism, proclaimed that 'the world is
formed of concepts' and rejected the correspondence theory of truth,
maintaining that a judgment's 'truth or falsehood cannot depend on
its relation to anything else whatever, reality, for instance, or the world
in space and time'.[21] Not so widely acknowledged is the apparent suit-
ability of this kind of view for an identity theory of truth;[22] and
although, a century later, Moore's claims seem incredible, even unintelligible, it may help to think of his view that the world consists of
concepts as the reverse side of the coin of Russell's doctrine of real
propositional constituents; moreover, while we have seen that that
doctrine appears to be inconsistent with a correspondence theory of
truth (p. 85*f*), it looks as though it may lend itself to an identity
theory. Further, it will be invulnerable to the problems which Bradley
claimed to surround the notion of judgment when this is thought of as
constituted of symbolism (p. 89*f*), and may thus help in arresting the
drive towards monism which begins from his pursuing those problems.

Russell made plain that the entities constituting propositions form
the widest possible ontological category – 'a man, a moment ... or anything else that can be mentioned' – and thus include quite everyday
things, such as cats and mats (1903 §47). And we saw in Chapter 3
(p. 53*f*) that his combination of this doctrine of real propositional constituents with that of the unity of the proposition entails that a proposition is a unified complex object belonging as firmly to the world as
the trees outside my window. Here it seems, we have the key ingredients of an identity theory of truth. Yet the theory remains merely

latent in Russell's thought, and for good reason: as all propositions are unified, the world contains both objective falsehoods and objective truths. Russell, in effect, held, as part of his inheritance from Moore, what we could call an identity theory of the proposition. And this excludes, it seems, an identity theory of truth: truths would not be distinguished from falsehoods by being identical with reality, since the view in *The Principles of Mathematics* is that all propositions are identical with reality. An identity theory of *truth* requires a non-identity theory of falsehood. This is presumably why Russell turned instead to primitivism: while all propositions have the same ontological status as trees, truth is an unanalysable property possessed by the true propositions and lacked by the false ones (*ibid.* §52).[23]

In effect, the central problem with an identity theory of truth, at least as far as any proposed Russellian version is concerned, is that the only reason for contemplating it is the doctrine of real propositional constituents, but this doctrine itself amounts to an identity theory of the proposition, which is in turn incompatible with a non-vacuous identity theory of truth and forced Russell to move to primitivism. However, primitivism has generally been thought so implausible that almost no one else has ever been able to take it seriously, and even Russell himself, despite what Peter Hylton has called his 'White Queen-like talent for believing the impossible',[24] could not manage to hold it for long.

Nevertheless, primitivism looks less implausible when re-badged and allowed resources only subsequently available. Ernest Sosa has pointed out that when contemporary deflationists distinguish themselves from their predecessors by emphasizing that truth is a property, this brings them very close to primitivism. Field (2001) and Horwich (1998), for example, both maintain that truth is a property without a constituent structure, which cannot be analysed by providing necessary and sufficient conditions for its instantiation. Moorean/Russellian primitivism is an early version of these claims, and moreover, despite pre-dating it, looks compatible with the use of Tarski's equivalence schema:

> On this view [Moorean primitivism], what you cannot do either with *good* or with *yellow* or with truth is to define it, to give an illuminating, compact, at least surveyable, Moorean analysis of it. It is in *this* sense that you cannot philosophically 'explain' any such 'simple' concept. And this leaves it open that you should have *a priori* knowledge of infinitely many propositions constituted essentially by such concepts.
>
> (Sosa 1993, p. 11)

Field and Horwich provide explanations of what it is to grasp the concept of truth, rather than merely urging that it is too simple to be analysed, but this does not suffice to distinguish them from primitivists. To suggest what it is to grasp a concept is quite different from offering a definition of the concept. To suppose otherwise would be like thinking one could not be a primitivist about yellow if one claimed that fully possessing the concept of yellow involves being disposed to deploy the concept in the presence of yellow things.

As Sosa argued, to go beyond primitivism, deflationists must commit themselves to strong versions of their official claims, for example that there is and can be no theory of truth beyond the instances of the equivalence schema.[25] The primitivist can accept Tarskian biconditionals as *a priori* propositions essentially involving truth without needing to suppose that they are *the only* such propositions. Similarly, primitivists did not anticipate the standard (and hard to defend) deflationist claim that truth plays no explanatory role. In this way it may well seem that primitivism is *more* plausible than some currently popular views of truth. Certainly it is difficult to see why deflationists think these strong conclusions should follow from their basic position, which seems to be just that of the primitivist.[26]

But even if primitivism can be rescued from implausibility by appeal to resources only subsequently available, we should consider the possibility that Russell need not have adopted it in the first place. The identity theory of the proposition requires merely that propositions are identical with facts; it is not obvious that a given proposition must be identical with the fact that it states. This leaves open the possibility of a theory, different from Russell's, according to which each proposition, true or false, is identical with some fact or other, but only a true one is identical with its truth-maker. Thus, for instance, the proposition that Charles I died in his bed should not be identical with the fact that Charles I died in his bed, for there is no such fact, but according to the identity theory of the proposition it should at least be identical with some other fact; the proposition that he died on the scaffold, however, is identical with the fact that he did and is true by virtue of that identity. On this kind of view, to learn whether a proposition is true or false is to discover its identity.

The problem now, though, is to make anything of the identity theory of the proposition, since unless we can specify which fact a false proposition is identical with, we lose all grip on the identification of false propositions: for anything we have said so far, all of them might be identical with the same fact and hence with each other. As Russell's personal horror of idealism began to fade, he could have tried to evade this problem by stipulating that each proposition is itself a representational fact, perhaps a mental or linguistic one, so that the requirements of an identity theory of the proposition can be met without violating the requirements of an identity theory of truth in this way: the fact with which each false proposition is identical is not an extra-mental (most generally, extra-representational) fact, whereas the fact with which a true proposition is identical is precisely one outside the representational system. This, however, would require him to relax the doctrine of real propositional constituents so that it would apply in full only to true propositions, thus imposing an alarming asymmetry between the true and the false. And this in turn would demand a radical revision of Russell's views concerning acquaintance: either acquaintance would not be the full perfect knowledge he supposed, or it would have to be possible to be mistaken about whether or not one was acquainted with something. In a sense, the nature of our thoughts would be opaque to us. But one might think this a price worth paying for an account of both truth and falsehood. An identity theory of truth, then, might have been available to Russell after all.

Russell, the multiple relation theory, and correspondence

In Chapter 3 (p. 73*f*) we saw that Wittgenstein was able to acknowledge the unity of the proposition by eliminating the idea of the relating relation's (or some symbol thereof) being itself a constituent of the proposition, without this elimination's appearing to be, as Russell had feared, the beginning of the slippery slope to monism. This was what I there called 'the second step', of the two necessary for the devising of a workable theory of judgment within the framework comprising logical atomism.

An interesting feature of the second step is that it is independent of the first, the move away from the doctrine of real propositional constituents towards a conception of the proposition as symbol. It makes no difference whether one thinks of the proposition as being a (quasi-)linguistic, representing entity or, on Russellian lines, as something whose constituents are the things represented: in the first case, any conventional expression for the relation will not function as the name of an object and is in principle eliminable from the propositional sign; in the second case, the problem Russell faced, of one thing's having to do double duty as both a constituent to be linked to other constituents and as the linking principle itself, is solved by the elimination of the first duty altogether and assigning the other to a different (generally mental) relation between non-relational constituents. That is, if we wish to express in writing the fact, say, that the thing *a* is to the left of the thing *b*, we may do this either, for instance, by employing the sign '*ab*' exactly as written, with the spatial ordering of the signs functioning as the representation of the fact (that is, the representing relation of left-to-right adjacency between the signs is shown, not named); or, if the real things *a* and *b* are themselves, as Russell supposed, constituents of our thoughts, by putting them into a mental relation, such as thinking of them sequentially – unlike *actually* being to the left of, one not requiring psychokinesis – whose function is to symbolize *that* the thing *a* is to the left of the thing *b*.

Russell had in fact been given by Wittgenstein (what had previously though less transparently been available to him from Bradley) the materials which would have enabled him to have retained much of the 1910/1912 theory of judgment without the difficulties which led to the formulation of the 1913 theory. For on this view the relation which unifies the propositional constituents into a representation of a fact is not the relation which unifies those constituents into the represented fact (if there be one, which there does not have to be). Objects can be their own names, as befits Russell's earlier account of propositional constituents, but can form two different facts, one of which can represent the other. A correspondence theory can, after all, be combined with Russell's view that the constituents of representations are the constituents of the represented. Of course, there remain other better-known objections to the multiple relation theory of judgment at least as serious as those which we have just seen may perhaps be overcome (see Chapter 3 p. 72*f*). One of these, which may now loom large again, is Wittgenstein's own. Another is that Russell abandoned the theory before attempting to generalize it to quantified propositions, and it is by no means easy to see how this could be done. And even were these objections to be surmounted, what we would have so far is still merely the sketch of a possible theory and thereby, as Ramsey said, 'miserably inferior' to the Theory of Descriptions. Nevertheless, others have since taken seriously the governing idea behind the doctrine of real propositional constituents, the idea that thought encompasses the extramental. Its current version, which has developed through the work of Gareth Evans and Hilary Putnam, is the notion of 'broad content'.[27] We may add this to the two mentioned in Chapter 3 (pp. 76–7) as a third current approach to the study of belief which has its roots in the arguments of the period we are examining.

There does, then, seem to be a possibility of rescuing a fraction of the standard contrast between Bradley's and Russell's views about truth. But, as we saw Bradley himself saying in another context, we have reached this goal 'with a struggle, distressed by subtleties, and perhaps in some points disillusioned and shaken'.

5
Grammar and Ontology

'Distrust of grammar is the first requisite for philosophizing.'
Wittgenstein (1913b), p. 93

The transparency thesis, the theory of descriptions, and the usual story

Although study of *The Principles of Mathematics* helps free one from the stereotypical picture of the dispute which is our focus, an unwary reader risks immediately falling victim to another of Russell's putative contrasts between himself and Bradley. This is one that did not appear in the list I presented in Chapter 1; it does not belong there. However, though less often remarked, it underlies and helps to explain some of the more obvious supposed differences between them which inform that standard picture. It begins to emerge in this now fairly well-known passage:

> The study of grammar, in my opinion, is capable of throwing far more light on philosophical questions than is commonly supposed by philosophers. Although a grammatical distinction cannot be uncritically assumed to correspond to a genuine philosophical differ-ence, yet the one is *primâ facie* evidence of the other, and may often be most usefully employed as a source of discovery ... On the whole, grammar seems to me to bring us much nearer to a correct logic than the current opinions of philosophers; and in what follows, grammar, though not our master, will yet be taken as our guide.
>
> (Russell 1903, §46)

It is clear enough what Russell's principal claim is here. He sums it up himself later thus: 'But I had thought of language as transparent – that is to say, as a medium which could be employed without paying attention to it' (1959, p. 14). Although the title involves a measure of hyperbole (the needed qualifications are obvious), for the sake of having a starting point we may follow Russell's lead and think of it as the thesis of the logical transparency of grammar.[1] I shall call it, more briefly, the transparency thesis. What it amounts to in practice is a matter of some complexity; at present it suffices to say that the grammatical categories which Russell thought of philosophical importance are those of proper name, adjective and verb (plus one more, which I shall come to in the next section).[2] A little less apparent than this principal claim, though, but at least as important for our purposes, is the passage's gesture at Russell's defection from the ranks of the idealists. For these are the 'philosophers' whose common suppositions and current opinions are mistaken about the status of grammar, and from whom Russell is dividing himself in this profession of faith in grammar's general philosophical transparency. And the idealist who, as we have seen, figured above all in Russell's imagination as representative of the whole tribe was F.H. Bradley.[3]

The picture we are implicitly presented with in this passage, then, is of two philosophers with contrasting attitudes to grammar, whose major differences over logical matters can be diagnosed in terms of the fact that Russell subscribes to the transparency thesis while Bradley denies it. But matters are more complicated than that, and sorting out the differing attitudes of the two philosophers to grammar takes us to the heart of some of the tangled disputes which formed a turning point in twentieth-century philosophy.

The first complication is that Russell soon changed his attitude to the transparency thesis, yet without relenting in opposing Bradley. If one were to accept the usual story of the origins of the theory of definite descriptions, the change could be summarized like this: through the theory of descriptions, Russell moved from holding to abandoning the transparency thesis. (Even one who rejects the usual story is inclined to this version of events. See Hylton 1990, p. 269.)

What is that usual story? In the less unscholarly versions,[4] it begins by noticing some striking further remarks from *The Principles of Mathematics* itself (all further references in this section are to this book unless otherwise specified):

Whatever may be an object of thought, or may occur in any true or false proposition, or can be counted as one, I call a *term* ... [E]very term has being, *i.e. is* in some sense. A man, a moment, a number, a class, a relation, a chimaera, or anything else that can be mentioned, is sure to be a term; and to deny that such and such a thing is a term must always be false.

(§47)

I shall speak of the *terms* of a proposition as those terms, however numerous, which occur in a proposition and may be regarded as subjects about which the proposition is.

(§48)

Being is that which belongs to every conceivable term, to every possible object of thought – in short to everything that can possibly occur in any proposition, true or false, and to all such propositions themselves ... Numbers, the Homeric gods, relations, chimeras, and four-dimensional spaces all have being, for if they were not entities of a kind, we could make no propositions about them. Thus being is a general attribute of everything, and to mention anything is to show that it is.

Existence, on the contrary, is the prerogative of some only amongst beings. To exist is to have a specific relation to existence ... [T]he distinction between existence and being ... is essential, if we are ever to deny the existence of anything. For what does not exist must be something, or it would be meaningless to deny its existence; and hence we need the concept of being, as that which belongs even to the non-existent.

(§427)

Notice two things. One is that Russell's italicization in the second quote is misleading; he is in fact defining the notion *term of a proposition*. The second, and more important, is that amongst these claims is included what we have called the doctrine of real propositional constituents. Russell is more explicit about this doctrine at §51:

But a proposition, unless it happens to be linguistic [that is, about words] does not itself contain words; it contains the entities indicated by words.

And §47 has already shown us that these entities are not essentially mental or intensional but may include quite everyday objects, such as a man.

Makin (2000, p. 181) argues that the objects Russell recognized as constituents of propositions could not have been ordinary ones. He quotes, tellingly, a later part of §47: 'every term is immutable and indestructible. What a term is, it is, and no change can be conceived in it which would not destroy its identity and make it another term.' No ordinary object such as a man could meet these conditions. How, then, can we explain the co-presence of these remarks with 'A man, a moment ... or anything else that can be mentioned, is sure to be a term'? Makin's suggestion, in effect, is that the exposition of the doctrine of real propositional constituents through ordinary objects is purely illustrative or pedagogic. But while this is true of the kinds of examples given provisionally in Russell 1918, it simply does not fit the downright assertions of 1903; it seems that §47 either is just inconsistent or demands a radical revision of our conceptions of everyday objects.

I think that it is both, but not in such a way as to threaten the (qualified) attribution to Russell of the transparency thesis. The explanation is twofold. The first part is that Russell's emphasis on the immutability and indestructibility of terms is dictated by the views of time and change he came to in his study of Leibniz; it is not demanded by a directly ontological preconception. A temporal thing, such as a man, can, in his opinion, only be momentary, but is in all other respects not entirely different from a man as ordinarily conceived. The second part is supplied by Makin himself in another context: it is that Russell's metaphysics emerged only gradually in what was initially conceived as principally a mathematical exercise, namely the logicist project. Like many radical thinkers, he accepts a framework which the development of his own views eventually renders illegitimate, the process being unclear to the thinker himself at the time. But no matter which explanation is correct, for present purposes this is a side-issue. For Russell includes, crucially, in his list of examples, in §47, relations. And whether these are 'everyday' relations, like *being north of*, or the mathematical ones which are his main concern, like *greater than* (as in '2 > 1'), is neither here nor there when it comes to the dispute with Bradley, which can be adequately discussed in terms of either.

Whatever the ontology, the fact that Russell held the doctrine of real propositional constituents as well as the transparency thesis (not to mention his conception of logic as consisting of the most fully generalized truths) means that the philosophical significance of grammar will turn out to be ontological: grammar is a window on the world. Hence we see Russell freely using, for instance, the word 'verb' to refer to those constituents of propositions which correspond to the verbs of language.[5]

Why did Russell hold this unintuitive doctrine? It seems to have come to him from Moore, as he acknowledges (1903, p. 44n), but that is merely a diagnostic answer.[6] We have already seen, in one of his later articles, a hint of the role the doctrine played for Russell himself, when he says:

> But in this view [that 'judgments consist of ideas'] ideas become a veil between us and outside things – we never really, in knowledge, attain to the things we are supposed to be knowing about, but only to the ideas of those things.
>
> (Russell 1911, *CP6* p. 155)

This view, as we noticed in Chapter 3 (p. 53*f*), seems to have been at work in his thinking ever since his abandonment of idealism. We see it very prominently in the telling final sentence of the passage, already quoted in Chapter 3 (p. 54), from his correspondence with Frege:

> I believe that in spite of all its snowfields Mont Blanc itself is a component part of what is actually asserted in the proposition 'Mont Blanc is more than 4000 metres high'. We do not assert the thought, for this is a private psychological matter: we assert the object of the thought, and this is, to my mind, a certain complex (an objective proposition, one might say) in which Mont Blanc is itself a component part. If we do not admit this, then we get the conclusion that we know nothing at all about Mont Blanc [itself].
>
> (Russell 1904b)

The answer thus appears to be that, for Russell, the doctrine of real propositional constituents establishes a link between mind and world, uniting the symbol and the symbolized, which makes it possible for us to achieve knowledge and truth. (We shall see later that he came to believe that this link needed supplementation for categorical truths to be attainable.) Here we have, as we saw in the last chapter, one of the seeds of identity theories of truth, though now we are in a position to see an additional reason why the seed does not bear fruit in Russell: in accordance with the picture suggested by the transparency thesis of a one/one correspondence between words in the sentence and things in the proposition, his 1903 account of truth adds a simple, unanalysable, property to the world to correspond to the words 'is true'. In this way emerges Russell's primitivist theory of truth that we described in the previous chapter.

But it seems obvious straightaway that such views as these have stranger ontological consequences than the momentariness of real men: for example, that there is a present King of France, one who does not exist. The usual story is as follows. According to their surface grammar, utterances of the form 'The *F* is *G*' and '*a* is *G*' apparently pick out through the definite description 'the *F*' or the name '*a*' a single object that the proposition is about, in such a way that should this picking out fail, the sentence will lack meaning (so that the onto-logical consequences, as Russell recognized in §427 of *The Principles of Mathematics*, flow from the recognition of the meaningfulness of such definite descriptions and names). The discovery of the theory of defi-nite descriptions in 1905 was motivated by Russell's increasing wish to avoid such consequences; that discovery enabled the crucial distinc-tion to be drawn between, on the one hand, the surface grammar of both definite descriptions and at least many grammatically proper names, and, on the other, their true logical form; and the discovery of this logical form reveals that the grammatical form of utterances involving these kinds of expressions is purely a surface phenomenon which disappears under analysis, so that such picking out of a single object turns out to be inessential to the sentence's possession of meaning. This knocked a large hole in the transparency thesis.[7]

Some of Russell's own remarks have encouraged this story, and in various formulations it has been standard in the textbooks for years.[8] Nevertheless, the story is untrue, as well as muddled by assumptions about surface grammar; and the summary based on it, that Russell moved from holding to abandoning the transparency thesis, is both exaggerated and superficial. Let us see why.

The consequences of replacing the usual story

In fact, even in 1903 Russell had noticed problems generated by com-bining the transparency thesis with the doctrine of real propositional constituents, for he saw immediately that such expressions as 'all men', 'some man', 'any man', 'every man', 'the man' and 'a man', despite their ability to figure in subject position in sentences like 'All men are bald', cannot be regarded as introducing terms which the proposition is about in the same way as, say, 'Julius Caesar was bald' can be said to express a proposition about Julius Caesar. For instance, the idea that there is a term *any man* which is somehow a man but no particular one is untenable (Russell 1903, §§56, 60).[9] At this time, Russell's way of dealing with propositions formulated using these expressions was to regard them as containing not such paradoxical objects but rather denoting concepts (which he indicates by the use of italics). It is not necessary for present purposes to try to explain the tortuous detail of the theory of denoting concepts.[10] It is enough to indicate that the immediate purpose of the theory is to allow propositions to contain as constituents, in lieu of terms, things that they are not about, that is, to evade the full consequences of combining the doctrine of real propositional constituents with the transparency thesis.

Russell then points out that there are denoting concepts which do not denote anything (1903, §73). This makes it possible to explain – what the transparency thesis does not explain – how one can say both truly and unequivocally 'There is no such thing as the unique solution of the equation $x^2 = 1$.' Thus *The Principles of Mathematics* already included an account of expressions of the form 'the F' which permitted them to be an exception to the transparency thesis, since the function of that account was, by substituting denoting concepts for problematic objects, to allow for cases where combining that thesis with the doctrine of real propositional constituents would get Russell into trouble. For example, the meaningfulness of 'The present King of France is bald' is explained, not by the present King of France's being a constituent of the proposition, but by the proposition's containing instead the denoting concept *the present King of France*.[11] Hence the identification of propositional and sub-propositional entities was, even in 1903, not necessarily just a matter of naïvely reading off ontological commitment from the sentences of (uninflected) languages.[12] Consequently, the usual story of the origin of the theory of descriptions is false, and there is so far no reason to suppose that the theory marks a move from holding to abandoning the transparency thesis.

Nevertheless, the shift in 1905 to the new theory of descriptions does mark a decisive further move away from that thesis. For the denoting concepts themselves were still peculiar entities corresponding to and identified by the original grammatical structures which had made problematic the supposition that they corresponded to objects in the first place[13] – such concepts as *any man*, or *the present King of France*, for example. That is, although the proposition that the present King of France is bald does not contain the present King of France, it does contain *the present King of France*, so that the corresponding grammatical phrase is still of ontological significance; likewise, 'any man', for example, is still regarded as a grammatical unit which has meaning in isolation and thus introduces a corresponding distinct constituent of the proposition, a denoting concept. Even the apparent exception which Russell in 1903 allowed to the combination of the doctrines of transparency and of real propositional constituents did not fully break with those doctrines, then, and it was only with the new theory that the programme of eliminating dubious entities was fully carried through.[14] On the new theory, in its eventual form, these mysterious denoting concepts – and just how mysterious they are is revealed by the fact that on Russell's own principles they ought to be, like any other propositional constituent, language-independent entities susceptible of acquaintance and of being assigned logically proper names; and yet they cannot be, because they can be identified only through denoting phrases[15] – are replaced by a fragmented apparatus of separate propositions with quantifiers, variables and propositional functions, of which only the last could be said to bear much direct relation to the surface grammar of natural languages. The result is a strengthening of the doctrine of real propositional constituents by removal of the ontologically dubious denoting concepts; and, in consequence, an apparent weakening of the transparency thesis.

It is worth noting at this point that Russell's move to the theory of descriptions was followed in the next year by a tentative replacement of the primitivist theory of truth with the correspondence theory, a replacement we saw was finally consolidated in 1910.[16] This change, too, signifies Russell's apparently increasing estrangement from the transparency thesis, since on the correspondence theory the monadic truth-predicate conceals a relation.

It is time to pull all this together. The usual story of the origins of the theory of definite descriptions is false, and its implications for Russell's attitude to grammar are exaggerated and superficial. Moreover, in many versions of the story, the theory is not always distinguished from its applications: in some accounts it is even presented as a theory of the elimination of proper names. But the pure theory is *just* a theory of definite descriptions in surface grammar (a theory that they belong *only* to surface grammar, and disappear in the process of analysis which reveals their underlying structure). There is some excuse for the muddle: Russell himself was later inclined to call various of its applications 'the theory of descriptions', and even in 'On Denoting' itself we get at the end of the paper the first hint of its broader application to some uses of proper names, when he suggests that the grammatical names of non-entities 'are denoting phrases which do not denote anything' (1905b, *CP4* p. 425):[17] 'A proposition about Apollo means what we get by substituting what the classical dictionary tells us is meant by Apollo, say "the sun-god".' (This *application* of the theory, unlike the pure theory itself, involves a two-stage process. First, a grammatically proper name is eliminated, using not the theory itself but some sort of linguistic intuition, in favour of a definite description; then the definite description is in turn eliminated according to the rules of the theory. The result is thus two steps away from the original grammatical form.) Although he applied the theory in *Principia Mathematica,* it was not until 1911, under the influence of epistemological considerations, that Russell proclaimed the fully extended application of the theory to include ontologically non-reductive analyses in the philosophy of language, so that even the names of one's friends can turn out to be descriptions: 'Common words, even proper names, are usually really descriptions' (1911, *CP6* p. 152).[18] And it is later still, again for primarily epistemological reasons, that he gets the idea of extending its application to ontologically reductive analyses of everyday objects in favour of sense-data and *sensibilia* (Russell 1914a).

This move to reductive analysis does not mean that Russell abandoned the doctrine of real propositional constituents. Sense-data, on his view, are real extra-mental existents, and he continued to subscribe to the doctrine until he abandoned (in 1919) the reality of the mind (or ego) to which propositional constituents are presented in acquaintance and in consequence the whole conception of propositions of which these views form a part.[19] On this realist view of propositional constituents, propositions, then, are not intermediaries between the mind and the world: as we have observed, they belong firmly to the world, not only because their constituents do, but because they themselves are unities and hence entities in their own right.[20]

The realist doctrine, in combination with the transparency thesis, has the effect in Russell's thought of making grammar the criterion of ontological commitment, even if it turns out that denoting concepts must be added to our ontology. (This result, with the element of – limited – faith in ordinary language removed, was, much later, still evident in Quine's dictum that to be is to be the value of a bound variable.) And the effect defines a position which both precedes and survives the discovery of the theory of descriptions and indeed motivates its application in ontologically reductive analyses of propositions: what changes with that discovery is the conception of where a language's true grammar is to be found. The footnote appended to *Principles* §46, that 'The excellence of grammar as a guide is proportional to ... the degree of analysis effected by the language considered' now appears prophetic: for only a *fully* analysed language will reveal reality's structure and constituent entities. But what is a fully analysed language?

Grammar, descriptions and analysis

The answer to this question must wait until we look at another way in which Russell's attitude to the transparency thesis changed between 1903 and 1918. In the 1902 Preface to *The Principles of Mathematics*, he talks of philosophical logic in terms of achieving the mental scrutiny of entities:

> The discussion of indefinables – which forms the chief part of philosophical logic – is the endeavour to see clearly, and to make others see clearly, the entities concerned, in order that the mind may have that kind of acquaintance with them which it has with redness or the taste of a pineapple.
>
> (Russell 1903, p. xv)

What this comes to in practice can be seen in the remarkable discussion of the notion of *and* in *Principles* §71, where the fact that the word 'and' is meaningful is enough to motivate what is in effect a search for a corresponding thing, *and* itself.[21] This discussion is in keeping with the procedure recommended in the words omitted from the quotation with which I began this chapter:

> Moreover, it must be admitted, I think, that every word occurring in a sentence must have *some* meaning: a perfectly meaningless sound could not be employed in the more or less fixed way in which language employs words. The correctness of our philosophical analysis of a proposition may therefore be usefully checked by the exercise of assigning the meaning of each word in the sentence expressing the proposition.
>
> (*Ibid.* §46; Russell's emphasis)

Later, Russell apparently takes back the claim that 'every word occurring in a sentence must have *some* meaning'. With hindsight, he says of this remark: 'This way of understanding language turned out to be mistaken.' But such is the grip that this 'way of understanding language' had upon him that he still could not entirely free himself from it. For in explaining the mistake he goes on:

> That a word 'must have *some* meaning' – the word, of course, being not gibberish, but one which has an intelligible use – is not always true if taken as applying to the word in isolation. What is true is

that the word contributes to the meaning of the sentence in which it occurs; but that is a very different matter.

The first step in the process [Russell is describing his abandon-ment of Platonism in mathematics] was the theory of descriptions.

(Russell 1937, p. x)

The fact that Russell's comments imply that having meaning is some-thing which *some* words are supposed to have in isolation, others not, indicates that he was thinking in terms of his earlier contrast between names and other words, where a name is 'a simple symbol, directly designating an individual which is its meaning, and having this meaning in its own right, independently of the meanings of all other words' (Russell 1919a, p. 174).

This gives us some sense of how Russell's partial change of mind about meaning was likely to affect his views: we should expect to find that a language in its fully analysed form (or a language which is fully analytic in its own right) is supposed to contain both some symbols for which the old views hold, and others for which they do not. And this is just what we do find. In 'The Philosophy of Logical Atomism', for example, he says:

> In a logically perfect language, the words in a proposition would correspond one by one with the components of the corresponding fact, with the exception of such words as 'or', 'not', 'if', 'then', which have a different function. In a logically perfect language, there will be one word and no more for every simple object, and everything that is not simple will be expressed by a combination of words, by a combination derived, of course, from the words for the simple things that enter in, one word for each simple component. A language of that sort will be completely analytic, and will show at a glance the logical structure of the facts asserted or denied.
>
> (Russell 1918, *CP8* p. 176; *LK* pp. 197–8)

This passage reveals – as indeed do the 'Philosophy of Logical Atomism' lectures as a whole – Wittgenstein's prewar influence,[22] in particular what he later called the 'fundamental thought' of the *Tractatus* (Wittgenstein 1921, 4.0312), that the logical constants do not represent, or go proxy for, objects. For Russell, of course, it follows from this that the understanding of the logical constants (now consid-ered as expressions rather than as what is expressed) can no longer be thought of in terms of acquaintance with indefinables. Nevertheless, despite the gradual restricting of the model of understanding meanings in terms of acquaintance with objects, Russell's reluctance to abandon the idea of the philosophical significance of grammar remains obvious. Later in the same work (Russell 1918, *CP8* p. 234; *LK* p. 269), he even says that 'practically all traditional metaphysics is filled with mistakes due to bad grammar', and explains what he means with an example from the philosophy of arithmetic, denying that the numerals '1', '2', '3' and '4' are names and that 1, 2, 3 and 4 are objects. But while Russell's language seems to be that of someone who has the notion of something like a grammatical method in philosophy, his treatment of his example reveals that the talk of grammar is superficial. One would expect that someone who thought that metaphysical error was the result of bad grammar would say, perhaps, that the first mistake was to think of the numerals as names and that the consequent second mistake was to suppose that the integers are objects. But Russell's diagnosis of the errors here puts them in precisely the reverse order, with the interpretation of the grammatical role of the numerals appearing as a consequence of a mistaken conception of the ontological status of the integers. In a set of transcribed and semi-popular lectures this could of course be the result of carelessness, but even if this is so such carelessness reveals the lack of importance that he ascribed to the grammatical diagnosis of the error: he was inclined to conceive of philosophical discovery on the model of acquaintance with an object with suitable properties for the task in hand,[23] and natural language played the part either (as in *Principles*) of providing a usually-transparent medium of such acquaintance or (post-'On Denoting') of something whose surface structure turned out fairly systematically to fail to be such a medium. But in both cases grammar is conceived of as something which has to fit a set of facts to which there is (an unexplained) independent intellectual or even quasi-sensory access. So his attachment to grammar does not extend here to the employment of a distinctively grammatical method in philosophy.

Still, Russell wavers a bit. In the same lectures we find him using a method that might arguably be described as grammatical (one reminiscent of Moore's 'open question' argument in *Principia Ethica* §13):

> The fact that you can discuss the proposition 'God exists' is a proof that 'God', as used in that proposition, is a description and not a name. If 'God' were a name, no question as to existence could arise.
>
> (*Ibid.* p. 218)

But the point here remains *exclusively* grammatical, about the status of the word 'God', rather than one which uses grammar to make a philosophical claim, such as, for example, that that very status shows there to be something wrong with the ontological argument. One may wish to generalize the grammatical point, as Russell himself was willing to do, and say that most (uses of) natural-language proper names are not, logically speaking, (uses of) proper names since they do not in practice function according to the logical requirements Russell imposes on names – for example, it is possible to use them in denials of existence. In the end, though, it is epistemology which dictates Russell's characteristic agnosticism about the existence of certain entities (such as the ego); the function of his grammatical points is merely to make such agnosticism possible. Again, then, grammar is conceived not as something autonomous but as something whose job is to fit an independently identifiable reality.

Before we move on from the theory of descriptions, it is worth emphasizing that sometimes, with hindsight (for example, Russell 1959, p. 84), Russell himself subscribes to part of the usual story, when he presents the theory of descriptions as freeing one from the assumption that words must stand for entities in order to be meaningful: 'The central point of the theory of descriptions was that a phrase may contribute to the meaning of a sentence without having any meaning at all in isolation' (*ibid.* p. 85). But, as we have just seen, he puts the point thus because his conception of a name was precisely that of an expression which *does* have meaning in isolation. And in fact, just as such a conception of a name would lead one to expect, and despite this presentation of the theory of descriptions, the theory's real function as applied both in ontologically non-reductive and reductive analysis is to reinforce that assumption, to protect it against obvious counter-examples, by showing that, *rightly understood*, such words are in fact just codifications of more complex expressions, for each individual component of which the assumption holds true.[24] Although this function, if noticed at all as a separable feature of the theory of descriptions, is likely to be associated with the famous 'fundamental epistemological principle' of 'Knowledge by Acquaintance and Knowledge by Description' (Russell 1911: *CP6* p. 154; *ML* p. 159), it in fact appears much earlier, as does the principle, in 'On Denoting' itself:

Thus in every proposition that we can apprehend (*i.e.* not only in those whose truth or falsehood we can judge of, but in all that we can think about), all the constituents are really entities with which we have immediate acquaintance.

(Russell 1905b: *CP4* p. 427; *LK* p. 56)

This fundamental epistemological principle, when combined with Russell's increasing scepticism about the scope of what one could be acquainted with, led him by the time of the 'Logical Atomism' lectures to a historically significant view of the entities named in a fully analysed language:

> In a logically perfect language, there will be one word and no more for every simple object, and everything that is not simple will be expressed by a combination of words, by a combination derived, of course, from the words for the simple things that enter in, one word for each simple component. A language of that sort will be completely analytic, and will show at a glance the logical structure of the facts asserted or denied ... A logically perfect language, if it could be constructed, would not only be intolerably prolix, but, as regards its vocabulary, would be very largely private to one speaker. That is to say, all the names that it would use would be private to that speaker and could not enter into the language of another speaker.
>
> (Russell 1918: *CP8* p. 176; *LK* pp. 197–8)

> ... A name, in the narrow logical sense of a word whose meaning is a particular, can only be applied to a particular with which the speaker is acquainted, because you cannot name anything you are not acquainted with ... One can use 'this' as a name to stand for a particular with which one is acquainted at the moment. We say 'This is white' ... But if you try to apprehend the proposition that I am expressing when I say 'This is white', you cannot do it. If you mean this piece of chalk as a physical object, then you are not using a proper name. It is only when you use 'this' quite strictly, to stand for an actual object of sense [that is, a sense-datum], that it is really a proper name. And in that it has a very odd property for a proper name, namely that it seldom means the same thing two moments running and does not mean the same thing to the speaker and to the hearer.
>
> (Russell 1918: *CP8* pp. 178–9; *LK* p. 201)

> [I]n order to understand a name for a particular, the only thing necessary is to be acquainted with that particular. When you are acquainted with that particular, you have a full, adequate, and complete understanding of the name, and no further information is required.
>
> (Russell 1918: *CP8* p. 179; *LK* p. 201)

There is reason to believe that these passages helped to provoke Wittgenstein's so-called 'private language argument'.[25] And when we compare them with the fact that the *experience* which Bradley claims is the fundamental stuff of reality is not intended to be the subjective experience of an individual self, then, however puzzling we may find this notion of experience and Bradley's attempt to defend himself against the charge of solipsism (1893, *AR* Ch. XXI; 1914c), we may be led to wonder whether it is only the Absolute Idealist who risks shutting himself up 'in a subjective prison' (Russell 1959, p. 62);[26] indeed, Bradley's monism – if defensible – excludes the solipsism Russell fears, for it forbids the separation of subject and experience which gives solipsism its restrictive bite. If there is any form of solipsism to be found in Bradley's thought, it resembles the vestigial kind found in the *Tractatus*, which 'strictly carried through, coincides with pure realism' (Wittgenstein 1921, §5.64; my translation).[27] This is, of course, a vexed issue, too large to be settled *en passant*, on both sides of the question: the difficulty in making sense of absolute idealism's notion of experience which is not someone's is always going to make it prone to the psychologistic reading implied by Russell's criticism, and Wittgenstein's strictures on the idea of a private language remain controversial. My intention is merely to indicate that there is more room for argument than Russell's casual dismissal suggests.[28]

Be that as it may, however, the main point is that the theory of descriptions, with the proviso that the usual story about it is false, is one of the factors which led, not to the abandonment of the transparency thesis, but merely to the gradual transfer from natural to fully analysed language of Russell's faith in grammar as revelatory of ontology, together with a significant *increase* in the degree of that faith.[29] This transfer signifies the development in Russell's thought, under Wittgenstein's influence, of the notion of logical form, hidden from view in natural language but revealed by the process of analysis. Already, then, we have seen enough to demonstrate that the simple contrast with which we began is a serious distortion of the truth. Let us now move on to examine another factor.

Negative propositions

At the time when Russell is proclaiming adherence to the transparency thesis, he has surprisingly little to say about negation. *The Principles of Mathematics* contains a formal definition in §19, but it is nothing like the 'analysis of an idea into its constituents' which, as we saw above

with respect to 'and', Russell thought to be genuine philosophical definition. On the face of it, someone who thinks, as he did, that grammar
is a guide to a correct logic and that logic is not separate from ontology, should find negation a problem, and owes a solution. One would
expect unease over negation to lead to unease over the transparency
thesis.

Given, however, that Russell's self-proclaimed 'abandonment' of the
transparency thesis amounts, as I have said, to no more than a shift
from ordinary to fully analysed language as the vehicle of the relevant
grammar, it is not at all surprising that, after he has made this shift, he
has a good deal to say about negation. An important part of it is contained in the remarks quoted in the previous section about a 'logically
perfect language' from the logical atomism lectures. But there is more
from the same source. To see what is at issue, we need to go back to the
start of them:

> The first truism to which I wish to draw your attention – and I hope
> you will agree with me that these things that I call truisms are so
> obvious that it is almost laughable to mention them – is that the
> world contains *facts*, which are what they are whatever we may
> choose to think about them, and there are also *beliefs*, which have
> reference to facts, and by reference to facts are either true or false ...
> When I speak of a fact ... I mean the kind of thing that makes a
> proposition true or false. If I say 'It is raining', what I say is true in a
> certain condition of weather and is false in other conditions of
> weather. The condition of weather that makes my statement true (or
> false as the case may be), is what I should call a 'fact'.
>
> (Russell 1918: *CP8* p. 163; *LK* p. 182)

Two paragraphs later, he adds,

> It is important to observe that facts belong to the objective world.
> They are not created by our thoughts or beliefs except in special cases
> ... The first thing I want to emphasise is that the outer world – the
> world, so to speak, which knowledge is aiming at knowing – is not
> completely described by a lot of 'particulars', but you must also take
> account of these things that I call facts, which are the sort of things
> that you express by a sentence, and that these, just as much as par-
> ticular chairs and tables, are part of the real world ... When we speak
> falsely it is an objective fact that makes what we say false, and it is an
> objective fact which makes what we say true when we speak truly.

Notice that on this account the fact that the chair is under the table is 'a part of the real world' just as the chair and the table are. In his third lecture Russell classifies the different types of fact corresponding to the different types of declarative sentence. It soon appears, though, that not every type of sentence has its own corresponding type of fact. Only 'atomic' sentences, the ones which contain a single verb, such as 'Mary grows onions', have corresponding facts to make them true or false: the truth and falsity of the 'molecular' sentences, which are built up out of the atomic ones, can be accounted for without postulating molecular facts as well as atomic facts. Russell puts the point like this, using disjunctive propositions as an example:

> But when you take such a proposition as 'p or q', 'Socrates is mortal or Socrates is living still', there you will have two different facts involved in the truth or the falsehood of your proposition 'p or q'. There will be the fact that corresponds to p and there will be the fact that corresponds to q, and both of those facts are relevant in discovering the truth or falsehood of 'p or q'. I do not suppose there is in the world a single disjunctive fact corresponding to 'p or q'. It does not look plausible that in the actual objective world there are facts going about which you could describe as 'p or q' ... Generally speaking, as regards these things that you make up out of two propositions, the whole of what is necessary in order to know their meaning is to know under what circumstances they are true, given the truth or falsehood of p and the truth or falsehood of q.
>
> (*Ibid.*: *CP8* p. 185; *LK* p. 209)

Russell goes on to explain, for the benefit of an audience unfamiliar with the propositional calculus, that 'p or q' is the proposition that is false when p and q are both false but is true otherwise. He then adds this significant comment:

> You must not look about the real world for an object which you can call 'or', and say, 'Now, look at this. This is "or".' There is no such thing, and if you try to analyse 'p or q' in that way you will get into trouble.
>
> (*Ibid.*: *CP8* p. 186; *LK* pp. 209–10)

That is, on Russell's view, 'p or q' could be a fact only if 'or' were an object. So there are none of these implausible molecular facts, there are just atomic facts. However, Russell is prepared to acknowledge other kinds of implausible fact, in particular, negative facts:

Are there negative facts? Are there such facts as you might call the fact that 'Socrates is not alive'? I have assumed in all that I have said hitherto that there are negative facts, that for example if you say 'Socrates is alive', there is corresponding to that proposition in the real world the fact that Socrates is not alive. One has a certain repugnance to negative facts, the same sort of feeling that makes you wish not to have a fact '*p* or *q*' going about the world.

(*Ibid.*: *CP8* p. 187; *LK* p. 211)

But what exactly is it that is repugnant about negative facts? One possibility is that they just seem unnecessary, in the way that disjunctive facts do. We might think that the theory of truth-functions can provide all we need: not-*p* is the proposition which is false when the proposition *p* is true, and is true when the proposition *p* is false. We don't, it may seem, need a negative fact: the truth of not-*p* can be accounted for via the truth of *p*, and the truth of *p* can be accounted for by the presence of the corresponding positive fact.

There are two problems with this answer. One is that there is more than being unnecessary to being repugnant. So this explanation of what Russell is after is insufficient. But the deeper problem is that the answer is muddled. It *begins* by quite satisfactorily accounting for the truth of not-*p* via the *falsehood* of *p*, but it *ends* by saying that we can account for the truth of not-*p* via the *truth* of *p* without justifying the shift in the explanation from the falsehood of *p* to the truth of *p*. And while the truth of *p* can be accounted for by the presence of the corresponding positive fact, its *falsehood* cannot be accounted for in the same way. Rather, its falsehood needs the *absence* of the corresponding fact.

Russell is aware that appeal to truth-functions will not answer his question.[30] The fundamental reason for postulating negative facts is the need for a truth-maker for negative statements, and what will work for disjunction will not work for negation. On the face of it, Bradley's clearly anti-transparency view that the truth-maker is some other fact incompatible with the falsehood of the negative statement – for example, what makes it true that my blood is not at 100°C (and not at 99.99°C, and not at 101°C, and not at 101.5°C, and not at 102°C, and so *ad infinitum*) is the fact that it is at 37°C – is more plausible than the Russellian alternative of continuum-many negative facts. Russell's complaint about this is, as he goes on to say, that 'it makes incompatibility a fundamental and objective fact, which is not so very much simpler than allowing negative facts' (*Ibid.*: *CP8* p. 189; *LK* p. 213). Let us allow this objection to stand, and ask, given that Russell would not accept the Bradleian account, why does he not instead maintain that what makes it true that my blood is not at 100°C is the absence of the corresponding fact? Why does he opt for the view that negation is a fundamental feature of the world? I think Russell would have said that the absence of a fact is the existence of a negative fact (and he certainly was saying this when he returned to the matter a little later[31]). But as Russell would understand negative facts, this should have worried him, for, when rejecting disjunctive facts, he said, as we saw, 'You must not look about the real world for an object which you can call 'or', and say, "Now, look at this. This is 'or'." There is no such thing ...'. If Russell rejected disjunctive facts in these terms, but was prepared to admit negative facts, then one might reasonably conclude that you may look about the real world for an object which you can call 'not', and say 'Now look at this. This is "not".'[32] If he wanted us to think that there are negative facts, then by his own words, this is just what he should have been doing. How has he got himself into this predicament? An answer might be: it is the lingering effect of the demand for a one word/one thing correspondence characteristic of the transparency thesis.[33] In the discussion appended to the third of his logical atomism lectures we see Russell's faith in the grammar of his 'perfect logical language' being tested to destruction.

Russell's discussion of negation and disjunction, is, however, significant in another way. It helps to illustrate another problem concerning his continuing faith that grammar maps ontology in a fully analysed language. An examination of this problem reveals that further elements of the standard Russell/Bradley story need major revision.

Universal propositions

The problem originates with the treatment, in 'On Denoting', of the universal proposition as hypothetical: 'Consider next the proposition "all men are mortal". This proposition is really hypothetical and states that *if* anything is a man, it is mortal', Russell says, adding in a footnote 'As has been ably argued in Mr. Bradley's *Logic*, Book I, Chap. II' (1905b: *CP4* p. 420; *LK* p. 43). Although Russell's acceptance of this view and his acknowledgment of Bradley are well-known, it is not usually remarked that it too constitutes a change from the account of universal propositions in *The Principles of Mathematics*, where they are handled in terms of denoting concepts. Thus the proposition that all numbers are either odd or even is, on the 1903 view, about all numbers but does not contain all numbers as constituents (otherwise under-

standing the proposition, which requires acquaintance with its constituents, would be beyond the power of the human mind), containing
instead the denoting concept *all numbers* which 'though not itself infinitely complex, yet denotes an infinitely complex object. This is the
inmost secret of our power to deal with infinity' (Russell 1903, §72).[34]
Accordingly, although the complications are fewer because there is no
settled myth to be demolished, much that has already been said about
the shift from denoting concepts to the theory of descriptions applies
here too, in particular the remarks concerning the extent to which the
change represents a departure from the transparency thesis.

By 1905, then, Russell agreed with Bradley that universal propositions containing nothing but general terms are not, despite their
surface grammar, categorical truths; and, because of the familiar interdefinability of the universal and existential quantifiers in propositions
via negation, he accordingly was committed (at least in his own eyes)
to the view that *no* universally or existentially quantified propositions
containing nothing but general terms are categorical – all turn out to
be hypothetical.[35] That *in effect* committed him to the existence of
intrinsically hypothetical facts, though only in effect, because Russell
did not at this stage address the question what kinds of facts are truth-
makers for hypothetical propositions: for his ontology did not yet
include facts. Once he adopted the correspondence theory of truth,
however, the issue of the nature of hypothetical propositions' truth-
makers naturally arose.

What, then, are these truth-makers? On the one hand, Russell
rejected the view that universal propositions (which are hypotheticals)
have *non*-hypothetical atomic facts as truth-makers, on the grounds
that 'All men are mortal' cannot be analysed as 'John is mortal and
James is mortal and ...', since this needs completion with the universal,
and hence hypothetical, proposition 'All men are among those I have
enumerated' (1918: *CP8* pp. 206–8; *LK* pp. 234–7). But the upshot was
not, after all, an ontology which included intrinsically hypothetical
truth-makers for universal propositions; rather – to borrow Bradley's
words from the chapter to which we saw Russell referring at the beginning of this section – it was that 'Truth will then refer to fact *indirectly*'
(Bradley 1883, p. 46). For Bradley thought, and Russell, once he had
adopted an ontology which included facts, came to think, that there
are no hypothetical facts (*ibid.*, p. 46; Russell 1918: *CP8* pp. 186–7;
LK pp. 210–11). In Bradley's case, there are no hypothetical facts
because in his ontology there are no facts at all; in Russell's, this was
because he thought that, via techniques now familiar through the

propositional calculus, hypothetical propositions are definable truth-functionally as disjunctive propositions. This position over-determines the elimination of hypothetical facts: first, their definability in terms of disjunction and negation reveals that there is no need to postulate *sui generis* hypothetical facts; second, as we observed in the previous section, Russell thought too that there are in any case no disjunctive facts (because he could not believe that there is anything in reality corresponding to the disjunctive 'or'); and third, the theory of truth-functions made it otiose to posit the existence of any molecular facts at all, disjunctive or otherwise. Russell himself acknowledges the difficulty, and contemplates the readmission of molecular facts.[36] But the result is that his position on truth-makers for hypothetical (and so also for universal) propositions became subject to a fundamental unclarity: are these truth-makers hypothetical or not? Neither answer, it seems, is satisfactory.

The problems do not, however, end there. Once one has adopted the view that universal propositions are made true by universal facts – as we have just seen, the precise nature of these facts is unclear, but we can at least say that they are non-singular – and then adds the view that ordinary singular propositions turn out, by application of the theory of descriptions and the interdefinability of the quantifiers, to be universal ones, singular facts are likely to disappear from one's ontology altogether, and language threatens to become decoupled from the world by reason of its consequential inability to express truths which are guaranteed not to apply to more than one case (a view which Bradley accepted with equanimity). This brings out something which had not occurred to Russell in 1903: that the doctrine of real propositional constituents, though it is precisely designed to make truth and knowledge possible, does not on its own guarantee that this will involve categorical truths about singular facts, and so does not on its own yet guarantee a genuine connection between language and world. The doctrine needed supplementation with something that would guarantee this. In *The Principles of Mathematics* the matter is just taken for granted.

Although Russell came to follow Bradley in supposing that universal propositions are hypothetical, he did not endorse Bradley's wider claim that *all* apparently categorical statements are really hypothetical in form, an anticipation of Quine's modification of the theory of descriptions to exclude all singular terms.[37] Bradley anticipated too a feature of the theory of descriptions, namely the ambiguity of the denial of a statement containing a definite description:

'The King of Utopia died on Tuesday' may be safely contradicted. And yet the denial must remain ambiguous. The ground may be that there is no such place, or it never had a king, or he is still living, or, though he is dead, yet he died on Monday.

(Bradley 1883, pp. 124–5)

But while the example is strikingly similar to Russell's own treatment of the denial of 'The present King of France is bald' (and gives the lie to his well-known jibe, 'Hegelians, who love a synthesis, will probably conclude that he wears a wig'), it differs in its significance. First (like the theory of denoting concepts), it is not part of a worked-out account which enabled the clear and justificatory depiction of the inference from 'The man who came to dinner is an impoverished aristocrat' to 'The man who came to dinner is an aristocrat'. In this respect it is massively inferior to the Theory of Descriptions.[38] Second, unlike Russell, Bradley does not contrast the example with a case where language goes directly to the world rather than employing general terms to capture reality indirectly. Both philosophers held that, where the world/ language relation goes through descriptions, it is indirect and vulnerable to error, and that unless there were cases where the relation is *not* mediated by descriptions, language would not be unambiguously linked to the extra-mental world and there would be no absolute, unconditional and complete empirical truths. Bradley accepted the consequence (indeed he devoted much space in *The Principles of Logic* to arguing that there is no possibility of unconditional, context-free, unambiguous designation – this is one of the roots of his claim that truth has degrees), but its intolerability for Russell motivated him to maintain that there are indeed such exceptional cases.[39] These exceptions are precisely those involving logically proper names. This notion provides the needed supplementation for the doctrine of real propositional constituents: it enables the formation of sentences expressing definitely categorical judgments concerning spatio-temporal particulars with which the mind doing the judging is acquainted.[40] Further, Russell seems to have held that if language were not unambiguously pinned to the world by names then the only account of truth available would be a coherence theory, to which, as we saw in Chapter 4 (p. 79*f*), he thought there was the overwhelming objection that there could be mutually inconsistent sets of coherent and thus true propositions. Logically proper names thus rescue the correspondence theory of truth. Further, as they are linked to their bearers by acquaintance, a relation unmediated by concepts or descriptions, they provide the possibility of absolute, unconditional and complete empirical truths which would contain those bearers as constituents.

Bradley, by contrast, denies that we can ever make the subject of our judgments into a constituent of propositions: '[I]n every judgment there is a subject of which the ideal content is asserted. But this subject of course can not [*sic*] belong to the content or fall within it ...' (Bradley 1883, p. 13). Further, the claim that the logical form of universal propositions is hypothetical functions quite differently in Bradley from the way it functions in Russell, for Bradley's view that the terms of relations are unreal and his consequent rejection of the Russellian idea that the world contains simple nameables allows no corresponding conception of a logically perfect language. In fact, on Bradley's view, grammar is a doubly bad guide for philosophers. In the first place, surface grammar misrepresents thought for the reasons he, through Russell, made familiar to us all in his treatment of the universal proposition; but, in the second place, even logical grammar is misleading, because its structures, however useful they may be for inference and proof, are utterly inadequate to the nature of experience, since according to Bradley discursive thought imposes distinctions on reality where none exist. This view that surface grammar is misleading has extensive ramifications throughout his philosophical logic, such as his suggestion that judgments contain just one idea (an extreme solution to the problem of the unity of the proposition), as against predecessors like the Port-Royal *Logic*,[41] and his hostility to the idea that the surface grammar's subject expression picks out the logical subject which the proposition is about: 'In their ordinary acceptation the traditional subject, predicate and copula are mere superstitions' (*ibid.* p. 21).

Subject–predicate grammar and the status of relations

Here it is helpful to recall the simple contrast we saw presented in *The Principles of Mathematics* and which may be summarized as follows: 'Russell subscribes to the transparency thesis, while Bradley denies it.' We have already noted the shortcomings of this simple contrast with respect to Russell himself. But what about Bradley? It is certainly true that Bradley denied the transparency thesis. But did he do so for the reasons which were attributed to him by Russell and his followers? Although, as we noticed, the simple contrast is not itself part of the stereotype, these reasons most certainly are. There are two connected versions of them, both highly influential, in Russell himself, in the commentaries and elsewhere. One is that Bradley 'rejected relations'. Another, usually given as grounds for the former, is that he subscribed to the view that all propositions are of subject–predicate form.[42]

Recent commentary by authors sympathetic to Russell's side of the dispute with Bradley provides representative examples of both versions.

The first version is expressed clearly by Nicholas Griffin (1991, p. 183):

> Although it was Russell who made this distinction [between grammatical and logical form] famous, such a distinction (though not so described) is to be found in Bradley; indeed, it is forced on Bradley by (among other things) his rejection of relations, since, from the point of view of overt grammar, some judgements are undeniably relational. Such judgements have to be reformulated in a way which eliminates the relation.

The dispute over relations is nearly always discussed by means of slack formulations such as the 'acceptance' or 'rejection' of relations by various philosophers, obscuring the details of an extended and tangled debate and making it all too easy to present the idealists as perverse. In this case, Griffin's remark encapsulates some common misunderstandings of the dispute over relations. The talk of Bradley's 'rejection of relations' obscures the difference between rejection (i) of the possibility of ordinary relational judgments' being true, and (ii) of a philosophical account of the world's variety and relatedness which is supposed to underpin the possibility of truth for those judgments. Further, it blurs the complexity and development of his views over time.[43]

Such talk is too common, however, to be entirely baseless. And it is hard to avoid when giving a summary account: I have, unwillingly, employed it myself earlier in this book, and even the scrupulously careful Peter Hylton (1990, pp. 11–12) allows himself the phrase 'Bradley's denial of relations', before moving unremarked through 'his denial of the reality of relations' to 'his denial of the ultimate reality of relations'. So we should ask: in what sense then, *does* Bradley reject relations? Interpretation (i) has no basis in Bradley's text. And it was not candid of Russell (nor would it be wise of Russellian critics) to try to use it as a stick with which to beat him on the basis that metaphysical doctrines can simply be discarded if they conflict with everyday truths: for this strategy would have the effect of condemning Russell's rival extreme pluralist views as much as Bradley's monism.[44] Interpretation (ii), on the other hand, does make sense of Bradley's text: what he consistently rejected for most of his philosophical career was the *reality* of relations; and since for Bradley, as we saw in Chapter 2 (p. 27*f*), to be real is to be substantial, the claim of relations' unreality is simply that they are not substances.[45] As relations are not substances, there are no names of relations (contrary to Russell's assumptions from 1903 to his abandoning of the multiple relation theory of judgment in 1919). This claim, which has been found so objectionable in Bradley, attracted no such vilification when it was made by Wittgenstein in a remark we have noticed already:

> Not 'The complex sign "aRb" says that a stands to b in the relation R', but rather, that 'a' stands to 'b' in a certain relation says that aRb.
>
> (Wittgenstein 1921: 3.1432, my translation)

It is thus not true that 'such judgements have to be reformulated in a way which eliminates the relational expression' (which is presumably what Griffin meant by his last sentence). All that is needed to do justice to Bradley's belief that relations are unreal is that relation-expressions not be construed as names; they might nevertheless, for all sorts of reasons, not be eliminable. Indeed, to discuss the matter in the way that Griffin does – and this is not to suggest any particular fault on his part, for this way is now standard – is to employ a method of doing philosophy which Russell himself helped to establish: that is, the attempted re-parsing of sentences which apparently commit one to the existence of something into a form in which no such commitment is suggested. If such re-parsing turns out to be impossible, then the item in question is taken to exist or be real.[46] The point may be expressed in Wittgensteinian fashion: the surface grammar of relational statements is misleading, for it suggests a false picture of reality.[47] And this is a view which Russell, under the influence of Wittgenstein, came to share.[48]

Admittedly, there are complications here, concerning just which features of the polymorphous notion of substance each philosopher accepted, and when. Confining these features, for the sake of simplicity, to independence and permanence (counting atemporality as a kind of permanence), then we may say that Bradley accepted both, Russell moved from accepting both (1903, §46) to accepting independence but rejecting permanence (1918: *CP8* p. 179, *LK* p. 202); and Wittgenstein accepted permanence but – with qualifications – not independence (1921, §§2.011–2.0122, 2.024–2.0272; and cf. Fogelin 1976, p. 6).

Common to all three, however, is that, were the world to contain substances (however emasculated) then to these substances would correspond names; and these complications do not make the dispute over the status of relations less of a muddle.

The second version can be found in a recent book by Anthony Grayling (1996, p. 33): 'One lesson he [Russell] had learned from arguing against idealism is that the surface grammar of language can mislead us about the meaning of what we say.' This remark suggests that the idealists took surface grammar at face value (a striking inversion of Russell's actual position on transparency in 1903), and that Russell arrived at the opposing position by arguing against them; when in point of fact he learned that lesson from Bradley himself. Grayling goes on, it seems, to concur with Russell's view that the idealists took 'all propositions to be fundamentally subject–predicate in form'. (Russellian accounts of early twentieth-century disputes have soaked deeply into the collective memory of subsequent philosophers.) But it is hard to make sense of this combination of complaints: if Russell's view were correct, it would sit ill with the former suggestion, since, as Bradley himself observed,

> the doctrine [sc. that all propositions are of subject–predicate form] ... is erroneous. 'B follows A,' 'A and B coexist,' 'A and B are equal,' 'A is south of B' – in these instances it is mere disregard of facts which can hold to the doctrine. It is unnatural to take A or B as the subject and the residue as predicate. And, where existence is directly asserted or denied, as in, 'The soul exists,' or, 'There is a sea-serpent,' or, 'There is nothing here,' the difficulties of the theory will be found to culminate.
>
> (Bradley 1883, *PL* p. 13)

Obviously, then, Bradley recognized that the surface grammar of some propositions (or judgments, to use his word) is not of subject–predicate form. Nevertheless, perhaps he thought that matters are different with their deep grammar, even though in this passage he is talking about ideas rather than words. And this is indeed how Russell got it into his head that Bradley's view was that all propositions are 'fundamentally subject–predicate in form', for Bradley regarded judgments not as linguistic but as ideal entities,[49] and, many times, says things like these: '[A]ll judgments predicate their ideal content as an attribute of the real' (1883, *PL* p. 50), and 'in every judgment there is a subject of which the ideal content is asserted ... We shall see that the subject is ... always reality' (*ibid.*, p. 13). The 'ideal content' is that which belongs to thought, the real vehicle of judgments.

But it is easy to overlook the fact, as Russell did, that for Bradley this logical subject could not be (as Russell's own logical subjects were) a constituent of the judgment. The content of judgments, according to Bradley, is at bottom entirely predicative, and the reality which is their subject does not figure as part of that content; although for Bradley reality is substantial, 'Reality' is not its name. When he says – in effect, for his language is different – that the logical form of a grammatically subject–predicate judgment is 'Reality is such that *S* is *P*', where '*S*' and '*P*' both function predicatively, his view is even closer than we have already noted (in the previous section) to an informal anticipation of Quine's modification of the theory of descriptions to exclude all singular terms. It is closer because the expression 'Reality is such that ...' functions in Bradley's thought as a predecessor of the formal logician's quantifier and variable.[50] This is entirely consistent with the position we saw him taking (Chapter 3, p. 50*f*), that all parts of a judgment are, equally, unsaturated, that is, in his terms, unreal: all being ultimately predicative, all are incomplete.

Despite these complications, perhaps Russell's most noticeable use of grammatical notions is his frequent appeal to the unqualified allegation that various philosophers, especially idealists, just assumed that all propositions are of subject–predicate form. This allegation turns up over a number of years, beginning in 1900 with his *Critical Exposition of the Philosophy of Leibniz*, where Russell argues both that the assumption is false and that its falsity is a matter of utmost philosophical significance.[51]

Why does Russell think this grammatical doctrine so significant? The main reasons appear to be two. First, he claimed that the doctrine is peculiarly widely held:

> In the belief that propositions must, in the last analysis, have a subject and a predicate, Leibniz does not differ either from his predecessors or from his successors. Any philosophy which uses either substance or the Absolute will be found, on inspection, to depend upon this belief. Kant's belief in an unknowable thing-in-itself was largely due to the same theory. It cannot be denied, therefore, that the doctrine is important. Philosophers have differed, not so much in respect of belief in its truth, as in respect of their consistency in carrying it out.
>
> (Russell 1900, p. 15)[52]

To Kant and Leibniz, Russell explicitly adds Descartes, Spinoza and Bradley as having held to the subject–predicate account of propositions (and repeats the list, except for Kant, in the second paragraph of his 1924), but it is clear from the above that he thinks that almost every philosopher has done the same. This would indeed be a remarkable discovery: that most philosophers have, often presumably inadvertently, committed themselves to a particular grammatical doctrine. What is the explanation of the prevalence of this commitment? One might expect here the sort of explanation in terms of grammatical illusion with which we are familiar from Wittgenstein; but Russell offers none.[53]

Second, he held that the doctrine is an error. This on its own does not explain why it is significant. There is something special about the error. What is it? Hylton offers the following diagnosis:

> Russell, then, takes the subject–predicate view of propositions to be philosophically crucial because he identifies this view with the doctrine that relations are not real, objective, non-mental entities.
>
> (Hylton 1990, p. 155)

There is something right about this, but the explanation is hardly sufficient. For why should Russell have made this not exactly obvious identification? The answer to this question must surely be found in his adherence to the transparency thesis and the doctrine of real propositional constituents. Adding the subject–predicate view to these, would, in Russell's mind, entail the conclusion that relations are not real entities. And this, he thinks, would make all relational judgments false. Given his other commitments, the subject–predicate view has to go.

This diagnosis is borne out by the fact that over several years Russell used his allegation (that almost every philosopher had taken propositions to be, ultimately, of subject–predicate form) in an attempt to refute a range of different views on the subject of relations. Here is its occurrence in *Our Knowledge of the External World*:[54]

> Traditional logic, since it holds that all propositions have the subject–predicate form, is unable to admit the reality of relations: all relations, it maintains, must be reduced to properties of the apparently related terms. There are many ways of refuting this opinion; one of the easiest is derived from the consideration of what are called 'asymmetrical' relations.

After explaining his classification of relations, Russell goes on to produce his refutation. The argument is on pages 58–9, and concludes thus:

> Asymmetrical relations are involved in all series – in space and time, greater and less, whole and part, and many others of the most important characteristics of the actual world. All these aspects, therefore, the logic which reduces everything to subjects and predicates is compelled to condemn as error and mere appearance. To those whose logic is not malicious, such a wholesale condemnation appears impossible. And in fact there is no reason other than prejudice, so far as I can discover, for denying the reality of relations. When once their reality is admitted, all *logical* grounds for supposing the world of sense to be illusory disappear.

The most obvious feature of these remarks is the significance claimed for Russell's argument in the last sentence quoted. Only slightly less obvious a feature is how reminiscent of Moore Russell's strategy is: undercut *an* argument for a view, and then maintain that the view's being held must be attributed to sources other than rational ones. What is not so obvious is just how the argument is meant to work, for it is very casually stated.

Prior to the quotation, Russell's argument is that 'the question whether all relations can be reduced to predications' is to be answered in the negative, since it is clearly impossible to express propositions concerning asymmetrical relations (such as '*a* is greater than *b*') in terms of properties:[55] the best attempts we can make at such expression, for example, through propositions such as 'The whole *ab* contains difference in magnitude', are 'formally incapable of explaining the facts' because they lose the information as to which of the objects is greater. Restoring this information requires that we say which of the magnitudes is greater, and this means that the original relation, which was to be reduced, reappears.

Russell attached a great deal of weight to this argument. In somewhat less casual form (though in fact much of the wording is the same), it is given a prominent place in Chapter XXVI of *The Principles of Mathematics*. It represents Russell's attack on what he called the 'monistic' version of the reducibility thesis, which he attributed to Bradley. (He also attacked a 'monadistic' version, which he attributed to Leibniz.[56]) It has been a formative influence on how later philosophers have conceived the dispute between the two. Whatever one thinks of the argument – and we shall try to come to a verdict on its significance in the next chapter – it is clear that it involves a point of grammar – this time of deep grammar, where syntax is designed to display semantic function and logical form is manifest – which is that claims about asymmetrical relations cannot be expressed as predications.[57] And this grammatical point gets its philosophical importance for Russell by being given an ontological significance: it shows that the relation is real, in the sense of being an independent substance. We see here an anticipation of the notion of a logically perfect language as we saw it introduced in 'The Philosophy of Logical Atomism' (Russell 1918: *CP8* p. 176; *LK* pp. 197–8): the ineliminability of a relational expression shows the relation to be some kind of elementary object.

This realism regarding relations is characteristic of Russell's post-idealist phase, and disappears, as a result of Wittgenstein's influence, only after the Great War. For example, in the *Critical Exposition of the Philosophy of Leibniz*, Russell moves unhesitatingly from noting that Leibniz regards relations ('in this third way of considering them') as 'mere ideal thing[s]' (1900, p. 13), through saying that Leibniz is 'denying the independent reality of relations' (*ibid.* pp. 14–15), to claiming that Leibniz is committed to 'the denial of relations' (*ibid.* p. 15). What this so-called denial of relations comes to in Russell's mind, even though he does not here explicitly say what it means for a relation to be unreal, can be gleaned from the fact that he does not consider the possibility that relational propositions may be true even if relations are ideal. But his working criterion of reality seems to be grammatical, in at least one sense of that word. After all, no amount of empirical study of two unequal objects will cast light upon the ontological status of *greater than*, and Russell's view is clearly that the question of its status is settled entirely by the question of whether, say, '*a* is greater than *b*' can be represented in subject–predicate form without crucial loss of information.

Despite the fact that Russell's criticisms of Bradley often missed their target, this represents a point in common between the two philosophers, but one obscured by their divergence in its application. The point in common is their employment of grammatical criteria for adjudicating the issue of the reality of relations. The question of relations' reality is the question of their individual substantiality. For Russell, this is settled by deciding whether or not relational expressions are eliminable. If they are not eliminable, they must be taken to be names of some kind of objects, and his view (at least prior to his post-Wittgenstein change of mind on the subject) is that they are not eliminable. But Russell's argument is weakened both by his assumption that the only way in which they could be eliminated is by reduction to predication (whereas *Tractatus* 3.1432 displays another possibility),[58] by his pre-Tractarian naïvety about what it is to be a *symbol*, and by his tendency to regard grammatical criteria as merely reflective of a reality to which he has independent access; moreover his argument gets simplified in its application by his conception of a logically perfect language, whose categorematic expressions will have uniform semantic roles.

Bradley's view is both more complex and more extreme: even if elimination of relational expressions in favour of predication were possible (a view to which Bradley himself does not adhere), this would not amount to an elimination of relations, since, Bradley thought, predication involves a relation between subject and predicate, a relation indicated by the copula;[59] but in any case, given that he would have rejected the notion of a logically perfect language (for he held thought, and hence language, to be in principle inadequate for the presentation of reality), the ineliminability of a relational expression would still in principle leave open the question as to whether it had to be interpreted as indicating a substance; and, most extremely, he argued that terms of relations are unreal themselves, so that even if a language's relational expressions were ineliminable and shared with its term-expressions a uniform semantic role, this would show only that relations and their terms were on a par in all being unreal.[60] However, despite the importance which both Bradley and Russell accorded to grammar, in both philosophers it is put at the service of underlying metaphysical visions. In this way they stand out sharply from Frege, whose semantics was driven by syntax.[61]

Subject–predicate grammar: substance and attribute

Given the common view that the surface grammar of at least many sentences of English is subject–predicate in form, and the long tradition of finding an ontological counterpart in the substance–attribute distinction,[62] it is perhaps surprising that Russell even at the time of his closest adherence to the transparency thesis was hostile to the notion of substance. There is some evidence that the seeds of this hostility may have been sown in the historical study he undertook, as part of his work towards the Moral Sciences Tripos in 1894, of the seventeenth-century philosophers (Descartes, Spinoza, Geulincx, Leibniz, Locke) who in their different ways make such prominent use of this notion, in which he evinces an acute awareness of the problems arising from those uses.[63] The seeds did not immediately germinate, however: in his 1897 book *An Essay on the Foundations of Geometry*, Russell adheres to a substance–attribute ontology, moreover drawing no distinction between properties and relations.[64] It seems to be in the work he did on Leibniz from 1898, and which culminated in the *Critical Exposition* of 1900, that he began to think the notion irrevocably flawed. Of the various problems he associates with it, two are particularly relevant in the present context. Each concerns one of the principal (and standard) features he attributes to the role of substance in Leibniz's thought. First, substance is that through which one can account for change: 'Change', he says, 'implies something which changes; it implies, that is, a subject which has preserved its identity while altering its qualities' (1900, p. 42). Secondly, it is the logical subject of predication while itself not predicable of anything else (*ibid.* p. 43). He summarizes the view thus:

> Substance, then, is that which can only be subject, not predicate, which has many predicates, and persists through change. It is, in short, the subject of change.
>
> (Russell 1900, p. 43)

He immediately goes on to infer that

> The different attributes which a substance has at different times are all predicates of the substance, and though any attribute exists only at a certain time, yet the fact of its being an attribute at that time is eternally a predicate of the substance in question.
>
> (*Ibid.* p. 43)

Although Russell puts objections specifically to Leibniz's monadism, that is, to his view that there are many substances, he makes it very clear that he thinks the entire notion of substance is confused. Russell alleges three major inconsistencies. He finds the relation of the substance to its attributes unintelligible: a substance, must be, yet cannot be, 'the sum of its predicates' (1900, pp. 48–50). He finds time 'necessarily presupposed in Leibniz's treatment of substance', but 'denied in the conclusion' (*ibid.* p. 53). There is a parallel problem with space: 'Monadisms ... since they work with substance, must deny the reality of space; but to obtain a plurality of coexistent substances, they must surreptitiously assume that reality' (*ibid.* p. 126). Immediately Russell draws his devastating conclusion:

Spinoza, we may say, had shown that the actual world could not be explained by means of one substance; Leibniz showed that it could not be explained by means of many substances. It became necessary, therefore, to base metaphysics on some notion other than that of substance – a task not yet accomplished.

(loc. cit.)

Russell's hostility to the notion of substance appears on various occasions. For example, in *The Principles of Mathematics* (1903 §443), during his discussion of motion, he says:

The notion of change has been much obscured by the doctrine of substance, by the distinction between a thing's nature and its external relations, and by the pre-eminence of subject–predicate propositions. It has been supposed that a thing could, in some way, be different and yet the same: that though predicates define a thing, yet it may have different predicates at different times. Hence the distinction of the essential and the accidental, and a number of other useless distinctions ...

In this passage we get a hint that he thinks of the philosophical notion of substance as no more than an ontological shadow cast by the grammatical subject–predicate distinction. This view, as we remarked, does not sit easily with a commitment to the transparency thesis. And as §443 continues, this thesis in effect shifts, moving from the naïve version he had announced earlier, in §§46 and 47 (and quoted at the start of this chapter), to something closer to the version we described as requiring a fully analysed language. What forces the shift, it becomes clear, is that giving an account of change requires Russell's 'terms' to be 'eternal, timeless, and immutable' and hence not to be thought of as substances. The notion of substance and the grammatical distinction not only go together, but eventually are linked with the so-called 'axiom of internal relations', where Russell's first objection to the notion of substance is given wider significance in a cogently written passage:

A more searching argument against the axiom of internal relations is derived from a consideration of what is meant by the 'nature' of a term. Is this the same as the term itself, or is it different? If it is different, it must be related to the term, and the relation of a term to its nature cannot without an endless regress be reduced to something other than a relation. Thus if the axiom is to be adhered to, we must suppose that a term is not other than its nature. In that case, every true proposition attributing a predicate to a subject is purely analytic, since the subject is its own whole nature, and the predicate is part of that nature. But in that case, what is the bond that unites predicates into predicates of one subject? [Russell then goes on to argue that no account of such a bond can be given, and concludes ...] Thus we get into equal difficulties whether we affirm or deny that a subject is other than its 'nature'.

(Russell 1907, pp. 144*f*)

And at this point he refers us back to his Leibniz book.

We have already seen, in Chapter 2 (pp. 27*ff*, and especially p. 42*f*), that Bradley is not averse to thinking in terms of substance. So Russell clearly has a *prima facie* case. But we also saw in the latter section that Bradley, despite his reputation, rejected the axiom of internal relations, and (p. 37*f*) that he was fully alive to the problems Russell raises in the last quote and indeed derives his own doctrines in part from the view that he shared with Russell, namely that these problems are unsolvable. The case, then, is only *prima facie* at this stage. We shall see in the next chapter just how successful was Russell's attempt to develop his rejection of subject–predicate grammar into a searching criticism of Bradley's position.

In the meantime it is worth noting that, although Russell persisted in efforts to construct an ontology which avoided the admission of substance-like entities – for example, the fundamental ontological category of his later neutral monism (Russell 1919b, 1921) is that of *events* – there is a period when his logical atomism allows them in. They are the particulars, which are, as we saw earlier (p. 115*f*), the bearers of logically proper names:

Particulars have this peculiarity, among the sort of objects that you have to take account of in an inventory of the world, that each of them stands entirely alone and is completely self-subsistent. It has that sort of self-subsistence that used to belong to substance, except that it usually only persists through a very short time, so far as our experience goes. That is to say, each particular that there is in the world does not in any way depend upon any other particular. Each one might happen to be the whole universe; it is a merely empirical fact that this is not the case.

(Russell 1918: *CP8* p. 179; *LK* pp. 201f)

The fleeting nature of these particulars – they are the offspring of Russell's earlier attachment to sense-data, and it seems that any change counts as replacement[65] – frees him from having to worry about some of the objections he had made to Leibniz. But he has some difficulty maintaining the non-propositional character of acquaintance which is necessary for the avoidance of the need to distinguish between, as he put it, 'the essential and the accidental'.[66] It is more relevant in this context, however, to notice once more something that he and Bradley have in common: as Passmore (1969, p. 25) perceptively observed, 'Instead of rejecting the whole concept of "what stands alone" and "the self-subsistent", what Russell has done is transfer these properties from Bradley's Absolute to atomic particulars.' Amongst the differences between these particulars of 1918 and the terms that are their 1903 ancestors in Russell's ontology, one thing is very prominent: the former are ultra-temporary, the latter eternal. Both kinds of entity originate in Russell's sense that nothing can be the persisting subject of change. In this respect, he and Bradley are at one: change is unreal.

Coda

I have been concentrating on the grammatical aspects of one of the most significant and misunderstood periods of change in the recent history of philosophy, and I have tried to bring out the explanation of one superficially odd feature of twentieth-century analytic philosophy. In part, and through the self-presentation of Russell and Moore, analytic philosophy has defined its origin in terms of a reaction against idealism, presenting itself as a beacon of clarity and precision against the preceding mirk. Now that original reaction, as we have seen, had as an ingredient something which the idealists had rejected: the placing of trust in the surface grammar of natural languages. Yet analytic philosophy itself, through its demand for clarity and precision, and in particular its association with the attempt to mathematicize everyday reasoning, followed Russell in reacting against that trust, and returned to one of the negative tenets of idealism: that ordinary language does not reflect in its grammatical structures the way the world is. Although, unlike idealism, analytic philosophy came to be influenced by the conception that this reflection can nevertheless be found in logical form, the stark contrast with which we began has to be replaced by a much fuzzier picture.

6
Relations

'Sherlock Holmes closed his eyes, and placed his elbows upon the arms of his chair, with his finger-tips together. "The ideal reasoner", he remarked, "would, when he has once been shown a single fact in all its bearings, deduce from it not only all the chain of events which led up to it, but also all the results which would follow from it".'

A. Conan Doyle, 'The Adventure of the
Five Orange Pips', 1892

The significance of relations

Even to a philosopher who has perhaps just opened this book at the current page and has no special interest in the late nineteenth-century monistic idealism which so marked British philosophy in the late nineteenth century and beyond, it is perhaps no longer news that the picture of those idealists bequeathed to us by Moore and Russell and displayed in Chapter 1 stands in *some* need of correction. But how distorted is that picture, and what should take its place? The earlier chapters of this book have begun answering these questions. In this chapter, I hope to complete the process, by focusing on perhaps the most central matter of all, the topic of relations. But despite what I have said so far, the ground for this completion has still not been entirely cleared: there are still confusing factors at work. Many of these belong to that Moore/Russell legacy, such as the effect of their presenting the idiosyncratic Bradley as representative of so-called 'Hegelians' in general. This effect can take two forms. What is rightly attributed to Bradley we may wrongly attribute to other idealists. But it has been more common to attribute to Bradley what is true only of others. So for many years we had a picture of Bradley which was liable to mislead us about not only him but everyone else too. The potential for confusion is compounded by the picture's power and simplicity, and by the fact that there is textual support for crucial parts of its detail, so that it seems to survive an independent check. And, as we have seen, there is as well its constant availability in writings far more accessible and readable than those of the idealists themselves – for example, Russell's mass-selling *The Problems of Philosophy* and *My Philosophical Development.*

We can add to the list of confusing factors the persisting bad habit amongst commentators of treating Bradley's writings as presenting a philosophical position unchanging over time;[1] while, given his view that time is unreal, there might be a certain pleasing irony about that, and although he clearly was not the restless spirit that Russell was, it is asking for trouble just to assume, for example, that what he thought about relations near the end of his career in 1924 was straightforwardly the same as he had thought when writing the 1883 *Principles of Logic.*[2] Finally, there is another part of the Moore/Russell legacy: this is that certain anti-idealist conceptions characteristic of analytic philosophy (for example, that of the black/white character of truth and falsity) got so deeply embedded in the common philosophical consciousness that some idealist doctrines important to the intelligibility of their views looked so obviously illegitimate that they became almost invisible to readers looking for rational argument.[3]

I take it for granted that Bradley cannot be regarded as a typical idealist or Hegelian, if for no other reason than that, as he said himself, he rejects 'what seems [Hegel's] main principle'.[4] But because Moore and Russell wrote as though a refutation of Bradley would be a refutation of idealism, any answer to our original questions full enough to engage with the detail of their arguments will involve what has been undertaken in this book: comparison of analytic philosophy's inherited picture of Bradley with its original. Now, as a mere glance at Chapter 1 (p. 4*f*) will confirm, significant parts of that picture concern the subject of relations, and include such claims as these: first, Bradley was opposed to relations because he just assumed the only possible propositional form to be subject–predicate; secondly, his attempted *reductio* of relations treats them illegitimately as objects; thirdly, he believed that all relations are internal, and what this means is that all relations are reducible to properties, or alternatively that no relation holds contingently; fourthly, he held this view of relations as an axiom or dogma. This last ingredient may have been added in order to explain away Bradley's not recognizing that he had been refuted; presumably he was not open to argument on the matter.

In fact, there is much in what Bradley says about relations which seems to fit the summary presented in the previous paragraph,[5] and despite what has been said in earlier chapters, it cannot be merely dismissed. But what, then, is the truth about this matter? This is an historical question of some significance, for something like that summary has been important to analytic philosophy's self-image, an image which depends upon contrast with that of a benighted and vanquished predecessor, idealism. And one of the battlegrounds on which it did indeed seem for many years that idealism had decisively lost was that of relations. Many philosophers since have absorbed this story as undergraduates. And if not, this will not usually have been because it has been questioned, but because they were left ignorant of it, perhaps through the confidence of their teachers that the battle could never be rejoined, perhaps through that contempt for history, especially of the non-canonical sort, which has so disfigured much analytic philosophy. Only in such a way, it seems, can one explain the near-disappearance of the issue, despite its having been central to the idealist criticisms of empiricist accounts of knowledge and experience and despite the fact that Russell thought a correct account of relations to be critical for the vindication of mathematics.[6] This disappearance is particularly striking when seen in the light of the near-obsessive persistence of discussion in recent philosophy of other characteristically Russellian themes, such as proper names, definite descriptions, and acquaintance. But that very centrality to idealism of its treatment of relations must also be part of the explanation of the disappearance in the twentieth century, not merely of any serious discussion of relations, but also of idealism itself and even of the early realism which was its immediate successor. For it was principally the topic of relations over which the idealists differed from their empiricist predecessors – after all, they shared Berkeley's hostility to the independence of the physical world, to the point that nineteenth-century arguments for idealism could seem mere perfunctory repetitions of Berkeley's own – so that once *monistic* idealism had been made to seem wrong about relations, the natural reaction would have been to reopen the possibility of an *atomistic* idealism rather than to move to realism. The eventual result was, as we know, a return, via a brief detour into Moore's and Russell's early realism, to the empiricism Bradley had so much despised.

Both disappearances are graphically illustrated by subsequent events. In 1924 Russell could still say this:

The question of relations is one of the most important that arise in philosophy, as most other issues turn on it: monism and pluralism; the question whether anything is wholly true except the whole of truth, or wholly real except the whole of reality; idealism and realism, in some of their forms; perhaps the very existence of philosophy as a subject distinct from science and possessing a method of its own.

(Russell 1924: *CP9* p. 170; *LK* p. 333)

Russell goes on to make clear that, although he has preceded these remarks with reference to 'arguments for and against the reality of relations', what he means by the 'question of relations' is the question which is preferable: his own 'doctrine of external relations', that is, 'what Mr Bradley denies when he asserts the doctrine of internal relations', or Bradley's view. Despite Russell's own judgment of the importance of the-atter, however, by 1935 the symposiasts at a Joint Session already 'found the doctrine of internal relations absurd'.[7] (It is not insignificant that these symposiasts were Ayer and Ryle, both with many years of influence ahead of them.) And the infrequent subsequent commentators have found it hard to understand what all the fuss was about, as Bradley seems so obviously in the wrong. Yet as soon as one begins to read the original texts, it is hard to retain the artificial clarity of hindsight; this was surely one of the most baffling disputes in the history of philosophy. One of the reasons for this is that the participants themselves appear to have been confused about what is at stake.

I intend to sort this matter out for good and all. Yet it might be thought that this task is impossible. For example, Hylton (1990, p. 11) says: '[I]t is ... absurd to suppose that we can discuss the dispute over relations while leaving the nature of truth as an open question, to be resolved later.' But this remark is almost ludicrously pessimistic as it stands. (What further questions must be resolved before we can discuss differences over the nature of truth? And where do we stop?) Even were we to substitute 'settle' for 'discuss', the claim is still an exaggeration, for there is much about this dispute that can be settled, and even settled in Bradley's favour while baulking at his notion of truth. And the claim is contrary to Hylton's own practice, for he himself believes, rightly, that Russell did not succeed in straightforwardly refuting Bradley's view of relations. Of course, what Hylton was probably after was the more plausible idea that we cannot, as it were *sub specie aeternitatis* and in isolation from other philosophical commitments, answer the question 'Who was right about relations, Bradley or Russell (or neither)?' But the trouble with this question is merely that it is too coarse-grained: it can be treated as a compound of several others which may not all get the same answer, and as we shall see in this chapter, some of them at least can be settled. To say this is of course not to deny, what I shall try to show, that in order to *understand* Bradley's views on relations one has to take into account some of his views about truth.

I begin with the question of whether Bradley did in fact hold that all relations are internal. (Practised readers of Bradley will appreciate that the presence of a quantifier in this sentence imports a precision to the doctrine which could easily be lacking in any original. But we must start somewhere, and what exactly it comes to, and whether it was indeed an axiom or dogma for Bradley, are secondary to some such question as this.) It appears to be clear (to fill out and emphasize a point already made in Chapter 2) that at least in the later part of his life he did not, as several remarks indicate.[8] The unfinished essay on relations (Bradley 1924) is perhaps the most outspoken. Referring to the very notion of the reality of internal relations, he says, for example (*CE*, p. 642): 'The idea, I would add, that I myself accept any such doctrine as the above seems to myself even ludicrous.' Awareness of this fact has recently begun to filter through into the literature. For example, Thomas Baldwin's *G.E. Moore* (Baldwin 1990), in its treatment of Moore's early retreat from idealism, contains a very fair and non-stereotypical account of Bradley's views on relations which acknowledges the problems in supposing that Bradley adhered to the doctrine of internality; but even there, the notion that there was some commitment on Bradley's part to internal relations still survives.

Logic, metaphysics and internal relations

The idea persists, too, even in work whose avowed purpose is to make us radically rethink our opinion of Bradley. A striking example is Manser's *Bradley's Logic*, whose treatment of Bradley's discussions of relations I shall briefly examine, because doing so reveals some features of those discussions which are both significant and generally overlooked. Manser opens the chapter to which we have already referred thus: 'It is generally accepted that Bradley believed that all relations were internal. To many recent philosophers this has been enough to show that he was either confused or silly .' Manser, although he regards his task as one of showing that Bradley was neither confused nor silly, does not go on to dispute this 'general acceptance', but instead appears to concur with it. What he does do is distinguish between two interpretations of the doctrine, an initial 'logical' view of how judgments are to be analysed which finds expression in the first (1883) edition of *The Principles of Logic* (Bradley 1883), and a later 'metaphysical' interpretation, associated with *Appearance and Reality* (Bradley 1893), which Manser describes as 'a falling away from the interesting and probably correct analysis of the nature of judgment and language which he gives in the *Principles*' (Manser 1983, p. 134). Given what we have already seen of Bradley's views on truth, this idea makes sense: it would be quite characteristic of him to defend initially some more or less plausible view only to abandon it later for something extreme and highly implausible. And it is certainly true that in the *Principles*, as he indicates in the Preface to the first edition, he attempted to write a book on logic with as little metaphysical content as he could manage, so that Manser's view is plausible enough to deserve consideration.

According to Manser, then, there are two doctrines of internal relations in Bradley's writings, the first of which, that of the first edition of *The Principles of Logic*, is a sensible one concerning the analysis of the proposition. But, as we have seen in Chapter 2, Bradley appeared at the end of his life to disclaim any adherence to internal relations. What, then, was he dissociating himself from at this stage? If we are to believe Manser, it could have been either or both of the logical and metaphysical doctrines. However, the later essays give us no reason for believing that it was anything specifically logical – as opposed to metaphysical – at that later stage. What are we to make of this? Had Bradley forgotten about the earlier doctrine? Manser suggests that he had lost interest in logical issues by this stage; but another possible diagnosis is that there was no such earlier doctrine at all.

So let us have a look at the pages in which it is supposed to appear. Manser cites page 21 of *The Principles of Logic* as a crucial text (and one could add, using Bradley's own index, pages 10–11 and 22 as well). And it is true that Bradley uses the phrase 'internal relation' on page 21. But a careful reading shows that it is clear that any impression that there is a commitment on Bradley's part here to anything which could in any interesting sense be called a doctrine of internal relations is merely the result of a kind of linguistic accident.

To see this, we should ask first how Bradley himself thought of what he had done. One way to come at this is via the index to the *Principles* (which he compiled himself for the second edition; there is none to the first). This contains a separate entry under 'Relations, internal', and this sole entry is to a footnote belonging only to the second edition of 1922 and expressing the sort of view which Manser has described as a 'falling away'. The references in the index to the sort of view which Manser praises are under the heading 'Relation, in judgment'. This leads to my second point, that the two occurrences of the phrase 'internal relation' on page 21 are both in the context of a discussion of the relations holding among the material contained *inside the judgment* (not the reality about which the judgment is made, but the ideal matter, as Bradley himself calls it, the kind of intermediary between language and reality whose existence Moore and Russell came to deny in their early writings).[9] That is, the force of the word 'internal' in this context is no more than to distinguish between, on the one hand, relations within the judgment and, on the other, relations of the ideal matter to things outside the judgment. The same is true of the other occurrences of the word cited in the previous paragraph. In other words, the fact that Bradley uses the phrase 'internal relations' here indicates nothing at all about what sort of analysis of the proposition he is offering. It is a phrase which with equal justification and the same sense could have been used by the authors of the Port-Royal *Logic*, by Mill, by Frege, by Russell, indeed by any of those with whom we might regard Bradley as in actual or potential disagreement over logical matters.

We have seen that if we search in the text of the first edition of *The Principles of Logic* for a doctrine of internality that is restricted to judgment, we find nothing that is identified as such. The same holds if we search for a denial of external relations in judgment: for example, in discussing analysis and synthesis in inference, Bradley says (1883, pp. 471–2): 'In one case the whole precedes and is followed by its internal relations; but in the other case external relations come first and so produce the whole.' And in a later endnote (1922, *PL* p. 494, n. 5) glossing this remark, he adds: '"External relations." "External" means here "not falling within our *datum*."'[10] Even much later in his career Bradley continued on occasion to use 'external' and 'internal' in this non-technical sense, especially when speaking of judgment; and sometimes it takes very careful reading to discern this fact. Two significant examples, which seem to be universally unnoticed for what they are, occur on page 26 of *Appearance and Reality*, right in the middle of the famous chapter on relations![11] It would be hard to imagine a more effective way of causing confusion. I shall say more about this chapter later.

On the other hand, if we start to look in *The Principles of Logic* for a doctrine on relations which is not restricted to judgments, practically the first thing that we find (on page 96) is an early version of Bradley's argument against, not the *externality* of relations, but the *reality* of relations (with no restriction as to type), in a full-bloodedly metaphysical version:

> If relations are facts that exist *between* facts, then what comes *between* the relations and the other facts? The real truth is that the units on one side, and on the other side the relation existing between them, are nothing actual. They are fictions of the mind, mere distinctions within a single reality, which a common delusion erroneously takes for independent facts.

In the light of this, it is perhaps no surprise that Manser says, 'There is a sense in which the doctrine of internal relations can be seen as a denial of relations' (1983, p. 129), for this remark expresses concisely a confusion between two different theses about relations which have both been attributed to Bradley: namely, that all relations are internal, and that all relations are unreal. (The previous section showed Russell making the same mistake. We shall find that there is an explanation for this confusion.) And in doing this, it grafts onto the second thesis a controversial interpretation of its meaning. As we have seen, the second thesis is certainly expressed in *The Principles of Logic*, although not in the passages Manser refers to; while the first, construed as 'the issue of the internality or externality of relations, as far as Bradley was concerned at this time of his life' (*ibid.* p. 127), is just not an issue at all.[12]

If we are going to identify how a 'metaphysical' question of the internality of relations ever arose for Bradley, we must look elsewhere. Certainly, when Manser comes to the question of how the later doctrine arose from the earlier logical point, he can find nothing better than 'a confusion between sense and truth', a rather crude error for any reasonably sophisticated philosopher to make (*ibid.* p. 132). The merest charity should prompt us to look further.

There is of course an objection to the points I have made so far in this section. It is that I have been making a lot of fuss about what is an essentially verbal issue. What does it matter, one might say, what label we apply to Bradley's theory of judgment? The point is surely that he had such a theory, and, as we saw in Chapter 3, that it worked by denying that judgments are made by relating distinct ideas. It is this which is of philosophical interest and which Manser has got hold of.

Whether we choose to call this a doctrine of internal relations or something else is essentially trivial.

There is some justice in this objection. Nevertheless, the matter is not trivial. For if we think of Bradley's theory of judgment in terms of internal relations, we are likely to assume, as Manser himself did, a more general commitment to internality when (as, we observed in passing in Chapter 2 and I shall shortly show in detail) Bradley's relation to that doctrine was at least problematic. And we may start looking, as Manser did, for a way in which the earlier doctrine could have developed into some later doctrine which might with more justice be thought to be one of internal relations; whereas, as we just saw, one must attribute grossly fallacious reasoning to him in order to maintain that what is thought to be his later doctrine grew out of the supposed earlier one. Moreover, thinking this way is likely to lead us to misunderstand the earlier doctrine, which in fact is more obscure than the claim that the ingredients of a judgment are internally rather than externally related. Indeed, it is on the face of it hard to see how this claim could be an expression of Bradley's central assertion about judgment, namely, that in a judgment, 'The relations between the ideas are themselves ideal' (1883, *PL* p. 11); whereas, reminding ourselves that Bradley is consciously working with two senses of the word 'idea' (opposing the conception of the idea as a psychological entity to that of the idea as a logical unit), and remembering that he opposes the ideality of the logical unit to reality (this, in one version or another, is a constant theme in his writings over most of his life), it is much easier to see how this assertion amounts to a suggestion that, in a judgment, there are no real relations of any kind between independent logical units. This is what is right about Manser's view, but we shall always be tempted to misunderstand its significance if we think of it in terms of internality rather than in terms of unreality. The account of judgment in the early pages of *The Principles of Logic* is in fact just an early appearance of the later doctrine of the unreality of relations and of their terms, applied to the ingredients of judgment. Its later extension beyond the ingredients of judgment needs no particular explanation. Indeed, given Bradley's commitment to the identity theory of truth, already evident in the *Principles*, he could hardly have drawn the firm distinction between judgment and fact which Manser's distinction between the logical and metaphysical version of the doctrine of internality requires. What needs explaining is the initial confining to judgment, and the explanation is simple. It is that Bradley was, as he said, trying to write a book on logic without getting involved in metaphysics.

But the problems with thinking of Bradley's theory of judgment in terms of internal relations do not stop there. For *clear and unequivocal* expressions of the doctrine of internality, whether in an application restricted to judgment or not, are not common in his writings; and, lacking them, in our efforts to gain understanding we naturally turn to the interpretations of Bradley's remarks which have become established in the literature as both demonstrating the presence of the doctrine and simultaneously giving its nature. These interpretations have some at least of their roots in hostility to the doctrine – they are presentations of it as ripe for refutation – and if we then understand Bradley's theory of judgment in their light, that theory may in consequence become as obscured as his position on relations has been.

I have discussed this issue at some length, for two reasons. One is that to do so brings out some of the sources of the widespread confusion concerning Bradley's views on relations. The other is that Manser's was the first concerted attempt to secure Bradley a place in analytical philosophy's pantheon;[13] not only must it thus stand as exemplary, but any errors it contains increase the risk that previous misapprehensions about Bradley will simply be replaced by new ones.[14] And if he is eventually reinstated as a philosopher whom we can argue with rather than merely wonder at, it is important that this should proceed on a secure basis.

Interpreting the doctrine of internal relations

I remarked a moment ago that Bradley's position on relations has been obscured. That observation inevitably poses the question of how the doctrine of internal relations should in fact be understood. There are two standard interpretations in the literature. One is that to assert the internality of all relations amounts to asserting that no relational statement is contingently true; and this in turn is treated as entailing that all are necessary. This version is usually associated with Moore, but Russell too (in a letter to Bradley of 9 April 1910[15]) interpreted Bradley as making the same claim. Given that any subject–predicate statement can be cast in the form of a relational statement, and that, as might well have been assumed at the time, there are no other irreducible propositional forms, this version amounts to the assertion that there are no contingent truths at all, and hence that all truths are necessary. The other interpretation, this time associated solely with Russell, has it that the doctrine is that apparent relations are reducible to properties. (This, as we saw in Chapter 5, is connected with Russell's often-repeated charge that, for Bradley, the only possible propositional form was subject–predicate, a charge which sits uneasily with another standard Russellian allegation that Bradley's arguments sometimes rested on the 'trivial confusion' of subject–predicate statements with identity-statements – that is, the former are interpreted as the latter.)

There are remarks in *Appearance and Reality* which can seem to express a commitment to the doctrine of internal relations in general, and then more specifically in both these senses. Moore, for example, begins his famous and influential essay 'External and Internal Relations' by quoting from its Index, 'Relations are all intrinsical', which looks hard to gainsay[16] – it is perhaps the clearest apparent commitment to the doctrine of internality to be found in Bradley. While it is worth noticing, in view of what I said earlier about the interpretation of the word 'internal' in the chapter on relations in *Appearance and Reality*, that none of the references under this index heading is to that chapter, we do find, when we pursue them, such remarks as these:

> That which exists in a whole has external relations. Whatever it fails to include within its own nature, must be related to it by the whole, and related externally. Now these extrinsic relations, on the one hand, fall outside of itself, but, upon the other hand, cannot do so. *For a relation must at both ends affect, and pass into, the being of its terms.*
>
> (1893, *AR* p. 322, my emphasis)

Now this lends itself to the second, Russellian, interpretation: first, its special subject matter seems to be external relations, and secondly, it can be read as entailing the reducibility of relational propositions to subject–predicate propositions, in that monadistic version where the subject is one or other of the related items. It is also possible to find in the same work (for example, on pp. 125–6) remarks seeming to endorse the monistic version, that is, which make it appear that the subject should really be the complex whole formed by the related objects taken together in their relation. On the other hand, the first, Moorean, interpretation is obviously supported by such claims as this: 'There is a like self-contradiction in absolute chance. The absolutely contingent would mean a fact which is given free from all internal connexion with its context. It would have to stand without relation, or rather with all its relations outside' (*ibid*. p. 347).

One thing that may strike us here is that these two accounts seem not to amount to the same thing, for on the face of it a subject–

predicate statement that a certain object has a certain property can be just as contingent as a relational statement. In order to make them the same thing, one would apparently have to maintain also that every property of a thing belonged to it essentially, something which it is difficult to hold without some elaborate justificatory machinery such as we find, for example, in Leibniz. And even Leibniz attempts to draw back from the consequence that contingency is an illusion, 'our ignorance set up as reality' (to use Bradley's words from *AR* p. 517). But in so far as they are present in Bradley, he seems to move from one to the other quite indiscriminately, as though he himself saw no significant difference between the two (this is evident, for example, as one continues to read down page 347 from the quotation just cited), and he is openly hostile to the notion of contingency.

Perhaps the first thing that needs to be said at this point is that even if Bradley had thought that any relational proposition is logically equivalent to some subject–predicate proposition – and we should recognize that attribution of such a thought is itself likely to be anachronistic (depending on our criterion of logical equivalence), and anyway goes well beyond in precision anything that he actually does say – this would not have meant that he believed that relational propositions were reducible to non-relational ones, for he thought that subject–predicate propositions themselves involved relations between subject and predicate, so that any problems with relations would hardly be solved by attempted elimination of them in favour of subjects and predicates.[17] Noting this important qualification, let us assume for the sake of argument that remarks like those just quoted are an expression of a commitment to some sort of equivalence between relational and subject–predicate propositions.

Given his hostility to contingency, then, did Bradley think at this time that every property of a thing belonged to it essentially? Alas, the situation is much more complicated than that, and to understand what it is, we must begin by examining the important note B to the Appendix to *Appearance and Reality*. There is much in this note that is helpful in the understanding of Bradley's position on relations, but also much that is downright confusing, and we shall have to handle it delicately. In it, he considers the claim that spatial relations are external. His examples are a man and a billiard ball, and he imagines an opponent urging that it is just common sense that these are unaffected in themselves by a mere alteration of place. His response is of the first significance for our topic:

But an important if obvious distinction seems here overlooked. For a thing may remain unaltered if you identify it with a certain character, while taken otherwise the thing is suffering change. If, that is, you take a billiard-ball and a man in abstraction from place, they will of course – so far as this is maintained – be indifferent to changes of place. But on the other hand neither of them, if regarded so, is a thing which actually exists; each is a more or less valid abstraction. But take them as existing things and take them without mutilation, and you must regard them as determined by their places and qualified by the whole material system into which they enter. And, if you demur to this, I ask you once more of what you are going to predicate the alterations and their results. The billiard-ball, to repeat, if taken apart from its place and its position in the whole, is not an existence but a character, and that character can remain unchanged, though the existing thing is altered with its changed existence. Everything other than this identical character may be called relatively external ... but absolutely external it cannot be.

(Bradley 1897, *AR* pp. 517–18)

It is very hard to assess this reply: conflicting pictures of the nature of the world are in play, and it may be that nothing more can be said *in argument* by either side to resolve the stalemate.[18] But one point can be made, if not exactly in Bradley's favour, then at least helping to make his view intelligible. It is this. What for him is at stake is the justifiability of the grammatically-based categories in which the common sense advocate of external relations unhesitatingly conducts his discussion. Of course this advocacy implicitly relies on those categories, such as term, subject, predicate, relation, attribute and so on, so that its points, which are in effect points about how those categories work, will appear so obviously true as to make scepticism concerning their applicability ludicrous. But for this very reason the victory is hollow. To be worth having, it must be attained using a vocabulary which is neutral between the disputants, one which will at least allow Bradley to make himself understood. But there is no such vocabulary: we simply have no words for a billiard ball, or a man, taken *not* 'in abstraction from place' (or from some other background). And this is no accident, which could be remedied by the introduction of technical terms, for the difficulty is systematic, and the examples given are merely representative.[19] The stalemate, then, amounts to this: that one side attempts to conduct the argument in terms whose very legitimacy the other side is questioning, while the other side is unable to provide any other terminology in which the question can be framed non-self-defeatingly.

It is sometimes suggested that Bradley's reply is fallacious, moving from the essentiality to a material object of some spatial relations or other, to the essentiality of the particular relations it happens to be in.[20] What is said in the foregoing paragraph may be regarded as a rejection of this charge. Bradley's claim, which the English language itself hinders him from making clearly, is that to think of the total particular situation in terms of *a billiard-ball* is already to have abstracted without argument, to have divided that total situation into object plus (possibly unmentioned) surroundings. Once we have made that abstraction, then of course some relations will be external to the object; but unless we do, none can be singled out in any principled way as external. But the crucial point is that the very process of abstraction involved in thinking this way itself relies upon some relations being external to the object, for without such externality, no conception of an object, at all, is possible. As an argument for the externality of some relations, this appeal to common sense is plainly circular.

Now that we have observed Bradley's distinction between existences and characters, we are in a position to say something useful about the connection between the two interpretations of internality. For there is such a connection, and it is given in that distinction. How? Well, suppose that relations are indeed reducible to properties. The question I asked earlier is, why should these properties be any more essential to their terms than the original relations were? And the answer is, of course, that they need not; but this lack of necessity depends on a division of the properties of the object in question into the essential and the non-essential. And to make the assumption that this division is possible is already to employ Bradley's *bête noire*, abstraction, and to treat the object 'as a character', not as an existence. (It is worth comparing Bradley's hostility to the analytic/synthetic distinction, already evident in his 1883.) If we refuse to make this division, then we can plausibly be supposed to be committed to the denial of contingency (though it should also be added that we are equally committed to the denial of necessity, at least in any of its common understandings). And there is no doubt that Bradley does so refuse; albeit with a vital qualification whose significance we have yet to make clear.

The qualification is this. As Bradley insists again and again, he is not opposed to such division for practical purposes; he is just not prepared to regard it as the final truth about things.

The development of Bradley's views on relations

We have seen that, of the two interpretations of the doctrine of internal relations, Russell's is unjustified, and that the remarks which appeared to justify it support, at best, a claim of equivalence between some relational statements and others, a claim which cannot amount to reducibility but instead is closely connected to the Moore interpretation. The Moore version does at least seem to reflect Bradley's hostility to contingency. What we have yet to see is that Bradley rejects the doctrine, why he does, the way that he does so, and, given that we have found passages which appear to express a commitment to it, what his relation to it actually was.

My thesis, briefly expressed, is this. Bradley does appear to be explicitly committed to the doctrine in the first and second editions of *Appearance and Reality* in 1893 and 1897.[21] We have seen reason to suppose that this commitment does not begin until after 1883, the year of publication of the first edition of *The Principles of Logic* (although a general hostility to separateness, which can be regarded as later finding expression in the doctrine of internal relations, is already present in *Ethical Studies*, published in 1876[22]). By the time we get to the essays of the period 1909–11 which make up a substantial part of *Essays on Truth and Reality*, whatever commitment there was is over and the doctrine is rejected (1909a, *ETR* p. 190; 1909c, *ETR* pp. 238–9; 1911a, *ETR* pp. 290–1; 1911b, *ETR* p. 312), albeit in qualified fashion, and this rejection is maintained until the end of his life, as the unfinished essay on relations in *Collected Essays* shows (see, for example, 1924, *CE* pp. 641, 646, 665 and 667–8). Further, I shall argue that Bradley's commitment to the doctrine was based to a significant extent on a confusion with another doctrine about relations which he did hold to from 1883, at the latest, until the end of his life, namely the doctrine of the unreality of relations; that in *Appearance and Reality* he moves from one to the other and back again and perhaps was never clear that he had done this; that this confusion is understandable in the light of genuine logical relationships between the two doctrines (no wonder that we find the same confusion in later commentators); and that it is over-attention to *Appearance and Reality* which, from Moore and Russell onwards, has given Bradley the reputation of being the archetypal theorist of internal relations. (Though we should not forget the effect produced by controversy: Bradley, holding Russell to be committed to the reality of external relations, criticized him for this.[23] It would only be natural, even if fallacious, to infer from this criticism some commitment on Bradley's part to the doctrine of internality.)

We have seen already that in *The Principles of Logic* there is no commitment to a doctrine of internal relations, even in the sanitized form devised by Manser, and that the impression that there is is based on a pun, but that matters look importantly different in Bradley's next major publication, the 1893 first edition of *Appearance and Reality*. Yet the chapter of that book which is normally assumed to be an argument for the doctrine of internality, Chapter III, is in fact not easy to read that way. To begin with, it is not a treatment of relations and terms in general at all; rather, it arises directly out of the previous chapter's argument that reality is not captured by the attribution of adjectives to substantives, and argues further that the situation is not improved by dropping the substantives and treating reality as consisting of qualities in relation. (The terminology in the original exhibits this sort of fluctuating between language and the world.) However, Bradley himself occasionally substitutes 'term' for 'quality', so there is some justice in generalizing his argument and taking it to be a reflection of what he would say about terms and relations without specification of what the terms are, and I shall not press this point.

So, allowing that Bradley's discussion may be treated as one of relations and terms, we can turn to my second point, which is that most of what he says is about relations in general, without qualification.[24] The following remark when read in context, is surely definitive:

> The object of this chapter is to show that the very essence of these ideas [i.e. 'the arrangement of given facts into relations and qualities'] is infected and contradicts itself. Our conclusion briefly will be this. Relation presupposes quality, and quality relation. Each can be something neither together with, nor apart from, the other; and the vicious circle in which they turn is not the truth about reality.
>
> (Bradley 1893, *AR* p. 21)

However, in the middle of the discussion we already see signs of confusion about what it is supposed to be proving:

> It is possible for many purposes to accept and employ the existence of processes and relations which do not affect specially the inner nature of objects. But the very possibility of so distinguishing in the end between inner and outer, and of setting up the inner as absolutely independent of all relation, is here in question.
>
> (Bradley 1893, *AR* p. 23)

The first sentence in this second quotation suggests that it is external relations which are in question, and that the conclusion is going to be that all relations are internal, but in the second sentence we immediately return to part of the original issue: whether there can be terms without any relations at all.[25] If we read carefully, though, we can see that the main theme here is that there is something in principle wrong with the whole distinction between the external and the internal. He never resiles from this suggestion, and it recurs in his writings right up to his death. But it needs to be carefully separated from one easy to confuse with it, that there is such a distinction but necessarily all examples fall on one side of it.

Unfortunately, such care is not always exhibited by Bradley himself, as for example in the following passage:

> But the 'this' certainly is used also with a negative bearing. It may mean 'this one', in distinction from that one and the other one. And here it shows obviously an exclusive aspect, and it implies an external and negative relation. But every such relation, we have found, is inconsistent with itself (Chapter iii). For it exists within, and by virtue of an embracing unity, and apart from that totality both itself and its terms would be nothing. And the relation also must penetrate the inner being of its terms.
>
> (Bradley 1893, *AR* p. 201)

And this looks like an unequivocal affirmation of the doctrine that all relations are internal, via the assertion of the inconsistency of *external* relations. Moreover, it refers to the very chapter of *Appearance and Reality* which specially dealt with relations as proving this. Given the index entry that we have already noticed as introducing Moore's classic paper, it is no cause for wonder that Bradley was credited with the doctrine by both followers and opponents.

Any lingering doubts would now surely be removed by reference to the 1897 note B to the Appendix, where Bradley not only is explicitly hostile to external relations (and does not remind us that this hostility might be based either on the belief that all relations are internal or on the belief that there is something wrong with the internal/external distinction, for he seems at this point himself to have lost sight of the difference between these alternatives[26]), but also comes out with the notorious assertions about the red-haired man, assertions which seem to go even further than Holmes's remarks about the ideal reasoner in my epigraph to this chapter, and which look as though they amount to the claim that starting from, say, one's own red-hairedness one would, in principle, be able to infer every other truth about the universe, which implies that everything is internally related to everything else.

But in later years Bradley gets clearer about what he wants to say. In a letter to Russell of 28 January 1901 he insists 'I don't hold *any* relational system can be consistent', and at least from 1909 onwards, he resolutely adheres to the view, most vehement and explicit in the 1923–24 essay 'Relations', that his hostility to externality is based on a rejection of the external/internal distinction, so that now he is openly hostile to internality as well:

> Criticism therefore which assumes me committed to the ultimate truth of internal relations, all or any of them, is based on a mistake.
>
> (1909c, *ETR* p. 239)

> Mere internal relations, then, like relations that are merely external, are untenable if they make a claim to ultimate and absolute truth. But taken otherwise, and viewed as helpful makeshifts and as useful aids in the pursuit of knowledge, external and internal relations are both admissible and can be relatively real and true.
>
> (1924, *CE* p. 645)

In other words, Bradley might even accept the view of, for example, Ayer (1971, pp. 158–9), that relations are external or internal according to how a thing is described. And it is in the light of such remarks as those I have just quoted that we need to view claims like the following:

> And Pluralism, to be consistent, must, I presume, accept the reality of external relations. Relations external, not relatively and merely in regard to this or that mode of union, but external absolutely must be taken as real. To myself, such relations remain unthinkable.
>
> (1909c, *ETR* p. 237)

The odd thing about Ayer's comments is that he seems to take himself to be offering a view which is a rival of Bradley's. Perhaps the explanation of this is that Ayer, unlike Bradley, would not have committed himself to the unreality of all relations, a view which, as we have now finally seen confirmed, Bradley held to from the publication of *The Principles of Logic* in 1883 until the end of his life. But what does this doctrine amount to?

I take it that no one *these days* would suppose that it amounts to the claim that no relational statement is true (and we have Wittgenstein to thank for helping *us* to get clear about this, for the monists themselves were by no means so clear, and were inclined to the sort of exaggerated rhetoric with which Moore – conflating it, understandably, with the doctrine itself – took issue[27]). Or at least, if one wants to suppose that, then one has to do so on the basis of general considerations about metaphysics which as we shall see will have the effect of condemning rival pluralist views as much as Bradley's, though Russell's anxiety over relations and their importance for mathematics may still have been based on some such idea, even though we associate it with Moore. Rather, as I pointed out in Chapter 2 (p. 42*f*), Bradley's claim of unreality is simply that relations are not objects, which he conceives of as independent substances.[28] As relations are not objects, there are no names of relations. This far (with some cavils about the notion of substance, to be canvassed in the next section), Bradley and the early Wittgenstein might be regarded as being at one over relations, as we saw in Chapter 5 (p. 128*f*):

> Not 'The complex sign "aRb" says that a stands to b in the relation R', but rather, *that* 'a' stands to 'b' in a certain relation says *that* aRb.
> (1921: *Tractatus* 3.1432, my translation)

Wittgenstein's remark concerning how relations are to be symbolized is one expression of the idea as applied to external relations,[29] and the Tractarian view that internal relations are shown and not said is another expression of it in the other application, as we see in the sections beginning at 4.122 and culminating in this remark:

> The existence of an internal relation between possible states of affairs expresses itself in language by an internal relation between the propositions presenting them.
> (*Ibid.* §4.125, Ogden's translation)

All this said, however, it remains that Bradley was more sympathetic to internal than to external relations, and he was careful to deny only their *ultimate* reality. The following remark reveals this: 'As to what has been called the axiom of internal relations, I can only repeat that "internal" relations, though truer by far than "external", are, in my opinion, not true in the end' (1911b, *ETR* p. 312). In view of this lingering sympathy, and of Bradley's own inclination to confuse the doctrine of internality with that of unreality, a confusion which others have been only too willing to adopt, one may wonder whether there is some close logical connection between the two doctrines. Indeed, Baldwin, in discussing this question (1990, pp. 32–4), begins by quoting an explicit rejection of the doctrine of internality, and ends by alleging that Bradley is committed to both doctrines. What is the explanation of this?

In a metaphysical system one of whose governing concepts is that of reality in the sense of substantiality, the doctrine of internality is an inherently unstable position. It is unstable because things that are internally related do not have – by definition – the kind of independence that is logically required of substances, and yet without such independence they cannot be thought of as related *things* at all. The Russell of 1918 reminds us that each of his particulars 'stands entirely alone and is completely self-subsistent', having 'that sort of self-subsistence that used to belong to substance', so that 'each particular that there is in the world does not in any way logically depend upon any other particular' (1918; *CP8* p. 179, *LK* pp. 201–2). There are, broadly speaking, two ways in which such independence can be achieved. One is Russell's logical atomist way: extrude complexity from objects into facts, so that complexes lose their status as objects and the substances are independent in virtue of their simplicity. Another is Bradley's: absorb complexity, so that the eventual sole substance has its independence in virtue of there being nothing else. (There are, of course, also attempts to have it both ways, such as Leibniz's.) But the point is that what systems of both kinds agree on is that internal relations not only are unreal themselves because all relations are, but also undermine the reality of their terms, even if not everyone would like this idealist way of putting it. (Though it took Russell many years to come around to acknowledging this even implicitly, and then it was Wittgenstein's influence, not Bradley's, that brought about Russell's change of mind on the reality of relations. Russell never acknowledged that Bradley had been right: the account of relations in the essay 'Logical Atomism' (Russell 1924) is quite different from that of 1903 in *The Principles of Mathematics*, and in that essay Russell, recounting Bradley's criticisms of his 1903 views as though they were directed towards those of 1924, simply conceals the change of mind and wrongly implies that Bradley misrepresented him.[30])

Once we see that the internality of relations entails their unreality, it need no longer surprise us that Bradley was more sympathetic to internality than externality, for internal relations wear the unreality of themselves and their terms on their faces, so to speak, because their necessary mutual connectedness precludes independence; nor that he was at one stage inclined to confuse the two, and sometimes seems indifferent as to whether he is trying to show that relations are internal or that they are unreal. For the former is but an indirect route to the latter. It should be no surprise either that he eventually got clear enough on the point to be able to make it explicit that the rejection of the claim that there are external relations did not commit him to the doctrine of internality, and that, when rejecting the doctrine of internality, he does so by stipulating carefully that it does not express the 'ultimate truth' about things, is not true 'in the end'. Even when, as we saw, he dismissed as 'ludicrous' the idea that he would accept the doctrine of internality, the doctrine is described as that of 'a relation which is asserted to be real ultimately and internal merely' (1924, *CE* p. 642).

An analytic philosopher is likely to get irritated around this stage, and ask brusquely, 'Does Bradley maintain that all relations are internal or not?' But the only accurate answer here, when we are dealing with his mature beliefs, would have to be, 'He does and he doesn't.' He does on a superficial level, as having a greater degree of truth than 'All relations are external', a rarely-held view which does on occasion feature in Bradley's writings as the target of his attack. (We saw, in Chapter 3 (p. 53*f*), that Russell is committed to it in *The Principles of Mathematics*.) But he doesn't, if the comparison is to be with 'Some relations are external and some are internal', for this last, *in so far as it is uncontroversially true*, expresses something about the realm of common sense which is not even in the same race as the doctrine of internality – the comparison itself is ill-judged. Nor does he maintain it if the comparison is to be with this genuine rival: 'The division of relations into the external and the internal is not exclusive and exhaustive.' He says these things himself – for example, 'No relation is *merely* intrinsic or external, and every relation is both' (1924, *CE* p. 667) – but we are blind to such remarks, or dismiss them as unintelligible, frustrating or evasive. Yet when we are not being philosophers, we allow such manoeuvres without hesitation. Few of us, for example, would find it difficult to rank 'France is hexagonal' higher than 'France is triangular' in terms of degrees of truth, but who would want to say that either was completely accurate? And a person totally innocent of post-Fregean philosophy but versed in facts about sport might well rank 'A cricket pitch is 20 yards long' as more true than 'A cricket pitch is 30 yards long' and less true than 'A cricket pitch is 21 yards long'.

So it is hard for those philosophers reared in the analytic tradition and imbued with the ideology of classical logic, who probably absorbed without question the assumption that the truth/falsity distinction is a matter of black and white and learned to put on one side awkward sentences such as 'A handkerchief is an article of clothing',[31] to keep in mind in more than a token way the fact that the idealist account of truth includes such a doctrine of partial and temporary truths which suffice for the business of daily life, and for the practice of science, logic and mathematics, but which may nevertheless be metaphysically inadequate in that they lead to contradiction when fully thought through. And even an idealist would hardly have embraced a metaphysics which treated the statements 'Australia is chronically short of potable water' and 'Australia is not chronically short of potable water' as both just plain false, with nothing to choose between them when it comes to making a practical decision on, say, population policy or recycling. Thus Moore's saying that it is just obvious that there are contingent truths, and even Russell's demonstration that propositions expressing transitive asymmetrical relations are irreducible and essential for mathematics, are neither of them direct refutations of Bradley's considered views on relations. Baldwin (1990, pp. 34–5) tries to maintain that Bradley can, nevertheless, be condemned on the basis of his methodology's coming into conflict with common sense and lacking independent support. But to this it can be said, first, that Bradley's methodological requirements grow naturally out of those which common sense and scientific practice take for granted;[32] and secondly, that, as we have seen, he is careful to take steps to ensure that his metaphysics is not in competition with common sense or any of the disciplines.

All the same, as soon as one leaves the level of common sense and gets into metaphysics at all, some doctrine which has the same purpose as this idealist one of partial truth is going to have to be brought into play somewhere. Russell pretended to believe that it was just plain false 'that there are no relations and that there are not many things, but only one thing', jibing that 'Idealists would add: *in the end*. But that only means that the consequence is one which it is often convenient to forget.'[33] But thus hunting with the hounds of common sense, he could have had no realistic expectation that he would be allowed to run with the hare of metaphysics himself, and *in the end*, he too, who said 'I do not believe in complex entities of this kind', a kind exemplified by 'all the ordinary objects of daily life',[34] had to face the task of giving an account of their status that would preserve (at least many) ordinary truths about them while discarding ordinary falsehoods. And I think it may fairly be said that his attempt to bring this off, the programme of logical constructions, has proved, in the long run, no more satisfactory a working philosophical tool than the idealist notion of partial truths. But things must have looked different at the outset, and the eclipse of the latter by the former must be explained at least in part by the notion of the logical construction's at least appearing to offer a workable programme, which its predecessor did not, completely lacking as it did a metric with which even a rough estimate of the degree of truth of an individual proposition might be reached. (The examples concerning the shape of France and the length of a cricket pitch involve merely ordering a few easy cases, and anyway cannot readily be generalized, even using its own examples – is 'France is hexagonal' more true or less true than 'A cricket pitch is 20 yards long'? But it must not be forgotten that things may have looked different to an idealist. Here is Bradley on Hegel: 'No one who has not seen this view at work, and seen it applied to a wide area of fact, can realize its practical efficiency', 1909c, *ETR* p. 223.)[35] And the long run is always arguably not yet over, so that even today the crucial test for the programme of logical constructions, the one which was supposed to demonstrate unequivocally the power and superiority of the new method – that is, the logicist account of arithmetic – and which was so spectacularly failed right at the outset, still seems to many philosophers merely to await the overcoming of a few difficulties for success to be attainable. (Even radical logicians like the paraconsistentists are inspired by the hope of rescuing this account from the paradoxes.)

Russell, internality and unreality

We saw in the last section that Bradley himself suffered temporary confusion about the nature of his own views on relations. By the time he had freed himself from this confusion, it was too late: the controversy with Russell had become irrevocably, indeed fatally, muddled. To reinforce this point, and bring out the consequences of what I have shown, let us look again at the best known, and probably the most historically influential, of Russell's arguments against Bradley. (He has of course other arguments, including one he describes as 'more searching'. But this one is the most straightforward, and it will anyway become clear that it does not matter which we choose, since, as we shall see, the two men were at cross-purposes.)

This argument is the appeal to asymmetrical relations, that is, those of which, for example, if it is true that *a* bears the relation to *b*, then it is false that *b* bears the relation to *a*. As we saw, Russell uses it repeatedly. This is not surprising, for the notion of an asymmetrical relation is essential to Russell's account of order, which itself is vital to his account of mathematics.[36] It is at the heart of the crucial anti-Bradley argument in *The Principles of Mathematics* (1903, Ch. XXVI); it is deployed again in *Our Knowledge of the External World* (1914, Lecture II). It is rehearsed, very briefly and obscurely (for Russell had let himself get behind and was in a hurry), in the famous lectures on logical atomism (1918, Lecture III). It also occurs in his Aristotelian Society paper (1907), from which Russell reprinted the relevant passages in his 1959 book *My Philosophical Development*. And he uses it, too, in his contribution to Muirhead's collection *Contemporary British Philosophy: Personal Statements* (Russell 1924). We may take the 1903 version as representative; it involves Russell's favourite example, *greater than*:

> The monistic theory holds that every relational proposition *aRb* is to be resolved into a proposition concerning the whole which *a* and *b* compose – a proposition which we may denote by (*ab*)*r* ... We are told, by those who advocate this opinion [Russell has previously identified Spinoza and Bradley], that the whole contains diversity within itself, that it synthesizes differences, and that it performs other similar feats. For my part, I am unable to attach any precise significance to these phrases. But let us do our best.
>
> The proposition '*a* is greater than *b*', we are told, does not really say anything about either *a* or *b*, but about the two together. Denoting the whole which they compose by (*ab*), it says we will suppose, '(*ab*) contains diversity of magnitude.' Now to this statement ... there is a special objection in the case of asymmetry. (*ab*) is symmetrical with regard to *a* and *b*, and thus the property of the whole will be exactly the same in the case where *a* is greater than *b* as in the case where *b* is greater than *a*.
>
> (Russell 1903, Ch. XXVI, §215)

Modern logicians, as we observed, are less impressed with this argument than Russell was. But let us put that on one side, and grant for the moment that the argument refutes what Russell calls 'the monistic theory' of relations. Two questions are pertinent in this context. First, what exactly is this theory? And second, did Bradley hold it?

Given what we observed in the last section, it is not surprising to find that Russell himself wobbles on the answer to the first question. In some places (Russell 1907, 1924, 1959), what is under attack is the view that all relations are internal. In others (Russell 1903, 1914), it is the view that all relations are unreal. On occasion (Russell 1918), the matter is entirely unclear.

We have seen already that the internality doctrine is not a view to which Bradley subscribed except for a temporary muddle which was sorted out by 1901, so that the 1907, 1914 and 1959 versions of the refutation are apparently misdirected. Bradley did, on the other hand, subscribe to the unreality doctrine. But this latter is interpreted by Russell as the monistic account given, for example, in the above quotation from *The Principles of Mathematics*. And in fact this is also how Russell interprets the internality doctrine (which explains why I inserted 'apparently' into the previous sentence). But we have already seen that Bradley, in holding that relations were unreal, was not committed to maintaining that relational propositions were reducible to subject–predicate propositions. To repeat: there are two reasons for rejecting the attribution to Bradley of such a commitment: first, he held firmly that subject–predicate propositions require a relation between the subject and the predicate so that relations turn out to be ineliminable even if a particular relational proposition were to be replaceable by a subject–predicate proposition; second, as we noticed in Chapter 2 (p. 37*f*), he held also that in any case subject–predicate propositions too are problematic, so that no problem with relations would be resolved by reducing them to predicates. He makes this plain in his most considered treatment of relations, which directly addressed Russell's argument, but was unfortunately left unfinished at his death, appearing in print too late to make any serious contribution to the debate:

> Asymmetrical relations are said to disprove Monism, because Monism rests on *simple* inherence [i.e. predication] as the only way in which there is ultimate reality.
>
> The argument, if right, is improperly limited – because *any* relations, *if so*, disprove Monism.
>
> But Monism does not rest on simple inherence as the one form of reality. It even (in my case) says that that form is unsatisfactory (see *Appearance*).
>
> In short, far from admitting that Monism requires that all truths can be interpreted as the predication of qualities of the whole, Monism with me contends that all predication, no matter what, is in the end untrue and in the end unreal ...
>
> (Bradley 1924, pp. 670, 672; his italics)

What was at stake for Bradley was the ontological status of relations; and a *locus classicus* of the sort of view that he was rejecting in urging that relations are unreal, is Russell's *Principles of Mathematics*. What is in question, that is, is whether relations can be thought of as terms in the Russellian sense, the extreme realist view that we uncovered in Chapter 3. It is possible, as we shall see from Russell's own example, to reject the idea that a relation is a term in a proposition, on an ontological par with its other constituents, without embracing what Russell calls 'the monistic theory' of relations.

In the sense that Bradley intended the claim that relations are unreal, then, Russell's appeal to asymmetrical relations is neither here nor there. It is no concession of defeat for Bradley to admit that relational expressions are ineliminable from sentences like '*aRb*', nor can be converted into monadic predicates, without loss of information. What is at issue here is how such expressions function: do they function by introducing a kind of object into the proposition, or not? Russell held (at this stage) that they do; Bradley denied this. Russell thought that something important was at stake. In *The Principles of Mathematics* he opens §212 with a reference to 'the philosophic dislike of relations', and immediately goes on to describe this 'dislike' as the view that 'no relations can possess absolute and metaphysical validity'. It is not obvious what this means, but we can discern it in Russell's rehearsal of the same theme in his famous essay 'The Monistic Theory of Truth', where he glosses it as 'the denial that there are any relations' (1907, p. 142; 1959, p. 57). These telling phrases reveal his thinking far more clearly than his explicit arguments. It takes the form of a *reductio*: 'Both the internality and the unreality doctrines come to the same thing: there are no relations. Consequently, every proposition invoking a relation is appealing to something that does not exist. Hence, every such proposition (and mathematics is full of them) is false.' And this is an argument on which, as we saw in the last section, Russell came to change his mind, by changing his views about meaning. In fact, the real issue between the two philosophers, for which the confused dispute over relations goes proxy, is that of how to think about meaning.

Nevertheless, however justified it may be to say that Bradley remained unrefuted by Russell's argument, this still of course leaves open the possibility that his view is still mistaken, or at least undemonstrated, or even unmotivated. It is to the examination of this possibility that we must now turn.

Bradley's arguments for the unreality of relations and their terms

At this point we come to what is, after all, the real issue, to which all that I have said in this chapter until now is merely preliminary. This is the question of how good Bradley's arguments on the subject of relations and their terms are. Given the amount of effort I have devoted to the topic of relations so far, I shall spend less time on surveying this well-ploughed ground than one might expect; my defence for this apparent imbalance is that, without the removal of the undergrowth of confusion first, what is at stake here could never have been clearly identified, and that, once it is identified, matters can then be seen to be far more straightforward than the accumulation of commentary would have led us to expect. As we have just observed the doctrine of internality to be of secondary significance and a needless and perplexing distraction, we can concentrate on the question of the doctrine of unreality.

It is important to remember that Bradley's various arguments on this subject are a team effort. No one of them on its own is meant to show conclusively the unreality of relations or of terms, but each closes off one of the possible positions which an opponent might adopt.[37] The systematicity this allows is most evident in Chapter III of *Appearance and Reality*; but the presentation there is marred by the confusions already mentioned (though other versions are less tidily arranged). And it is important, too, to bear in mind that the question always lurking more or less visibly behind Bradley's arguments is, 'Are relations and their terms real?' I have said already that this question is the same as 'Are relations and their terms substances?' and that the linguistic counterpart of this question, for him at least, is 'Do names of relations and their terms figure in a language which accurately mirrors reality?'

Bradley's most notorious argument, which as we have seen occurs as early as 1883 and is repeated in *Appearance and Reality* (1893, pp. 27–8) as well as later writings, is the second member of a pair which works by excluding in turn each component of this disjunction: Either relations essentially relate their terms (in the sense that there can be no such thing as a term-free relation, one example of a 'floating idea' as he sometimes calls it) or they do not.[38] The first member alleges that if they do, then they do not exist independently of their terms and are thus obviously unreal. The second member alleges that if, on the other hand, we try to deny this conclusion and insist that relations are real, then they would be themselves extra terms which would require further relations in order to link them to the terms which they were supposed to be relating (and so on *ad infinitum*).

Given the technical sense which Bradley attaches to 'real', and the assumptions common to all participants in the dispute, it seems to me that he is unanswerably correct in this disjunctive contention, whether it is taken as a point in the philosophy of language about the analysis of propositions – that apparent names of relations are in principle eliminable – or as a point in metaphysics about the constituents of the world, that relations are not substances. Our modes of expressing relations are not names, and the relations themselves are not objects, and that is that. One may want to say that nothing is or could be a substance in the required sense; but to take this line is to repudiate the mutually agreed terms of the dispute as it was conducted at the time, and in any case it remains true that relations fall far shorter of the mark than do, say, material objects.[39] Anyone who studies the debate of 1910–11 between Bradley and Russell in the pages of *Mind* (both sides of which are now available in *CP6*), and compares Russell's 1903 commitment to the reality of relations in *The Principles of Mathematics* with the eventual conscious ontological parsimony of his 1924 essay 'Logical Atomism', can hardly disagree, and it is a source of continual wonder to me that Bradley can still be blamed for treating relations illegitimately as objects when it is *just that treatment that he is disputing*. It is surprising that, for example, when Wollheim (1969, p. 113) wrote that Bradley described relations as 'a second kind of real thing' he omitted to observe that this description occurred within the framework of a conditional whose antecedent Bradley rejected; and it has taken us too long to notice that when Russell wrote, 'Bradley conceives a relation as something just as substantial as its terms, and not radically different in kind',[40] he himself was writing in 1927 from the comfortable position of having abandoned not only the ontology of *The Principles of Mathematics* but also the multiple relation theory of judgment, in both of which relations are just so conceived. No wonder that Russell, having surreptitiously switched sides to become the new champion of the insubstantiality and unreality of relations, could make his long-standing opponent appear, *ex officio* as it were, to have subscribed to their substantiality and, via this, to the denial of ordinary facts. (Notice too that, despite the earlier fears which had fuelled his opposition to those who held relations to be unreal, Russell, perhaps because of his Wittgenstein-influenced shift away from a conception of logic as the most highly generalized description of reality to a 'linguistic' view, managed to change sides on the issue of relations without apparently encountering any catastrophic consequences for mathematics.)

The second component of the disjunctive argument is often thought to stand alone (as, for example, by Russell in the debate summed up in the last paragraph), and is described accordingly as 'Bradley's regress argument'. This is, of course, to misrepresent its function; it is giving only one half of an argument by dilemma. And there is a standard reply to it which originates with Russell and is endorsed by Wollheim.[41] It is that the regress is indeed endless but not vicious, being merely one of implication and not requiring the actual completion of an infinite series before anything can actually be related. (Thus '*A* and *B* are alike' implies '*A* is like something which is like *A*', which in turn implies '*A* is like something which is like something which is like *B*', and so on *ad infinitum* but unworryingly.) This reply, if it is to be effective, must be based on the idea that the goal of the argument is to prove the internality rather than the unreality of relations. (This is particularly obvious in Wollheim's treatment of the matter; though Russell is clear that Bradley's argument is against the reality of relations, his reply is so bound up with confused conceptions of meaning that it is hard to know what to make of it.) If we keep it in mind that the question at issue is whether or not relations are real, we can see that the argument's point is that an infinite series of actual *objects* is generated, not just an infinite series of possible names, so that even if the argument does not prove a vicious infinite regress, it still threatens to show that the reality of relations requires an ontology embarrassing to anyone even as easy-going as the Russell of 1903.

We can see the appropriateness of Bradley's argument to the ontology of *The Principles of Mathematics*, and accordingly in the context of his debate with Russell, by putting together the following two extracts:

> Among concepts, again, two kinds at least must be distinguished, namely those indicated by adjectives and those indicated by verbs ... [T]he latter are always or almost always relations.
>
> (Russell 1903, §48)

> [T]he theory that there are adjectives or attributes or ideal things ... which are in some way less substantial, less self-subsistent, less self-identical, than true substantives, appears to be wholly erroneous, and to be easily reduced to a contradiction. Terms which are concepts differ from those which are not, not in respect of self-subsistence ...
>
> (*Ibid*. §49; the rest is irrelevant to the present purpose)

Bradley's argument, then, is applicable to the target at which it was directed, even if Russell had abandoned the fortress before it collapsed; and the regress it demonstrates is in fact far from innocent. To see what the argument succeeds in demonstrating, let us take a familiar analogy. Suppose I am given the task of making a chain out of some loose metal rings, and when I come to join any two of them, I respond by asserting that we need a third ring to do the job, so that the most I can achieve is just the addition of more rings to the collection. It is quite clear that no matter how many rings I add, I shall never get a chain unless I do something 'radically different in kind' (to use Russell's own words) from merely collecting more rings, something that I could just as well have done with the first pair of rings as with any of those subsequently added. Now as long as we think of relations as real, that is, as substantial in the sense which was common ground between Russell and Bradley (and not only in 1903; see the remarks from 'The Philosophy of Logical Atomism' which I quoted above, p. 160), we are in an analogous situation. A relation needs to be something 'radically different in kind' from its terms.

A parallel analogy can be constructed to pacify those who want to protest with Wollheim (1969, p. 114) that things are in fact related and the problem is not to relate previously unrelated things but to understand actual relational facts: suppose I have a chain and I want to understand its principle of construction. It is clear that I am already barking up the wrong tree if I begin by pointing out that the two end rings of an existing chain are linked by the intervening ones, for this account of linking does *nothing at all* towards explaining how two adjacent rings are linked; and if I try to pretend that there is some further ring intervening between adjacent ones, once more an infinite regress appears.

I can see no good reason why this argument has had such a bad press.[42] (There are of course historical reasons, some of which I have brought into the open in the preceding pages.) It should now be obvious that it would be an *ignoratio* to suggest that the argument ignores the fact that it is a matter of sheer common sense that there are related things in the world; for this is not in contention. What *is* in contention is a philosophical account of the world's variety and relatedness, a fact obscured by the same word, 'relation', having to do double duty as identifying *both* the problem *and* an unsatisfactory solution to it. (It is hard to over-emphasize the importance of that point, for, as we remarked in Chapter 3, p. 59f, the phenomenon is a widespread source of philosophical confusion.[43]) But even if this argument continues to be perversely rejected, Bradley has others on the subject which seem to me to have been underestimated or even ignored.

One of them is very close to the regress argument I have just sketched, and is directed against an assumption he claims to find in *The Analysis of Mind* (Russell 1921), that 'every mental fact can be analysed in the sense of being shown to be a relational complex – where, that is, it fails to be an atomic unit whether as a sensation or a relation' (Bradley 1924, *CE* p. 656). Bradley takes this assumption to entail that all complexity must be treated relationally. And he asks, what of the relations themselves? They cannot be simple, for then they could have no internal provision for relating two or more objects, so they must be complex. Yet if they are complex, they must themselves be analysable relationally, but then the same question arises, and so on *ad infinitum*. The point resembles that which Wittgenstein made in the *Notes on Logic* against Russell's conception of logical forms in the period immediately prior to the production of the aborted manuscript 'Theory of Knowledge' (Russell 1913), a conception that as we saw in Chapter 3 was supposed to get around the problems posed by Russell's 1910 theory of judgment but which required the forms to be both simple and complex (Wittgenstein 1913b, p. 99). And both criticisms illustrate Russell's constant difficulties with the problem of unity and diversity and his continuing attempts to resolve them by means of finding extra objects of acquaintance to do a job which no object, however peculiar, could possibly do.[44]

So far these arguments have concentrated on relations themselves, and their conclusion is that relations are unreal. This means that they do not constitute elements out of which complex wholes are constructed but instead are 'abstractions' from those wholes, creatures of intellectualization. Provided that we do not forget that this conclusion is not that reality contains no differences, merely that these differences are not to be understood in the way that some philosophers have supposed, it can and should be accepted with equanimity. Russell, in asserting that 'the axiom of internal relations is incompatible with all complexity ... lead[ing], as we saw, to a rigid monism' (1907, p. 145), mistook his target. Bradley's view has a lot in common with those whom Russell thought of as allies: applied to judgment, then, apart from its generalization from some to all propositional constituents, it is reminiscent of Frege, and, as we saw in the last section, Bradley and Wittgenstein, despite their different ways of expressing the point, could be said to be at one on the unreality of relations. Of course Bradley and Wittgenstein diverge dramatically in their eventual conclusions: the one was a monist, the other a pluralist. But this is nothing to do with their views on relations. It is a consequence of their differences concerning the status of related objects. Wittgenstein, rejecting the tradition of thinking of objects in terms of independent substances, thought it possible to name objects even though they could occur only in combination with others so that this naming could be achieved only in the context of a proposition. Bradley thought this not possible: objects, no less than relations, turn out to be unreal. And his arguments to this effect cannot be accepted with equanimity by those who wish to draw back from monism. It is on his treatment of things, not of relations, that Russell should have focused his attention.

Consider, for example, this argument, which appears first in 1893 (*AR* pp. 25–7), recurs in 1924 (*CE* pp. 634–5), and is intended to prove the unintelligibility of related terms. (It is again the second of a pair of arguments whose first member is a proof of the unintelligibility of terms devoid of relation. I take it that this first one needs no special attention, if only because any two terms whatever are related by similarity or dissimilarity.) My grasp of the argument is tenuous enough for me to be able to give only a rough presentation of it, and I am afraid that even rougher presentations are all we ever get from Bradley himself. The key claim is that 'in order to be related, a term must keep still within itself enough character to make it, in short, itself and not anything diverse' (*ibid.*, *CE* p. 634). The point is, I think, this. Imagine two numerically different objects of which the same relational predicate holds true. By virtue of their diversity, they must differ in some other respect. (Bradley, at least as long as one is dealing with things at the term–predicate–relation level, held to the Identity of Indiscernibles.) That is, each term must have some other predicate holding true of it which the other lacks. (This other predicate, although it may itself be relational too, must hold independently of the original relational one, or the terms would have no character of their own.) But then the question of the relation between the relational predicate and the other predicate arises, and a familiar regress begins: an endless multiplicity of relations breaks out within the term itself. Of course, this way of putting the argument is very careless about use and mention, but not in any way that affects the question of its soundness. (Rather, I have tried to make clear that Wollheim's criticism of this argument (1959, p. 117; 1969, p. 115), that the regress does not even begin because there is no relevant diversity internal to the term, is wrong.)

This argument has a metaphysical significance far beyond that of the attack on the reality of relations. It attacks the reality of terms, albeit –

as Bradley himself saw – using the attack on the reality of relations as a model (so that the issue of relations could easily have had its significance overestimated), and its consequences are far-reaching. Of comparable significance, it may seem, is the logical atomist attack on the reality of complex objects;[45] but the comparison is inadequate, for the logical atomists remained content with simple objects while Bradley rejected the reality of these too. And notice that, after the reality of relations eventually became a non-issue for Russell because of his surreptitious switch of sides on the question, he had come round to the view that mathematics and logic can survive on the reality of terms alone. Hence, of course, a threat to the reality of terms would equally be a threat to Russell's class-based account of number (a threat which would have persisted despite all the twists and turns in that account in reaction to the discovery of Russell's Paradox: monism and the axiom of infinity are not natural bedfellows); and this, together with the idea that mathematical truths are at best less than wholly true, should have been the primary focus of his hostility which, in its early concentration on relations, misidentified its target. It is on the rejection of the reality of terms, rather than that of relations, let alone on his muddled and temporary commitment to the doctrine of internality, that we should regard Bradley's more extravagant monistic conclusions as being based.

Even on its most conservative interpretation, the outcome of the attack on the reality of terms will be that a language that tries to be faithful to reality by restricting its names to those of substances will have no such names. It will, as we saw in Chapter 5, resemble the language which results from the application of Quine's version of the Theory of Descriptions, with the word 'Reality' playing for Bradley roughly the same formal role as the quantified variable does for Quine.[46] But whether or not this particular analogy will take us very far, the point I want to stress is that, as Manser tried to prove, this is a game which analytic philosophers know how to play in philosophical logic, just as their debates in the philosophy of science still often concern the reality of space and time even if the vocabulary has changed. This, though, makes the near-total, if gradual, collapse of monistic idealism start to look puzzling.

7
Decline and Fall

> 'Some of Bradley's sentiments are strongly reminiscent of Nazi
> state-worship.'
>
> Peter Geach, 'A Philosophical Autobiography',
> in Lewis (1991), p. 3

Health warning

A very learned philosopher once said to me that he was puzzled by the
fact that arguments which seemed absolutely compelling to one generation of philosophers were often found utterly unconvincing by
another. It was clear that he did not think it sufficient explanation to
talk about, for example, the problems posed by translation, by meaning shifts, by obscurity and so on. This short, and admittedly inconclusive, concluding chapter begins from the sense that we should take this
puzzlement seriously. Those who are already convinced that we should
not, who think perhaps that philosophy is decided on the arguments
alone, at least in their own case, are advised to read no further.

The decline of monistic idealism

Russell describes the beginning of his 'revolt into pluralism' like this
(Russell 1959, p. 54): 'It was towards the end of 1898 that Moore and I
rebelled against both Kant and Hegel. Moore led the way, but I followed closely in his footsteps.' He goes on to identify the central point
upon which the rebellion was founded, common to himself and
Moore, as that of relations. In his autobiography, he repeats the story
(Russell 1967, p. 61).

Russell wrote this account about sixty years after the event, so perhaps it is not surprising that it is oversimplified. In fact, his break with idealism began earlier than he says, appears to have had little or nothing to do with Moore, and was not connected with such recondite matters of metaphysics. It had its roots in his abandonment of his early pietistic Christianity. But those who abandon a faith often need another, and, in common with others of his time, Russell had found in idealism a substitute for religion. But it was not long before he became dissatisfied. The cause appears to have been his confronting, in his early years in Cambridge, a problem that was already familiar from Reid. It consists in the need to reconcile the rational demands of private and of public interest. Reid had believed that the two could not clash. He maintained that because 'the world is under a wise and benevolent administration, it is impossible that in the issue any man should be a loser by doing his duty'. The problem may have filtered through to Russell in Cambridge via Henry Sidgwick, who was unable to avail himself of Reid's convenient theistic solution. Russell himself faced it in one of his undergraduate essays (Russell 1893), and attempted to deal with it by invoking McTaggart's optimistic idealism, according to which not only is 'reality exclusively spirit' but the 'universe and ourselves are implicitly in harmony – a harmony that must one day become explicit'. Our immortality guarantees that this harmony will at some stage be experienced, and the prospect accordingly affords something normally provided by religion, namely comfort in adversity. This long-run solution was unavailable to Russell once he rejected immortality, and in his next effort, this time in a very early paper to the Cambridge Apostles (Russell 1894), he abandoned McTaggart and entertained what he called 'a more Bradleian view', in which the harmony is no longer left to a future we shall not live long enough to encounter but is present in a timeless Reality of which individual selfhood is a merely partial aspect. In a later Apostles paper (Russell 1897a), though, Russell in effect argues that such a Bradleian metaphysical harmony belongs to Reality and not Appearance, accordingly still cannot be experienced, and hence can offer no consolation. The paper ends by canvassing the suggestion that metaphysics is the wrong place to look for comfort. In flight from the Victorian Christianity of his childhood, Russell found only a very temporary refuge in idealism.[1]

Despite, then, Russell's later autobiographical remarks, it is clear from this brief account that he had already prepared the ground himself with his growing dissatisfaction with idealist metaphysics as a basis for a philosophy of living. That is, Russell's break with idealism began earlier than is commonly believed, and is based not on metaphysical but on practical considerations. Only in ground already fertilized could Moore's strange early arguments (see, for example, Moore 1899 and 1903, which Moore himself later repudiated) have taken root. And even Moore's later and more sophisticated arguments, when they came, were generally question-begging, so that it is no surprise that, as we shall see, he resorted to mockery.

It may help to add some brief reminder of how unsatisfactory even the best known of those arguments are. Consider, for example, Moore's famous article 'External and Internal Relations' (Moore 1919). Quite apart from the issue on which I have laid so much stress, that of whether Moore even chose the right target in attacking the doctrine of internality, in the whole paper, despite its length and complexity, Moore's only *direct* argument against this doctrine was this: 'It seems quite obvious that in the case of many relational properties which things have, the fact that they have them is *a mere matter of fact*: that the things in question might have existed without having them'. Similarly, Moore's sole direct argument against idealism in 'The Refutation of Idealism' (1903) was: 'I am suggesting that the Idealist maintains that object and subject are necessarily connected, mainly because he fails to see that they are *distinct*, that they are *two*, at all.'[2] It is not always observed that the tendency to question-begging so noticeable in 'A Defence of Common Sense' (Moore 1925) and 'Proof of an External World' (Moore 1939) was there in 1903 as well.[3] Or again, one might look at the well known Russell allegation that Bradley could not reduce asymmetrical relations to predicates. We saw in Chapter 6 (p. 163*f*) above that this allegation involves an *ignoratio*, and that Bradley pointed this out, though too late to be noticed. (Not so well known are the problems non-symmetrical relations posed, ironically, for Russell himself.[4])

To explain the decline and eventual collapse of idealism, we have to look beyond the arguments: even if those arguments were accepted, there remains the question of how this could have come about when they were so palpably inconclusive. This kind of observation is of course not novel. Hylton (1990, p. 105), for example, says:

> My claim here is not that either [Russell or Moore] had a conclusive argument against Idealism ... [I]ssues at the most fundamental level of philosophy are not decided by conclusive argument ... It is not because of any one argument that Moore and Russell rejected

Idealism – though once they had done so they certainly employed arguments, which they held to be conclusive, against it.

Hylton goes on to suggest that idealism can 'seem to be in danger of collapsing under its own weight', and sketches two of its 'pervasive features' (its apparent psychologism and its willingness to condemn everyday truths as falling short of some impossible ideal) which can, to an 'uncharitable reader' seem to correspond to 'fatal weaknesses'. This is not wrong, but it is unsatisfactory. Should the acceptance of a philosophical system rest on charity? And, even if so, why in this case was such charity first exercised, and later withheld?

Warnock's remarks at the same point suggest an answer:

> It would ... be historically improper to give the impression that Idealism perished of *refutation*. It is true that some of Bradley's fundamental views, such as his doctrine of 'internal relations' or his theory of truth, were subjected to destructive criticism. But metaphysical systems do not yield, as a rule, to frontal attack ... The onslaughts of critics to whom, as likely as not, their strange tenets are very nearly unintelligible are apt to seem, to those entrenched inside, mis-directed or irrelevant. Such systems are more vulnerable to *ennui* than to disproof.
>
> (Warnock 1958, pp. 10–11)

There is insight here. But, left as it stands, it is a dispiriting one. What is the point of argument in metaphysics, if it is always inconclusive or can persuade no one inclined to disagree? And what about those who are not 'entrenched'? Moreover, the insight fades when we look at Warnock's crucial explanatory term, *ennui*. Even if there is *ennui*, the conditions under which it arises need exposure. Otherwise we risk portraying philosophers as sulky adolescents.

Looking beyond the arguments is on its own a major historical undertaking; all I shall do is mention a few crucial factors and invite the reader to consider them.

The first factor is the dramatic discoveries and changes in physics, on both sub-atomic and celestial scales, that were being made in the period we are dealing with, and the demanding mathematical techniques required for their expression and comprehension. I have already stressed that idealism had no particular veneration for mathematics, and indeed the sciences in general, regarding them as just another variety of human activity with no preferred status, and their truths, like all others, as merely partial. But even this point demands qualification, for it is quite clear, right from the early pages of *The Principles of Logic* (1883, Book I, Chapter II, §78), that Bradley had, admittedly from the standpoint of an outsider, a great regard for science, holding that scientific laws, because of their universality, stand high on the ladder of degrees of truth, a fact implicitly denied in item 6 of the stereotype depicted in Chapter 1 (p. 10*f*). We must beware, as I warned at the start of Chapter 6, of thinking of Bradley as *representative* of the British Idealists. That said, it remains that, for Bradley, science provided neither a model nor an inspiration for metaphysics. At a time of astonishing scientific progress, a metaphysics which, like Russell's, was put together with the explicit goal of accommodating mathematics and the sciences, and itself deploying scientific method – 'philosophy, in our own day, is becoming scientific', he remarks – could hardly fail to seem more appropriate to the intellectual life than one which seemed to draw on a mystical vision of the unity of being.[5]

Only slightly less obvious is that the advances in formal logic and set theory made around the turn of the century, and continuing beyond it, opened up, as Russell saw, the possibility of doing philosophy in a new way which would provide unparalleled precision of thought and expression (for example, the easy disambiguation made available through the device of multiple quantification, and the exact expression of mathematical theorems), definite discoveries, even provable results, with technical solutions to philosophical problems. It seemed, and to many still seems, natural to assume that Russellian metaphysics, or logical empiricism, or one of their pluralist descendants, had some special nexus with logic, that the nature of the calculus somehow dictated a certain kind of ontology. The idea that it is possible both to be a monist and to take advantage of the facilities of a formal logic is not self-evident, and we have seen Russell denying it.[6] Moreover, and vitally, the new predicate logic, introduced by Frege and notationally made more convenient by Whitehead and Russell, had sufficient expressive and deductive power to give rise not only to a new way of doing philosophy, but also to whole new disciplines, such as metalogic, new discoveries, such as Gödel's incompleteness theorems, and new projects, such as the axiomatization of (at least parts of) physics.

In the changing climate, how did Bradley look? Averse to the view that mathematics and physics hold the keys to a metaphysical understanding of the universe, himself a maddeningly imprecise writer, and not only a principled opponent of formal and technical methods but also self-confessedly incompetent in practising them, he could hardly avoid the appearance of a figure of the past. Even if one tries to set this aside, his own views leave one with a sense of stultification: nothing is true, no inference is valid, everything one normally takes for granted is mere appearance, but you can ignore these things and still manage perfectly well in any enterprise other than metaphysics. It is hard to see, if one were to become a convinced Bradleian, what, for a philosopher, other than contemplate the Absolute, there would be to *do*; the contrast with Russell is evident. The age of the programme had arrived, *The Encyclopedia of Unified Science* was just around the corner, and the fact that Wittgenstein was already subverting what was to become the new orthodoxy from within was as yet unrecognized.

Still, much of what I have just described lay in the future, and, just as we saw that there was a question (and an answer) as to how the Moorean influence could be exerted on Russell, there remains here this question: in what way was the ground already prepared to receive the Russellian seed?

Answering this question demands that we look not only beyond the arguments but to matters which most philosophers ignore. We may, however, take as precedent Russell himself: the often neglected subtitle to his *History of Western Philosophy* is, of course, *'and its Connection with Political and Social Circumstances from the Earliest Times to the Present Day'*. All I shall do is sketch some circumstances as examples of how non-philosophical background causes may have effects within a discipline that, as Russell himself – in some contrast with the invitation hinted at in his sub-title – illustrates in a revealing piece of the rhetoric of perfectibility, prides itself on making up one's mind on the arguments:

> A man imbued with the philosophic spirit, whether a professional philosopher or not, will wish his beliefs to be as true as he can make them, and will, in equal measure, love to know, and hate to be in error. This principle has a wider scope than may be apparent at first sight. Our beliefs spring from a great variety of causes: what we were told in youth by parents and schoolteachers, what powerful organizations tell us in order to make us act as they wish, what either embodies or allays our fears, what ministers to our self-esteem, and so on. Any one of these causes may happen to lead us to true beliefs, but is more likely to lead us in the opposite direction. Intellectual sobriety, therefore, will lead us to scrutinize our beliefs closely, with a view to discovering which of them there is any reason to believe true. If we are wise, we shall apply solvent criticism especially to the

beliefs that we find it most painful to doubt, and to those most likely to involve us in violent conflict with men who hold opposite but equally groundless beliefs. If this attitude could become common, the gain in diminishing the acerbity of disputes would be incalculable.

(Russell 1946, pp. 46–7)

This passage, which I and other academic philosophers employ to encourage the formation of ideals in our undergraduates, makes a powerful contrast with Bradley's more modest – even sceptically conservative – remark already quoted at the end of Chapter 2: 'Metaphysics is the finding of bad reasons for what we believe upon instinct, but to find these reasons is no less an instinct.' Not exactly an instinct, but not much of a reason which could be avowed in argument, is what seems to have been a genuine *fear* of idealism on Russell's part. This comes out again and again, for example, in the already-noted remark to the effect that any philosophy which deals in ideas will impose a veil between us and the world. And compare idealism's unenthusiastic assessment of the status of mathematics with this extract from one of Russell's letters (written in December 1901):

The world of mathematics ... is really a beautiful world. It has nothing to do with life and death and human sordidness, but is eternal, cold and passionless. To me, pure mathematics is one of the highest forms of art; it has a sublimity quite special to itself, and an immense dignity derived from the fact that its world is exempt from change and time. I am quite serious in this ... And mathematics is the only thing we know of that is capable of perfection; in thinking about it we become Gods. This alone is enough to put it on a pinnacle above all other studies.[7]

Because of his general influence, Russell's *feelings* – not only his fear of idealism but also his regard for mathematics – and his consequent loathing of a metaphysics which threatened to undermine the basis of that regard, must be included on the list of causal factors in idealism's decline. It would be an absurd exaggeration of this point to maintain that his arguments about mathematical relations are mere rationalizations – for example, of a need for certainty rooted, like his earlier attachment to idealism, in the loss of his early pietistic Christianity. But it is certainly true that the characteristic language of idealism is a vague, windy and moralizing rhetoric, almost intolerable to those whose standards of clarity are derived from mathematics and logic or even from the painstaking efforts of Moore. Even if idealism's subject matter is timeless, its style quickly became hopelessly dated.

Style, of a more general kind than merely literary, is a factor which it is easy to underestimate in pondering major intellectual change of the sort we have been examining in this book. David Stove, with character-istic wit and perceptiveness, attributes this kind of reaction against idealism to

> *horror victorianorum.* I mean by this, that horror which even nowa-days is felt, at least to a slight degree, by almost everyone who visits a display of Victorian stuffed birds under glass, for example, or of Victorian dolls and dolls' clothes. Such things as these, of course, now communicate at most the *quality* of the horror. They cannot convey anything like the intensity with which it was felt fifty or sixty years ago, or the historical importance of this feeling.
>
> (Stove 1985, p. 19)

Although he is discussing the rise of Karl Popper, not of Russell, Stove's point applies (as he himself said to me in correspondence) in this context too. A telling example occurs in this piece of heavily, even sneeringly, ironical self-depreciation in Moore 1903 (p. 24):

> It is, I think, owing to the vastness of this difference [between 'the Idealistic view and the ordinary view of the world'] and owing to the number of different excellences which Idealists attribute to the universe, that it seems such an interesting and important question whether Idealism be true or not. But, when we begin to argue about it, I think we are apt to forget what a vast number of arguments this interesting question must involve ... I say this lest it should be thought that any of the arguments which will be advanced in this paper would be sufficient to disprove, or any refutation of them sufficient to prove, the truly interesting and important proposition that reality is spiritual. For my own part I wish it to be clearly under-stood that I do not suppose that anything I shall say has the small-est tendency to prove that reality is not spiritual: I do not believe it possible to refute a single one of the many important propositions contained in the assertion that it is so. Reality may be spiritual, for all I know; and I devoutly hope it is.

Another factor I have in mind is the gradual fading of the need for a substitute for religion. It is a familiar observation that conventional Christian belief waned under the impact of Darwinism. A less familiar observation is that idealism, providing a natural outlet for vague spiritual longings and a defence against a bleakly Darwinian view of the world, waxed at the same time. Stove, again, is an acute describer of this phenomenon: '*In 1887*', he tells us (and the emphasis is his own), '*almost every philosopher in the English-speaking countries was an idealist*' (Stove 1991a, p. 97). Similarly, Quinton says, 'Until well into the 1920s idealists held nearly all the leading positions in the philosophy departments of British universities and continued to be the largest group in the philosophical professoriate until 1945' (1971, p. 4). But that dominance has passed, and it is difficult now to recover what it was like to be in an intellectual climate in which the immateriality of the universe could be just taken for granted. However, some idea of the degree to which idealism had obtained a grip upon the minds of educated people can be got from one of Thomas Hardy's descriptions of Tess in her natural environment:

> On these lonely hills and dales her quiescent glide was of a piece with the element she moved in. Her flexuous and stealthy figure became an integral part of the scene. At times her whimsical fancy would intensify natural processes around her till they seemed a part of her own story. Rather they became a part of it, for the world is only a psychological phenomenon, and what they seemed they were.
>
> (Hardy 1891: Phase the Second, XIII)

What makes the remark that 'the world is only a psychological phenomenon' so striking and revealing is its casualness, as though to make such an observation at that time were the merest commonplace.

Once the lessons of Darwin had been fully absorbed, the need itself began to wane; room became available for metaphysical views less overtly a substitute for religion. Not independent of this is the impact of the Great War, after whose mud and blood and slaughter (even without the subsequent social disruptions of depression, strikes and extreme political clashes) it was harder to believe in the spirituality of the universe. This too is a point worth illustrating.[8] By the time the war began, sunrise and sunset had for over a century provided Romantic poetry with stock 'tokens of hope and peace and rural charm', often described in religious vocabulary, to the point where they 'had become fully freighted with implicit aesthetic and moral meaning'. But, during the war's years of anxious stalemate, these moments signified the hours of 'stand-to', when those caught in the front lines of the trenches – from the mountains to the sea, without chance of escape – on both sides of the Western Front, were obliged to stand, silent and alert, looking for indications of an attack. Dawn, indeed, was the traditional time for an infantry attack to be begun, and from being symbolic of hope became the occasion of a 'daily routine of quiet terror', while dusk signified the possibility of harrowing bombardment as well as being a constant reminder that this might well be one's last night on earth. 'Dawn', says Fussell, speaking of English prose as well as verse, 'has never recovered from what the Great War did to it.'[9]

Connected in turn with the War's impact is the decline of British imperialism, whose moral and spiritual mission had been justified by some idealist philosophers and undertaken by their pupils, who included such well known and influential figures as Alfred Milner, Arnold Toynbee (both senior and junior), Asquith and Grey. Milner gathered around him in South Africa a group of young men from Oxford's Balliol and New Colleges, the 'main bastions of Neo-idealism', who were 'outstanding representatives of British imperialism's late phase: Leopold S. Amery, Lionel Curtis, Patrick Duncan and Philip Kerr (later Lord Lothian)'. Here is an example of the connection made between idealism and imperialism by another of idealism's Oxford products:

> If the British Empire is to fill its true place in the world it must first find its true place in the heart of its own subjects: they must have a reason for the national faith that is in them. That reason will be given by the analysis of the laws of British power and of the conditions which justify its exercise. This final inquiry will set out not from the assumption that might is right, which is the creed of despotism and the argument of caprice, nor from the theory that right is might, which is the mistake of shallow enthusiasts, but from the conviction that the universe is the manifestation of an intelligible order, inseparable from the order revealed in the processes of thought; that the laws of the material and of the moral world arise from the same sources, and are but different aspects of the same reality.[10]

While this passage reflects Hegel rather than Bradley, those who rejected the imperialist destiny, such as L.T. Hobhouse, were likely neither to accept the views claimed to underpin it nor to draw careful distinctions among them when complaining about the malign influence of Oxonian idealism:

The most popular philosophy of our time has had a reactionary influence, the extent of which is perhaps not generally appreciated. For thirty years and more English thought has been subject, not for the first time in its modern history, to powerful influences from abroad. The Rhine has flowed into the Thames, at any rate into those upper reaches of the Thames, known locally as the Isis, and from the Isis the stream of German idealism has been diffused over the academical world of Great Britain. It would be natural to look to an idealistic philosophy for a counterpoise to those crude doctrines of physical force which we shall find associated with the philosophy of science. Yet, in the main, the idealistic movement has swelled the current of retrogression. It is itself, in fact, one expression of the general reaction against the plain, human, rationalistic way of looking at life and its problems. Every institution and every belief is for it alike a manifestation of a spiritual principle, and thus for everything there is an inner and more spiritual interpretation. Hence, vulgar and stupid beliefs can be held with a refined and enlightened meaning, known only to him who so holds them.

(Hobhouse 1904, pp. 77–8)

And even those more sympathetic to imperialism than Hobhouse might in the aftermath of the war look askance at a metaphysics tainted by association with the ideology of the Prussian state.

Conclusion

We, decades later, are in the fortunate position of being more detached from these causal influences, so that it is easier for us to assess the arguments on their own merits. My verdict is that, whatever one thinks about the soundness of Bradley's arguments on relations and terms, it is clear that they were not refuted at the time, and that any decision to neglect them must be based on grounds other than their lack of substance. (Plainly the verdict with which this book began, that his work is 'a lot of nonsense', cannot be sustained.) Donald Davidson, in what seems to be a late conversion, is one of the few to have observed that Bradley left analytical philosophers with a problem which they mostly either ignored or, like Strawson, discussed in the slightly disguised form of the subject–predicate distinction: 'For the most part, though, contemporary philosophers have not even recognized that there is a problem' (Davidson 2005, p. 94).[11] But if we should begin to suspect that Bradley's arguments might be sound, the consequences for metaphysics will be unsettling: no longer will it be possible merely to invoke, as for instance Armstrong does on more than one occasion, Hume's doctrine of distinct existences as though this sufficed to prove a point,[12] and the comfortable pluralism now so often just taken for granted by philosophers will have to be reconsidered. No matter how much we would like to think otherwise, philosophy is always at risk of subversion by doctrines which reappear from the wrong side of its history.

To say this, of course, is not necessarily to agree that, although Russell was, historically speaking, the victor in the range of issues that defined the Russell/Bradley dispute, it should have been the other way around.[13] It is merely to say that, at the very least, the balance needs to be redressed: that at least in the central matter of relations, terms and the nature of propositions, Bradley's eventual reputation was the result of the effect of rhetoric, propaganda and external historical circumstance, not of argument; that he should once again be recognized, as he was even by his opponents at the time, as a major thinker engaged in a major argument over fundamental matters with the man who became the most influential philosopher of the twentieth century. And I do think, just as I have made plain that I do about Russell, that his views face serious internal difficulties.

One of them is this. It is clear from what has been said in this book that Bradley is sceptical of the value of many of the intellectual tools habitually wielded by philosophers. We have seen him suggesting, for instance, that one cannot rely, other than as a merely temporary expedient, on such notions as the internal/external distinction, the analytic/synthetic distinction, and the subject/predicate distinction (and others that we have left unmentioned, such as causality). Other philosophers, of course, have been similarly sceptical. They face a consequent methodological difficulty: how is one to get on without the tools of the trade? Wittgenstein, after the apparently self-defeating exercise of the *Tractatus*, eventually tried to solve the problem by constant appeal to questions and examples. But in Bradley's case, this scepticism exists alongside a willingness to employ some of these tools himself. Most obvious is his heavy use of the, surely equally dubious, distinction between the real and the unreal, which in turn (as we saw in Chapter 2) is connected, in the minds of both parties to this dispute, with another notion with a chequered philosophical past, that of substance. The employment of distinctions and concepts which are then abandoned looks unnervingly like sawing off the branch on which one is sitting.

Before I say more about this matter, there is a further point I need to make. Towards the end of Chapter 2, I argued that Bradley was committed to a form of the principle of sufficient reason, but had no defence or attack against a rival commitment to ultimate contingency such as we find in Wittgenstein's logical atomism: to use a phrase from my description in Chapter 6 (p. 153*f*) of a similar deadlock, 'conflicting pictures of the world are in play' and Bradley's strategy leaves neither side any room for manoeuvre. In one way, however, this is unfair to him. For we could say – and his strategy in *Appearance and Reality* bears this out – that, like his 'proof' of idealism, his real argument is one of best explanation: we need to examine the whole metaphysical view to see if it offers the most comprehensive and least problematic systematic account of the content of experience. Now this reminder of his 'best explanation' strategy may itself look like a defence of Bradley. Not so, for it is just as much a defence of David Lewis's rival views:

> The reader in search of knock-down arguments in favor of my theories will go away disappointed. Whether or not it would be nice to knock disagreeing philosophers down by sheer force of argument, it cannot be done ... Philosophical theories are never refuted conclusively. The theory survives its refutation – at a price. [It has been] said what we accomplish in philosophical argument: we measure the price. But when all is said and done, and all the tricky arguments and distinctions and counterexamples have been discovered, presumably we will still face the question which prices are worth paying, which theories are on balance credible, which are the unacceptably counterintuitive consequences and which are the acceptably counterintuitive ones. On this question we may still differ. And if all is indeed said and done, there will be no hope of discovering still further arguments to settle our differences.
>
> (Lewis 1981, p. x)

And in fact the appeal to this strategy is especially problematic for Bradley. To see this, let us take up again the discussion from the previous chapter (p. 162*f*).

At that stage, I had tried to show that, although Bradley has a defence against Russell's charge that his metaphysics is inconsistent with everyday facts, the price he pays for using this defence is very high. In essence, the problem, and his strategy for dealing with it, is the same as one we saw earlier, namely, the inconsistency which arises between his metaphysics and logic. What we are to make of a metaphysics which claims that theories whose truth is necessary for the practice of reasoning are ultimately indefensible is a question which is unavoidable in any assessment of the overall coherence of Bradley's views. On the face of it, of course, the metaphysics has to give way under pressure from that direction, and from science and common sense. This is partly for Moorean reasons: it is far more likely that there will be an error in some difficult and complicated doctrine than in the simple principles by which we successfully conduct our everyday business. But it is also because its conclusions appear to undercut the arguments which are intended to establish them. His strategy in the face of these difficulties is to appeal to the doctrine of degrees of truth; and the fact is that Bradley's metaphysics cannot be made even remotely persuasive without appeal to this doctrine. It enables him to resolve the problems by maintaining that the metaphysics is more true than the principles used in arguing for it but with which it is inconsistent, and that, nevertheless, those principles, while less true than the ultimate metaphysics, are more true than rival principles which would deliver a different metaphysics. If that is right, then the fact that the doctrine of degrees of truth appears to provide not even an approximate metric for the estimation of those degrees in any particular case, is a mortal blow to that metaphysics. Not necessarily because his views are incoherent – perhaps there is a way out of the worry that, if the best metaphysics is inconsistent with the principles used in arguing for it, those principles cannot be more true than their denials – but because they fail in his own terms: it is clear, as I have said, that what he, like Lewis, thinks is persuasive about his metaphysics is not any set of decisive arguments in its favour, but its ability to deliver the 'best explanation', something which reconciles the available data and to which there is no insuperable objection. But if he has no method for determining beyond a few straightforward cases whether one difficult proposition is more or less true than another, or a rival 'best explanation' more or less true than his own, then, given the essentially contestable nature of metaphysics, there is no reason to be persuaded by the views he presents. The deadlock is irresolvable.

Finally, another word of warning. Although the last two decades of the twentieth century saw a revival of interest in the work of Bradley, this has remained most definitely a minority interest. To a lesser extent, the same is true of the attention paid to Russell's *The Principles of Mathematics* – though here the situation has been affected for the better by the impact of Hylton (1990). Most philosophers, in so far as they have any impression at all of the formative events and people we have been considering, are still content to work with the stereotype sketched in Chapter 1, whose sources and accuracy go unexamined.

This stereotype is, as we have seen, inaccurate, and most of us accordingly, either misconceive these matters or have only to turn to the standard secondary sources to acquire such a misconception. Perhaps this would not matter much if the error had no serious consequences. The problem is, though, that it does have serious consequences, which I described in Chapter 1 (p. 18*f*). A further one is that we may overestimate our own originality. I said at the outset that this study was not meant merely to set the record straight on the historical matters on which it is focused, though naturally I hope to have achieved that. After all, setting the record straight should in principle lead to a re-evaluation, however gradually achieved, of where we stand now. But we should not underestimate the propensity of philosophers who are heirs to the analytic tradition to consign material to the pigeonhole labelled 'History', where it can be safely ignored while we get on with re-inventing the square wheel.[14]

But although I do think there are interesting ideas in Bradley which should serve at least to open the mind, I am not trying to argue that philosophy needs a Bradley revival. Perhaps I am most concerned to present these matters as a lesson. For the same kinds of processes which led to the acceptance of the stereotype and the consequent inclination to view Bradley's work as just 'a lot of nonsense' are of course still at work today. A prominent case is that of Wittgenstein. Although the *Tractatus* continues to receive sympathetic treatment, a comparably inaccurate and rigid stereotype of his later views became established in the 1960s and, except amongst specialists, persists as I write. For example, Wittgenstein's 'logical behaviourism' and his 'cluster theory' of the sense of proper names are pure artefacts, whose causes involve mistranslations, the reliance of commentators on early, unreliable and superseded secondary sources, and the ignoring of extensive primary material published too late to affect the general impression.[15] Yet the former at least is established, turning up regularly in textbooks on the philosophy of mind, while the latter is constantly reinforced by its appearance in John Searle's over-anthologized 'Proper Names' and Saul Kripke's much-studied *Naming and Necessity*. Although there is likely to be more resistance because Wittgenstein's style, unlike Bradley's, is not so much of its time that it is likely to be the victim of a cultural backlash, and a prolonged rearguard action is being fought by more recent contributors to reference works, we may be currently witnessing a comparable stereotyping of Wittgenstein. My examination of the process, and illustration of how much work has to be undertaken to undo its results, may assist in preventing a repeat performance.

Notes

1 The Stereotypical Picture of the Russell/Bradley Dispute

1 The Order of Merit is restricted to 24 members at any one time, plus additional non-UK recipients. At the time of writing there have only been 168 ordinary members of the Order (honorary appointments of figures outside the Commonwealth are additional).

2 Bradley's College Fellowship, obtained in December 1870 and terminable only on marriage or death, had no teaching duties attached. In June 1871 he suffered a severe inflammation of the kidneys which appears to have had permanent effects. It has been suggested, possibly with malice, that the Bradleys in general were disposed to hypochondria; be that as it may, he was prone thereafter to be incapacitated by cold, physical exhaustion or anxiety; hence his retired life. He took an active part in the running of his college, but avoided public occasions. Collingwood records of Bradley in his *Autobiography*, '[A]lthough I lived within a few hundred yards of him for sixteen years, I never to my knowledge set eyes on him.' But although the history of Bradley's public life is largely that of his books and articles, it is clear that his was not a narrowly bookish existence. To protect his health, he frequently escaped the damp chill of Oxford winters for the kinder weather of southern English and Mediterranean seaside resorts, where company perhaps more congenial than that of an all-male Oxford common room was available.

3 See, for instance, Hylton (1990), p. 1 and the title of Candlish (1998).

4 Recently there have appeared two collections of essays devoted to the philosophy of F.H. Bradley and largely sympathetic in their treatment of it (Bradley J., ed., 1996; Mander, ed., 1996). It is striking that philosophers at Canadian universities supplied nearly all the material for the first of these volumes. Admittedly it arose from a conference held in Canada. But they also supplied nearly half of that for the second. And this arose from one held in England, at which the Canadian contingent was the largest national group. My conjecture is that this persistence of interest is probably traceable to a much earlier filling of Canadian university positions by Scottish migrants; whatever the explanation, the phenomenon is as much social as philosophical.

5 The application of these terms, especially 'realism', has varied over the years. Some philosophers, for example, think that there can be realist idealists and that the proper contrast with idealism is materialism. I stick here with the idealist/realist contrast as that is in keeping with my epigraph. As that epigraph shows, it has certainly been standard at times to think this way. For illustration, see Russell (1924), *CP9* p. 170; *LK* p. 333; also quoted in Chapter 6, p. 144, and Paton (1956), pp. 341, 347.

6 Some hint of why this change should have come about can be gained from Stroud 1979.

7   For examples of this phenomenon in (once) widely used textbooks, see Warnock (1958), pp. 2–3; Ayer (1971), p. 25. To point this out is not to deny that more judicious historians have generally treated this matter with greater delicacy (for example, Passmore 1957, p. 59).

8   There is a well-informed and sensitive discussion in chapter 8 of Mander (1994).

9   Some philosophers say that Russell had a great deal of respect for Bradley. This may be true. Certainly in their private correspondence he is polite, even deferential. However, his published remarks are, as we shall see, often very different in tone.

10 Text books and contributions to standard works of reference which fit this description include the following: BonJour (1995); Dancy (1985), p. 110; Haack (1978), p. 86; Hamlyn (1970), p. 123; Kirkham (1998); O'Connor and Carr (1982), p. 166 (Bradley is here identified only by implication); Richards (1978), p. 139; Sprigge (1995); White (1967), p. 132; Woozley (1949), pp. 125 and 150. It would be very easy to add to this list.

11 For example: Blackburn (1984a), p. 235, and (1984b), pp. 155–6; Candlish (1981), p. 252, n. 6; Candlish (1984), p. 254; Candlish (1986), p. 245; Manser (1983), p. 133; Passmore (1957), p. 116; Walker (1985), p. 2; White (1971), p. 109; Wollheim (1959), p. 171; Wollheim (1969), p. 167.

12 For example, Acton (1967), p. 362; Wollheim (1959), p. 74 (1969), p. 71. In Wollheim's case what Russell calls an 'unintentional' confusion is presented as a deliberate though inexplicit Bradleian commitment.

13 Allard (2005). More general recent accounts of Bradley, both of them clear and well informed, are Mander (1994) and Basile (1999).

14 A good, though somewhat unwieldy, example of the genre is Sprigge (1993). It is not surprising that the dual focus is rare, for it is likely to confront this intractable problem:

> Nothing short of a cogent account of how it is possible to confront the philosophical past philosophically as well as historically will give us what we need. But such an account will have to explain how one large-scale philosophical standpoint can engage with another in cases where each standpoint embodies its own conceptions of what rational superiority consists of in such a way that there can apparently be no appeal to any neutral and independent standard.
>
> (MacIntyre 1984, p. 40)

15 MacIntyre, *loc. cit.*

2   Finding a Way into Bradley's Metaphysics

1   A similar view is expressed by Locke (1706), Book IV, Chapter XIV, §4, and, with names substituted for ideas, by J.S. Mill (1843), Chapter I §2.

2   Even Hume, who explicitly denied that judgments had to involve more than one idea (1739, Book I, Part III, §VII, fn. 1), conceived ideas in this way. It was essential to the account of reasoning in terms of the association of ideas, an account which Bradley vigorously rejected.

3 For examples of each, see Leibniz's *Discourse on Metaphysics*, and Reinhardt Grossmann, *Meinong* (London: Routledge & Kegan Paul, 1974). A good contrast with Leibniz in this respect is Berkeley.

4 For example, even serious scholars (see, for instance, Manser and Stock 1984, p. 26) have thought that Bradley was referring to Leibniz on page 25 of *Appearance and Reality* when, in criticizing atomism, he mentioned 'the most thorough attempt to build a system on this ground' without apparently thinking it necessary to identify this attempt more explicitly. The name of Leibniz comes naturally to a modern reader in this context but, as Bradley (1897), p. 539 makes clear, he was thinking of Herbart, who is now remembered, if at all, as an educationist. The error is corrected in the 1986 reprint of Manser and Stock (though not in the index). Perhaps it is indirect evidence of how Russellian the modern reader is that Russell himself made the same mistake: see Russell (1900), p. 15 n. 1.

5 I cherish a quotation from a *New Statesman* review printed inside the dust cover of my copy of *Our Knowledge of the External World*: 'This brilliant, lucid and amusing book which ... everyone can understand.'

6 In this chapter, whenever a citation date appears without an author's name attached, the name is to be understood as Bradley.

7 Nor is it, *pace* Wollheim (1959), p. 282 (1969), p. 277, feeling *especially* pleased about things.

8 Even this will not do ultimately, but 'ultimately' is the point at which his metaphysics reaches complete inexpressibility. Cf. (1883), *PL* p. 487, and below (p. 42*f*). Bradley came to be dissatisfied with the original 1883 text of this work, which even he described in correspondence as 'badly arranged & unnecessarily difficult', as is illustrated by the combination of the Additional Notes and Terminal Essays in the second edition. On this matter, see the excellent Keene (1999). I have tried not to rely on examples concerning which he changed his mind, unless I am drawing attention to this fact.

9 Contentious not merely in the sense that others readily dispute them, but also in the sense that what they are is itself a matter of dispute, as we shall see.

10 One may think here that in view of Bradley's attribution of the method of ideal experiment to Hegel, one should look to Hegel himself for explanation. But to find such an explanation in Hegel turns out to be even more difficult than finding one in Bradley. The interpretation offered below is corroborated in an entry in the Bradley papers in Merton College Library (Bradley Papers, III B 2, p. 115).

11 The point is complicated by the fact that Bradley's philosophical logic is constantly being undercut by his metaphysics. In this case, for instance, after his drawing of the distinction between the valid and the invalid in reasoning, it emerges that he thinks that, *ultimately*, all inference is invalid (1883, *PL* p. 588 and 1922, *PL* p. 621). This adoption of temporary positions is a perennial irritant for one attempting to expound his views, and one can understand how A.R. Manser was led to claim that Bradley (1883) was a book of pure and defensible philosophical logic uncontaminated by the later and mistaken metaphysics (Manser 1983). This claim will be examined in Chapter 6 (p. 145*f*), but that it must be mistaken can be seen from the

parenthetical dates earlier in this footnote. Indeed, Bradley's 'later' meta-physics is evidently influencing his moral philosophy as early as 1876 (Candlish 1978, §8).

12 To find the full story of Bradley's surprising response to this question, see Allard (2005), chapters 6 and 7.

13 More recent authors have also posited a close connection between argument and thought experiment. See, for example, Sorensen (1992), p. 214.

14 I am thinking, for example, of the discussion of rule-following in Wittgenstein (1953), §§185–242. For another anticipation of Wittgenstein, compare Bradley (1883) *PL* pp. 519–32 with the *Tractatus* doctrine of saying and showing.

15 Unlike Wittgenstein, however, he draws a parallel here in moral philosophy (1883) *PL* pp. 266–71. This is only one of several ways in which Bradley's work, despite some notable changes of mind, is all of a piece in a way that Russell's, for example, is not. For other parallels, see Candlish (1978), §8. It is this unity of Bradley's work which makes it sometimes possible to cite temporally widely scattered writings in illustration of a single thesis. Bradley did not change his mind a great deal (cf. 1893, *AR* p. 356, n. 1), and when he did, usually said so (cf. 1922, *PL* p. 38, n. 7). This does not mean that there is never unconscious drift in his opinions.

16 Herbart influenced both Bradley and Wundt.

17 Russell interpreted Bradley the same way (letter to Bradley, dated 2 March 1911, held in the Bradley papers at Merton). Bradley's reply (dated 15 March 1911, held in the Russell Archives at McMaster University) considers and does not reject Russell's interpretation. Both letters are reprinted in *CP6*, pp. 352–3.

18 It is worth noticing the extent of the time period over which Bradley is re-iterating this claim: we shall see in Chapter 6 below that the matter is significant when it comes to sorting out exactly what it is that Bradley wants to say about relations, and whether Russell's criticisms were appropriate.

19 Cf. Candlish (1981), §2 and n. 3.

20 It must be kept in mind that Bradley's use of the term 'contradiction' is considerably looser than that employed by philosophers influenced by formal logic. This should not be taken to imply that – with the notable exception of Frege – he was ignorant of the formal logic of his time; as we have already seen, he rejected, on philosophical grounds, the attempt to capture reasoning in abstract calculi.

21 It is wrong to suggest (Wollheim 1959, pp. 202–3 and 1969 pp. 199–200; Montague 1964, pp. 160–1) that Bradley's experiment confuses conceiving with picturing; there is simply no evidence that Bradley did any such thing. What the experiment may confuse, however, is the impossibility of conceiving that *P* with the conceiving that it is impossible that *P*.

22 Another part involves an assumption about the way in which language works, one involving, as we shall see in a later chapter, a certain highly contentious doctrine about the nature of relations. Roughly speaking, it is the picture displayed for criticism by Wittgenstein in the early passages of *Philosophical Investigations* (for example, §12).

23 At this stage of my exposition, I am permitting myself the unqualified use of such phrases as 'attack on predication' and 'rejection of external rela-

tions'. Such use is very common in descriptions of Bradley's work, and serves as a temporary signpost for the reader. But, as already suggested, it will emerge that this practice must eventually be abandoned.

24 There is a curious tension, usually unnoticed, between Russell's repeated charges that Hegelians (that is, Bradley) first, confuse the 'is' of predication with the 'is' of identity, in favour of the latter, and second, assume that every proposition is of the subject–predicate form. More on this later.

25 As far as I know, it was not clearly made until De Morgan (1847), pp. 49–50; and it is absent entirely from Russell's own writings before 1899.

26 According to Nicholas Griffin (in correspondence), to whom I am particularly indebted in this paragraph, it can be found in Herschel.

27 This is a summary of part of Bradley's own summary of the crucial parts of his reasoning (1897, *AR* pp. 504–6; 1909c, *ETR* pp. 226–9). Wollheim's view (1959, pp. 74–83; 1969, pp. 72–81) that Bradley thought that all subject–predicate statements are really identity statements can thus be seen to be a distortion of the truth.

28 This is a very close relative of a notorious Bradleian argument concerning relations. I shall come to a verdict on the matter in Chapter 6. Here I am concerned merely to describe and explain.

29 Wollheim (1959), p. 111; (1969), p. 109 says of this theory that 'it seems very unlikely that [it] engaged his interest'. But he gives no reason for believing this; and Bradley defines externality in this way in more than one place (including a letter of 5 February 1909 to Samuel Alexander, held in the John Rylands University Library, Manchester). Moreover, the second sentence in this quotation from 1924 implies, as do other remarks (1911a, *ETR* p. 291; 1897, *AR*, pp. 507 and 559), that Bradley came to conceive the relationship between the two conjectures, of the independent reality of terms and relations on the one hand, and of the absolute contingency of their combination on the other, to be one of mutual implication. Indeed, Wollheim's whole treatment of Bradley's discussion of relations is suspect, given that he believes, against what we shall see is the evidence – and indeed against his own admission of the contrary – Bradley to have adhered to the 'Doctrine of Internal Relations' (Wollheim 1959, pp. 104–9; 1969, pp. 102–7), and that he deploys some of Bradley's arguments out of context. On the so-called Doctrine of Internal Relations, see below (p. 42*ff*) and Chapter 6. Russell, too, noticed the essential connection between externality and contingency in Bradley's thought (letter dated 9 April 1910, Merton College Library; and cf. also Bradley Papers, III B 14, p. 97 [III B 14 now appears in pages 243–389 of Volume 2 of Bradley 1999]). In any case, we should give this uncompleted essay on relations great weight in interpreting Bradley, for it represents a mature and sustained attempt to give expression to his most considered views on the topic. Bradley was unlucky in that the essay was left unfinished to be published only after his death and when interest in his work was already on the wane.

30 I take the obscure last clause of the quotation to refer to Bradley's view that experience prior to contamination by the categories of thought is non-relational ('less'), while experience after the ascent to the Absolute has transcended the categories of thought is supra-relational ('more'). I shall not try to defend or explain such suggestions here.

31   A recent example comes in the few references to Bradley in R.M. Sainsbury's *Russell*, London, 1979, who presented a view of the matter still common amongst those who have come to this question through study of Russell. Even Wollheim, who noticed that Bradley rejects the Doctrine of Internal Relations, could not resist the temptation to say of all Bradley's arguments on the subject that they are 'arguments adduced in its favour' (1959, p. 109; 1969, p. 107). So strong, presumably, was the influence of Moore and Russell. However, for Bradley's contemporaries, there was some excuse, for all the clear and explicit statements (which I know of) on this matter come from the posthumously published papers in *Collected Essays*, except for 1909c, *ETR* pp. 238–40. (Russell admitted in a letter to Bradley dated 16 November 1900 that he had not read *Appearance and Reality* with the same care which he had devoted to *The Principles of Logic*, and had misinterpreted it in his *Leibniz*. There is no reason to suppose that he was more assiduous from 1909 onwards.) Perhaps the main original cause of the confusion is *Appearance and Reality*. I shall have more to say on this vexed issue in Chapter 6, where I shall try to explain my hedging phrase 'in some sense'.

32   Cf. Candlish (1982), §7. It is hard to overemphasize the importance of the notion of substance in Bradley's thought, as we shall see.

33   David Stove once suggested that on my account of the priorities in Bradley's reasoning, Bradley could just as well have turned out a materialist as an idealist. (What would a materialist monism be? Something like Descartes's dualism, including the physics but without the mind.) I think the point has to be admitted (it is not clear that it is an objection), provided that the materialism were not of an atomistic kind. However, the qualifications involved are heavy. Idealism, it is true, appears logically quite late in the canonical ordering of Bradley's views. But psychologically, I am sure, it appears early, as anyone familiar with any of the details of Bradley's education, reading and manner of writing will recognize. Idealism is present, even before it is proved, as a goal, something awaiting justification. In a very real sense, a materialist monism could not be *Bradley's*. Further, Stove's point requires a certain indifference to the question of whether Bradley's argument for idealism is sound. However, it has the great virtue of reminding us how resolutely unpsychological is Bradley's notion of experience.

34   The point will be illustrated further in Chapter 6.

35   Russell (1907) *PE* pp. 142–3. He made the allegation also in a letter to Bradley of 29 October 1907 (Merton College Library). But the letters (of the period near this date) from Bradley to Russell which are held in the Russell Archives contain no reply on the subject.

36   Campbell (1931), p. 25.

37   The Bradley papers in Merton contain other attempts to come to grips with the problem (I B 19, p. 149, and III A 24, pp. 11–19). But they can hardly be said to be successful; and he must have recognized this himself, for they form a large part of the material suppressed from Chapter I of *Essays on Truth and Reality*.

38   This defence originally came from Peter Forrest, who suggested an analogy with Bradley's views on deduction and the laws of logic (see above, p. 27f). 'A [logical] principle will neither demonstrate its applications nor can it be demonstrated *by* them. The principle is demonstrated when we see it *in* and as the function of, an individual act' (1883, *PL* pp. 530–1); likewise, *mutatis mutandis*, the Principle of Sufficient Reason.

3 Judgment

1 Some measured defence of Russell's stance as opposed to Frege's is given by Makin (2000), pp. 151–5.

2 Bradley (1914c) wrote a reply to 'Knowledge by acquaintance and knowledge by description'. Although it is mostly devoted to the rejection of Russellian assumptions about the ego, it opens with some remarks revealing a surprising point of overlap between him and Russell:

> Mr. Russell in a recent essay ventures on the following assertion: 'Returning now to Julius Caesar, I assume that it will be admitted that he himself is not a constituent of any judgement which I can make.' To my mind the opposite of this admission appears to be evident. It seems to me certain, if such an admission is right, that about Julius Caesar I can have literally no knowledge at all, and that for me to attempt to speak about him is senseless. If on the other hand I am to know anything whatever about Caesar, then the real Caesar beyond doubt must himself enter into my judgements and be a constituent of my knowledge. And I do not understand how Mr. Russell can suppose that on any view like mine a different answer should be given.

The matter is well-discussed by James Levine (1998).

3 Russell gets round the apparent exceptions posed by intransitive verbs like 'breathes' by claiming that in such cases the verb expresses a complex notion which 'usually asserts a definite relation to an indefinite relatum' (§48).

4 We should not take this to mean that a proposition is a matter of words: with some important exceptions (whose nature and significance are considered in Chapter 5 below), he thinks of English as, by and large, a transparent medium through which reality's ingredients may be inspected, and talks indifferently of 'verbs' whether he means words or the 'entities indicated by words' (§51), that is, terms.

5 Sainsbury (1996), pp. 140–1 suggests that the problem of the unity of the proposition can be thought of as composed of four related but distinguishable sub-problems. These are (in Sainsbury's words):

   (i)   How does one distinguish, among collections of meanings, between those which can be arranged so as to say something (e.g. Desdemona, love and Cassio) and those which cannot be so arranged (e.g. Desdemona and Cassio)?

   (ii) Given a collection of meanings (e.g. Desdemona, love and Cassio), how does one distinguish between those arrangements of that collection which do say something (e.g. that Desdemona loves Cassio) and those that do not (e.g. that love Desdemona Cassio)?

   (iii) Given a collection of meanings which can be arranged so as to say more than one thing (e.g. Desdemona, love and Cassio), how does one distinguish between the things (e.g. between saying that Desdemona loves Cassio and saying that Cassio loves Desdemona)?

   (iv) Given a collection of meanings arranged so as to say just one thing, what cements the meanings together in the required way? What is the nature of the further ingredient or entity involved, here referred to as 'arrangement', over and above the meanings themselves?

On the strength of Sainsbury's illustrative examples, I am not sure that any of these captures Russell's 1903 conception of the problem; perhaps (iv) is the closest. (We shall see as we proceed just how he did conceive it.) Certainly, not all of them played a part in the way Russell thought of the matter, but we shall see that he did address, and eventually separate, (iii) and (iv). Wittgenstein's objection to the multiple relation theory can be usefully understood as the claim that Russell neglected (ii), and Wittgenstein's own account of judgment as involving the claim that (i) is a non-problem. Bradley's account can be understood in terms of a denial of the assumption underlying all four, namely that there is such a thing as a collection of discrete meanings. What it is more important to point out here is that despite the potential for talking at cross-purposes which Sainsbury reveals, there was no misunderstanding between Russell and Bradley as to what was at stake.

6 In his (1979) study, Sainsbury seemed inclined to think it just the result of a muddle. Palmer (1988) thinks it extremely serious. Other recent writers who take one or other version of it seriously include Gaskin (1997, 1998), Gibson (2004), Read (2005) and Davidson (2005). The inclusion of this last name is ironic given Sainsbury's claim that 'The problem is absent from, for example, a Davidsonian approach to meaning' (Sainsbury 1996, p. 147).

7 It should perhaps be emphasized that the point requires a Russellian, not a Tractarian, notion of fact.

8 So much for Wollheim's suggestion that this conception of externality did not engage Bradley's interest.

9 This shift will be examined in detail in Chapter 5.

10 Graham Stevens argues this at length. For a full account of what is sketched only very briefly in the remainder of this section, see Stevens (2004).

11 In fact Russell first formulated a version of this theory in print in Russell (1907), but it was not until 1910 that he publicly committed himself to it.

12 The expression 'propositional act' appears to have been introduced by Claudio de Almeida, as acknowledged in Griffin (1993).

13 This appears to be a long-standing, if intermittent, conflation. It is present in Russell (1904), *CP4* p. 437; *EA* p. 28; and, as we shall see, is still dogging him in 1913. According to Mark Sainsbury (Sainsbury 1979, p. 225), the problem of the unity of the proposition is still interfering with Russell's discussion of other problems as late as 1918.

14 Another way of putting this point would be to ask the question why *S* rather than *judging* appears as a constituent of the diagram. This question shows something of the pressure on Russell to drop the ego from his ontology, a pressure to which he succumbed in 1919. (Adding *judging* as a node to the diagram, rather than replacing *S* with it, brings with it a return of the relational regress of which Bradley made so much and which Russell was also trying to avoid.)

15 Russell uses the word 'obnoxious' here in the now obsolete sense of 'liable'.

16 Stout himself, in the article just cited, percipiently fixed on the 1912 version's plausibility as deriving from a confusion between the view that *A* and love and *B* have no unity of their own in the judgment at all and the view that they form a subordinate unity.

17 Geach (1957), p. 51; Ramsey (1927), p. 142.
18 The 1913 version is in one way importantly different from the 1910 and 1912 versions: in what it is a theory of. It focuses on understanding rather than belief (as he is now inclined to refer to judgment). For this reason it is strictly incorrect to present it as a theory of judgment. But such presentation does no harm: it makes the theory slightly simpler to expound, and easier to compare with its predecessors. And of course the theory applies to judging as well as to understanding.
     The revised version is an improvement because, as Russell says (Russell 1913: pp. 108, 110), understanding is more fundamental than belief. But it tends to obscure the problem of false judgment, which motivated its predecessor. (Of course one could re-pose this problem as one of avoiding making all falsehoods unintelligible.)
19 Russell (1913), p. 118. As was said, strictly this proposition should be 'S understands the proposition that A is similar to B'. But this makes no difference here.
20 The former problem is well-discussed by Leonard Linsky (1992), pp. 257–9, and the latter by Peter Hylton (1990), pp. 355–6. Other problems are identified by Mark Sainsbury (1979), pp. 64 and 225, and by David Pears (1977), pp. 177–83.
21 The objection is summarized by Wittgenstein in a letter of June 1913 (Wittgenstein 1913a). The story of the emergence of this objection and its significance for Russell himself is told by Ray Monk (1996), pp. 293–9. I have omitted, as peripheral to the focus of my discussion, consideration of it here. The interested reader may consult, for example, Weiss (1995) and Stevens (2004).
22 See the second footnote, added in 1917, to Russell (1911), *CP6*, p. 154; *ML*, p. 159.
23 In an insightful article, Kilmister (1996), p. 275 suggests that this 'belief in the efficacy of technical investigations in solving philosophical problems [is] one of the hallmarks of analytical philosophy'. On this criterion, Russell in the period we are considering most certainly was, and Wittgenstein was never, an analytical philosopher.
24 Given that he described the 1912 version as 'a slight re-wording' of its 1910 predecessor, he probably thought of them as one theory and at this point it does no harm to let this pass.
25 This is the deeper of the two explanations of Russell's apparent inconsistency in the logical atomism lectures. On some pages, Russell talks about our believing propositions (*CP8*, pp. 191 and 199; *LK*, pp. 218 and 226); on other pages, he says we don't, because there aren't any to serve as the objects of belief (*CP8*, pp. 197 and 200; *LK*, pp. 224 and 227). The superficial explanation is that he talks carelessly in an ordinary language way when he talks about believing propositions, whereas when he denies that we believe propositions he is using his own sense from *Principles*. The deeper explanation reveals that the 'careless talk' is in fact unavoidable, as emerges in his own discussion of the impossibility of a spatial map of belief (*CP8* p. 198, *LK* p. 225).
26 See Russell (1919b), pp. 295–7.
27 Ramsey (1927), p. 145.

4   Truth

1   David Holdcroft is one, recognizing that Bradley only ever offers coherence
     as the (not a) test of truth; but he makes the mistake of taking him to have
     nothing to say on the nature of truth at all (Holdcroft 1984). Another is
     Nicholas Rescher (1973), p. 23; but he takes Bradley to endorse a correspon-
     dence theory of truth. We shall see how it is possible to gain this highly
     unstereotypical impression of Bradley. James Allard (1984) came close to
     recognizing the facts, in expressing the same view as Rescher but correctly
     restricting the correspondence theory's sway in Bradley to *The Principles of
     Logic*; but at that time he had nothing to say about Bradley's central idea
     about truth, the one he held to for most of his philosophical career. Susan
     Haack was unusual among writers of student texts in that she actually went
     into what Bradley said, apparently even to the point of reading him, and
     certainly sufficiently to realize explicitly that he is not a coherentist at all.
     Yet such is the power of accumulated tradition that her discussion of
     Bradley takes place under the heading 'Coherence theories of truth', and –
     although she perhaps came the closest of all to noticing what is going on –
     she too allowed herself to be distracted by the presence of talk of corres-
     pondence in *The Principles of Logic*, and thus missed Bradley's account of
     the nature of truth (Haack 1978, p. 89 and esp. pp. 95 and 97). A parallel
     vacillation can be found in Grayling (1982), by comparing p. 126 with
     pp. 132–4. In both cases the force of tradition combined with perceptive
     reading produces incoherence. Perhaps the same combination explains why
     Kirkham (1992) follows Haack in holding Bradley not to have a coherence
     theory of truth, but then oddly retreats to the standard view in his 1998.
     The only people I know of who discerned, unaided, Bradley's real theory are
     Max Cresswell (1985) – though the historical significance of this crucial
     insight went unrecognized – and Tom Baldwin (1991) – though his version
     of Bradley is justly criticized by Ralph Walker (1998). More recent commen-
     tary, though it is significant that it has so far usually been provided only by
     specialists on Bradley (for example, Sprigge 1993, Mander 1994, Basile 1999,
     Allard 2005), has profited from these earlier discoveries. The textbooks are,
     however, starting to give way under pressure: cf., for instance, Blackburn
     and Simmons (1999), p. 10.
2   There is an interesting and extended discussion of Walker's objection in
     Wright 1995. Prior to Walker, Wollheim offered a similar defence of Bradley
     (1959), p. 176; (1969), pp. 172–3.
3   Bradley (1883), p. 487.
4   For a fuller account, see Allard (2005), pp. 203–5.
5   In his elegant and judicious discussion, Walker (1998), p. 103, argues that
     Bradley was in his 1883 a correspondence theorist but not a copy theorist,
     on the grounds that he believed a copy theorist mistakenly 'think[s] it pos-
     sible to give an informative account of what "correspondence" consists in'
     and is committed to the idea that the world divides into a plurality of dis-
     crete facts. What Bradley says here shows that Walker goes against Bradley's
     own words in completely dissociating him from the copy theory while
     arguing that he held the correspondence theory; it is, I think, telling that
     Walker's discussion is very lightly grounded in the actual text of *PL*.

In 1907 Bradley, rather naïvely, complained, 'It did not occur to me that I should be taken there [sc. in *PL*] or anywhere else to be advocating the copy-theory of truth' (1907, *ETR* p. 109n). I think that this complaint explains why Walker wants a distinction for Bradley between correspondence and copy theories: he reads it, I conjecture, with emphasis on 'copy-theory'; I read it with emphasis on 'advocating'.

6   The later theory appears explicitly on p. 704; but this is in a Terminal Essay added by Bradley for the second edition of 1922, and thus does not on its own necessarily cast light on what he had meant in 1883.

7   There is no need for us to adopt the extreme view of Anthony Manser (1983), that there is none of the later metaphysics in the first edition of *The Principles of Logic* at all, to be able to acknowledge that Bradley was trying to keep it out. (For the reasons why we should not follow Manser, see Cresswell 1985 and Chapter 6, p. 150*f* below.) For example, one can see occasional surfacings of idealism. But this observation should not make us fly to the other extreme, Cresswell's claim (Cresswell 1977 and 1979) that idealism is everywhere presupposed in Bradley's work. (For the reasons why we should not follow Cresswell see Candlish 1981 and 1982.)

8   Russell (1907). The withering is more that of rhetoric than of content, however; Allard (1996), pp. 137–46, shows that Russell's argument is question-begging.

9   The passage occurs in the context of an attempt to prove that judgments do not consist in *syntheses* of ideas; but it is clear that Bradley took the problems to be not restricted to this false view of judgment.

10 In contrast, in his 2001 (pp. 150–1) work, Walker attempts to *show* that the regress is non-vicious for the correspondence theory while vicious for the coherence theory. The argument appears to turn on a confusion of the correspondence platitude (which all theorists of truth can agree to affirm, much as Bradley did in 1883) and the correspondence *theory*, which requires some serious account of the nature of the correspondence.

11 Although this is the most unequivocal statement of the idea that I have found, we have already seen that it is present in Bradley 1883; other expressions of it are in Bradley (1893) *AR*, pp. 150, 153 and Bradley (1911) *ETR* p. 343. The dates reveal that it is not a temporary ingredient of his thought.

12 The presence of the word 'knowledge' in Bradley's version of the slogan is to be explained through his idealism. I have dropped it to avoid taking on too many tasks at once.

13 For example, the correspondence theory is treated as a kind of default theory by Ralph Walker in his 1989 study; unlike the coherence theory, it gets the benefit of philosophical doubt.

14 Linguistic idealism is a natural-looking candidate for a basis from which to defend an identity theory of truth. But its association with postmodern attacks on the whole notion of truth makes the basis shaky.

15 I do not intend to assess this idea; my aim is merely to show how it can be thought plausible, by questioning things which most later philosophers just take for granted. I should add that, as James Allard has shown, even from an independent standpoint it can be demonstrated to involve an argument which one does not have to be a committed monist or idealist to take seriously (Allard 1980 and 1984).

16   Some version of this parenthetical point will still apply even if we start to imagine languages which function very differently from English, such as one in which adjectival modifications are expressed by inflections of the noun.

17   The misuse of the notion of identity has been rampant in metaphysics and philosophy of mind. A rare exposé is Johnston (2005), pp. 642–3.

18   This was half-seen by Haack, who said rightly of Bradley that 'the explanation of the success of coherence as the test derives from an account of reality as itself essentially coherent' (1978, p. 95), while still talking of the whole truth in terms of a 'belief set', which underestimates both Bradley's monism and its essential counter-rationalism.

19   For a deft description of reaction to the Sorites by appeal to degrees of truth, including its motivation, some bibliography, and a brief exploration of its ramifications for, for example, modus ponens, and assigning truth values to molecular propositions, see Chapter 2 of Sainsbury (1995). There is a connection here between the issues surrounding vagueness, and those surrounding paraconsistency: in both cases, the question arises whether the provoking phenomenon (vagueness, inconsistency) belongs merely to the language or can be found in the world itself.

20   In this book I am concerned with Bradley and Russell. I have explored the general outlook for an identity theory of truth in Candlish (1999a, 2003 and 2005), where more recent versions are identified and considered. See also Engel (2001, 2002) and David (2001).

21   Moore (1899); pp. 8 and 18, respectively.

22   An exception is Baldwin (1991).

23   Some do not follow me in discerning a difference between primitivism and the identity theory, and find the identity theory (though not labelled as such) in these early analytic writings of Moore and Russell – for example, Cartwright (1987a). I defend the view that there is a difference in my 1999b study, at p. 234. Russell appears to agree with me in his presentation of primitivism in his 1904 work (pp. 473–4), where, incidentally, that theory has mutated from one in which false propositions merely lack the property of truth into one in which true propositions have one property and false another. (The change is insignificant in the present context.) In any case, it is clear that primitivism is imposed by the failure of identity between representation and represented to provide a distinction between truth and falsehood.

This vacillation between identity theory and primitivism can be found also in Meinong, as described by Findlay (1933), ch. X sec. IX. Meinong's 'objectives', such as the being-white-of-snow and the being-an-integer-between-3-and-4, divide into two sorts, the factual (*tatsächlich*) and the unfactual (*untatsächlich*). There are no entities between our minds and these objectives, hence no propositions between our minds and the facts. Truth and falsehood are derivative properties of objectives, when these are considered as the objects of what we should now call propositional attitudes. Findlay says of this, 'Meinong's theory of truth is therefore a theory of *identity* or *coincidence*. The *same* objective which is factual ... reveals itself in a certain judgement or assumption ... the fact itself is true in so far as it is the object of a judgement' (1933), p. 88, italics in the original. What is it, though, for an objective to be factual? Factuality is, Meinong says, 'a fundamental property which admits of no definition' (quoted by Findlay on p. 76). Here another mutation – this time that of the identity theory into primitivism – occurs under our eyes.

24   Hylton (1984), p. 385.
25   Sosa (1993), p. 13f.
26   *Ibid.*, p. 14.
27   For an introductory account of this notion and the issues surrounding it, see Bach (1998).

5   Grammar and Ontology

1   The context of §46 of Russell (1903) shows that the grammar in question is that of, for example, ordinary English. The use of the expression 'transparency' in discussion of this matter is adopted by Hylton (1990), p. 171. Hylton is inclined to exaggerate the degree of transparency Russell proposes, and is, to some modest extent deservedly, taken to task by Makin (2000), pp. 74–5, who makes much of the obvious needed qualifications but ignores Russell's 1959 comment. Arguing against Hylton, Makin asks rhetorically (*loc. cit.*), 'If one could count on propositions always being perceived through a transparent medium, what role could there possibly be for analysis?' The answer is, of course, that the role of analysis is to deal with certain limited exceptions to the transparency thesis by translating them into a transparent form. Just what these exceptions were, and how transparent Russell thought language to be, is investigated below.

2   Harold Noonan says (1996), p. 72, 'In fact, at this time language is not a subject of interest to Russell ...'. There is a sense in which this is correct – Russell's propositions are, as we have seen, not linguistic, or even language-dependent, items – but it is misleading unless one points out too that the reason it can be said at all is not only because of the doctrine of real propositional constituents but also because of Russell's (admittedly qualified) adherence to the transparency thesis. See Hylton (1990), p. 171. There must be *some* avenue of access to these constituents, particularly if one is going to write or speak about them with the intention that others will understand what is said; language provides one (though not, in Russell's view, as we shall see, the only one). The point is especially applicable to Russell, for whom the primary motivation of the doctrine of real propositional constituents is epistemic, as we shall see below in Russell (1904b).

3   I described in Chapter 1 above how Bradley figured in Russell's imagination. For discussion of how representative Bradley actually was, see Mander (1994), chapter 8; see also the first section of Chapter 6, below.

4   That is, those which do not ignore *The Principles of Mathematics* altogether and do not merely present his 'vivid sense of reality' (actually a phrase from Russell 1918) or some instinctive reaction against Meinong's ontology as Russell's motivating force in 1905 when writing 'On Denoting'. An example of this anachronistic approach, including the giveaway phrase, is Pears (1967), p. 13. For a contrast, see Makin (2000), p. 60.

5   How can grammar be both 'nearer to a correct logic' and a window on the world? The reason is that 'logic, as Russell conceives it, is not separate from

ontology' (Hylton 1990, p. 205). In the surrounding pages, Hylton gives a fuller description than is appropriate here of Russell's conception of logic at this time.

6 We saw in the last chapter that one can get some insight into Moore's otherwise barely intelligible account (Moore 1899) of the world as consisting of concepts by thinking of it as the reverse side of the coin of Russell's doctrine of real propositional constituents.

7 One phenomenon which goes unremarked here is that Russell, like many philosophers since, seems to have just assumed that the surface grammar of names and definite descriptions is obvious and makes manifest their putative semantic function of picking out a unique object, so that those cases where this function fails need special explanation. (He then holds the cases of failure, in a characteristic philosophical move paralleled in common treatments of perception and action, to illuminate the cases of success.) Because the function is only putative, this assumption – let us call it the face-value assumption – is not the transparency thesis itself; it is something more deeply rooted (something like a notion that there are grammatical natural kinds), which motivates the problem requiring the theory of descriptions for its solution, and which survived the discovery of the theory of descriptions to continue to exert an incalculable influence on the development of analytic philosophy. Although the previous sentences in this note were written before I read Oliver (1999), I think that the assumption I am referring to here is one object of the criticisms made there.

8 See, for example, Russell (1905b), *CP4* p. 425 lines 30–2; Russell (1937), p. x; Russell (1959), p. 84; the multi-reprinted and highly influential Quine (1966), p. 305; Pears (1967), p. 13; Ayer (1972), pp. 53–5; Haack (1978), pp. 65–6; Grayling (1996), pp. 33–5. Those to whom we are indebted for recognizing the falsehood of the usual story include Richard Cartwright (1987b), Harold Noonan (1996), Gideon Makin (2000) and, above all, Peter Hylton (1990). Chihara (1972) anticipated Makin in realizing that 'It is the logicist enterprise, rather than latter-day concerns of the philosophy of language, that provided the motivation and the theoretical setting [for the theory of descriptions] at large' (Makin 2000, p. 4). Indeed, Russell said so himself (1959), p. 79, but did not explain the connection.

9 Not that Russell had ever explicitly held this view. Rather, it is something that he is pushed towards by the combination of the transparency thesis and the doctrine of real propositional constituents; but he sees that the push must be resisted.

10 This has in any case been skilfully done by Gideon Makin. See Makin (2000), chapter 1.

11 See Hylton (1990), pp. 237–44; Noonan (1996), pp. 65–8. I follow Russell in identifying denoting concepts by using italics. Of course I also use them for other purposes: the context removes any ambiguity.

12 The passage by Russell quoted at the beginning of Chapter 5 has a qualifying footnote appended to it: 'The excellence of grammar as a guide is proportional to the paucity of inflexions, *i.e.* to the degree of analysis effected by the language considered.' But even with this qualification the idea of reading off ontological commitment from the sentences of languages should not be understood as potentially providing theoretically unmediated

access to ontology via brute linguistic facts. Russell seems not to have recognized how contestable is the surface grammar of English – even more contestable, and contested, than I had realized when first writing this very note. Both Russell's earlier exceptions to, and his later rejection of, the transparency thesis are infected by logicians' myths about grammar. See the devastating Oliver (1999).

13 See, for example, Russell (1905a), *CP4* p. 487. Here, just prior to the writing of 'On Denoting', he is still working within the confines of the theory of denoting concepts: 'We have thus merely a defining concept for each [putative entity], without any entity to which the concept applies. In this case, the concept is an entity, but it does not denote anything.' Harold Noonan has also seen this point (1996), pp. 66–7.

14 And, as we shall see later, Russell uses even the theory of descriptions itself to maintain the integrity of the idea that meanings are real objects corresponding to words.

15 Cf. Russell (1905b), *CP4* p. 421, lines 27–31: 'But the difficulty which confronts us is ... also that the meaning [i.e. 'the denoting concept'] cannot be got at except by means of denoting phrases'. I owe this insight to Noonan (1996), pp. 79–81, 95. Makin (2000), appendix C is harsh on Noonan here. Makin (chapter 2) correctly observes that Russell's principal point is that denoting concepts are, as he puts it, aboutness-shifters and that this makes problematic the formulation of propositions about them. This does not exclude Russell's making other points in passing; the structure of Russell's own sentence makes it clear that what is considered in this footnote is not his main contention.

16 Russell (1910), *CP6* pp. 123–4.

17 In this early exposition of the theory, the expression 'definite description' does not appear. Russell instead retains his original vocabulary, 'denoting phrases', but abandons the idea that these introduce denoting concepts. The first version of the theory of descriptions would more accurately be called the theory of denoting phrases (and opposed to the theory of denoting *concepts*).

18 By 1918 grammatically proper names have become 'abbreviations for descriptions' (Russell 1918: *CP8* p. 178; *LK* p. 200).

19 This needs qualification to allow for the elimination of propositions in the multiple relation theory of judgment of 1910 onwards. But no claim about constituents is affected here, since under the multiple relation theory the constituents remain the same but are constituents of propositional acts rather than of propositions.

20 After Russell's adoption of the multiple relation theory of judgement, it is propositional acts that are meant to be the unities, but, as we saw in Chapter 3 above, propositions as unified entities keep turning up in the exposition of that very theory of how to avoid them. In any case, for several years at least, Russell subscribed to the principle *ens et unum convertuntur*. See Russell (1903), §47, and the 1910 letter to Bradley reproduced on p. 350 of *CP6*. On Russell's problems associated with the unity of the proposition, see also Gaskin (1997), §§1 and 2.

21 Although conjunction is definable, for example, within the propositional calculus, Russell distinguishes this kind of mathematical definition from

genuine philosophical definition which consists of 'analysis of an idea into its constituents' (Russell 1903, §108). There is no indication that he thinks logical constants like conjunction are susceptible of this kind of definition. Russell's approach to *and* is in accordance with the word/thing correspondence mentioned in the first section of this chapter. This may seem extreme, but note that he is prepared to suggest that the sentences '9 is greater than 7' and '9 exceeds 7' express different propositions; for the fact that the sentences contain different words requires that the expressed propositions contain different entities. Cf. also Makin (2000), p. 193.

22 The published version of the lectures was prefaced by a note announcing that they 'are very largely concerned with explaining certain ideas which I learnt from my friend and former pupil Ludwig Wittgenstein' prior to August 1914 (Russell 1918, *CP8* p. 160, *LK* p. 177).

23 See Chapter 6, p. 163*f* below. Negative discovery consisted in the lack of such acquaintance after searching.

24 This account appears to be endorsed by Makin (2000), pp. 67–8.

25 See Candlish (2004).

26 A good explanation of how a philosopher can come to posit the existence of Infinite Mind of which our own minds are in some sense parts can be found in the early chapters of Walker (1989).

27 An excellent exposition of this aspect of the *Tractatus* and its contrast with Russell is in Pears (1975). Pears makes a compelling case for believing that Wittgenstein was reacting to the account of the ego in Russell (1913). By the time of the 1918 lectures, of course, Russell was treating the ego as a logical construction.

28 Russell's accusation of subjectivity in *My Philosophical Development* (1959) may have been motivated by his recollection of his own work from his idealist period, in particular his risking psychologism in his attempt to be metaphysically agnostic in his treatment of space. See Russell (1897b), §§55 and 193, and Hylton (1990), p. 79.

29 Or 'fully analytic' rather than 'fully analysed' if one thinks of an ideal language rather than of a completely perspicuous rendition of a natural language's deep structure. Makin (2000) would want to claim that Russell's faith was never in the grammar of natural language. While conceding tensions in Russell's thought, I reckon this goes against his own words. See the opening section of this chapter above.

30 Or at least, not without some surrounding metaphysics. In the *Tractatus*, for instance, the avoidance of negative facts is achieved by the exploitation of the properties of elementary propositions understood as pictures of atomic facts. See Fogelin (1976), chapter IV, §1. It is clear from their correspondence that Russell did not grasp Wittgenstein's elusive treatment of elementary propositions, for he asked whether any of them are negative, and received a dismissive response (Wittgenstein 1919, p. 73).

31 1919b: *CP8* p. 280, *LK* p. 288.

32 This is, of course, not to exhaust all the possible treatments of negation within an ontology of facts. I have mentioned only those explicitly canvassed at the time. For a survey of the range of possibilities, see Oaklander (2005).

33 Makin (2000), p. 67, citing Russell (1903) §46, argues that this correspondence holds only of the result of analysing a proposition, not of its original
ordinary language version. Russell's text is potentially ambiguous, but I think
Makin's reading unnatural. In the present context, however, the issue makes
no difference, since we are now concerned with a fully analysed proposition.

34 This is an early exemplification of Russell's already-remarked tendency to
try to solve a philosophical problem by discerning an object of acquaintance (here, a denoting concept) which somehow possesses just the right
logical properties for the solution. Makin (2000), p. 201 defends the procedure; my view is that *acquaintance* is an idle wheel in its mechanism.

35 Most philosophers would now think that interdefinability alone would not
show Russell to be so committed. The work would have to be done by, for
instance, the arguments of Bradley which he mentions but does not
expound. Regarding interdefinability alone as sufficient to reveal logical
form results in absurdities, such as the one encountered in Russell (1918),
CP8 p. 208 (*LK* p. 237). It is clear, however, that Russell thinks he has a
problem to solve. For difficulties with the notion of logical form, see the
wrongly neglected Smiley (1982).

36 Russell (1918); *CP8* pp. 185, 208; *LK* pp. 209, 237.

37 See Quine (1953), pp. 7–8, 167.

38 Cf. Hylton (1990), p. 259.

39 I do not pay special attention in this book to Bradley's objections to, and
Russell's endorsement of, the possibility of unique designation. Although it
is a significant difference between them, it does not form a central part of
the stereotype in the way that the topic of relations does. Good discussion
is found in Levine (1998) and Allard (2005), pp. 79–81.

40 Cf. Hylton (1990), p. 271n.

41 It is worth quoting in full a passage of which we have already seen a frag-
ment (Chapter 2, p. 22 above):

> Once we have formed ideas of things, we compare the ideas. We unite
> those which belong together by affirming one idea of another; we sepa-
> rate those which do not belong together by denying one idea of another.
> To judge is to affirm or to deny. The product of judging is expressed by a
> sentence which must contain two terms – the one term is the subject,
> which expresses the idea of which we affirm or deny another idea; the
> second term is the predicate, which expresses the idea which is affirmed
> or denied of the idea expressed by the subject. In judging, the mind not
> only conceives two ideas but also unites or separates them. The result of
> this activity of the mind is a proposition expressed by a sentence in
> which the verb 'is' either alone or with a negative particle connects the
> terms that express the ideas that are affirmed or denied. When I say 'God
> is just', the idea of God is joined to the idea of just; and this idea is the
> attribute of the proposition expressed by the sentence. The word 'is' indi-
> cates my joining the idea of God with the idea of just. If we say 'God is
> not unjust', 'is not' indicates my separating the idea of God from the idea
> of unjust ... [E]very proposition is necessarily composed of three elements
> – the subject-idea, the attribute, and the joining of these two ideas ...
>   (Arnauld and Nicole 1662, Part II, Ch. 3)

42 Oliver (1999), pp. 251, 258, 260–2 has made me properly uneasy about expressions like 'the view that all propositions are of subject–predicate form'. But it is impossible to discuss the history of this matter without them for these are the terms in which the disputes I describe were expressed. Oliver and I, in so far as our discussions of Russell overlap, seem not to disagree, except that I think he oversimplifies the Russell story on p. 263.

$3 For another example, see Wilson (1996). For a less *1066-and-All-That* approach, see Chapter 6 below.

44 See Chapter 6, p. 155f below. Nevertheless, as Hylton (1990), p. 184, makes clear, Russell's temporary but intense anxiety over relations seems to have been based on the idea that monism, because of its denial of the reality of relations, is inconsistent with the ordinary truths of simple mathematics, while extreme pluralism with its insistence on the reality of relations is not.

45 This reading of Bradley depends upon a careful distinction of the claim that relations are unreal from the claim that they are internal. It is defended in detail in Chapter 6 below.

46 One example of the use of this method in a completely different context, taken at random, for the purpose of illustrating how it has become second nature to philosophers, is Jackson (1977).

47 The claim made in this paragraph is complicated by the fact that Bradley did think that in the last analysis, and in some sense, no relational statement is true. But this is not because of special problems with relations: it is because, as we saw in Chapter 4, Bradley thought that in the last analysis no ordinary statement is ever completely true, there being no expressible truth that is uncontaminated by falsehood.

48 See Russell (1924), and Chapter 6, p. 155f below.

49 'Ideal', as we saw in Chapter 2, in the sense of belonging to the realm of idea.

50 The suggestion, once put to me in discussion, that this cannot be true because for Bradley 'Reality' is the name of Reality, overlooks the fact that in Bradley's view of language there are no names (at least, no names as philosophers such as Russell commonly understand them to function).

51 Given this significance, it is a pity that Russell himself wavers over whether the assumption concerns surface or depth grammar, for on page 4 he states it unequivocally as 'Every proposition has a subject and a predicate', whereas on page 9 it becomes 'Every proposition is ultimately reducible to one which attributes a predicate to a subject.' It is, I think, pretty clear that the latter is Russell's considered version.

52 One should compare this remark about substance with the remarks about his own conception of particulars in Russell (1918): *CP8*, p. 179; *LK* pp. 201–2.

53 Peter Hylton (1990), p. 155 asks, 'Why, then, did Russell take the subject–predicate view to be a nearly universal philosophical error? The most plausible answer, I think, is that he equated this issue with the issue of the reality and objectivity of relations.' This might explain why Russell thought the view to be an error, but on its own it can hardly explain why he thought it 'nearly universal'. Hylton's question bundles two issues together.

54 Russell (1914b), p. 56. A fuller version of the argument appears in Russell (1903), §215.

55 'Clearly impossible': in fact Russell (1914b), p. 58 thinks that symmetrical relations cannot be expressed as predicates either, but that the point is easier to demonstrate in the case of asymmetrical relations. This appears to be a shift from his 1903 argument, one probably based on his recognition in 1913 that difficulties concerning the 'sense' or direction of a relation are not an essential part of the problems involved in discovering what is meant by 'understanding a proposition'. See Chapter 3 above. Later philosophers have doubted the special significance of asymmetrical relations in this debate. See Humberstone (1995).

56 Russell (1903), §§213–14. The monadistic version is not relevant in the present context.

57 Some may think this not a point of grammar, since it brings in semantic matters. But, as Oliver shows, there is 'an instability in the grammatical categories due to the varying prominence of three, often not clearly distinguished, criteria of classification: the formal, the semantic and the syntactic' (1999, p. 255).

58 This aspect of Wittgenstein's thought is well-discussed by Ian Proops (2001).

59 Bradley (1893), *AR* p. 17; 1909a, *ETR* p. 239.

60 Bradley (1893), *AR* pp. 25–7; 1924, pp. 634–5.

61 See, for example, Frege (1892), p. 45. This verdict would be disputed by Makin. About this, I would repeat, *mutatis mutandis*, what I said in the opening section to this chapter about a similar disagreement concerning Russell.

62 Perhaps the most distinguished recent contributions to this tradition are those of P.F. Strawson (1959, 1974).

63 See *CP1*, Part IV.

64 Griffin (1991), pp. 216*f*.

65 Perhaps this should be 'perceptible change', but the nature of the particulars seems to make this addition superfluous.

66 There is a good brief discussion in Hylton (1990), pp. 368*f*.

6 Relations

1 This is the approach taken in, for example, Mander (1994); perhaps forgivably, in what is intended as an introductory text. Although, as I said at the outset, Bradley's views are relatively stable across time, this does not mean that they don't change at all, as we shall discover.

2 An illustration of movement in Bradley's thought, if any be needed, is his remark to Russell in a letter dated by Russell as November 1908 (now in the Russell Archives, to whom I owe thanks both for a copy and for permission to quote), 'I do not now hold the view which I accepted from Hegel that any truth can be developed into all truth by us through its own dialectical incoherence.' The point is made in Bradley (1909c), *ETR* pp. 223–4.

3 I owe this last observation to the insight of Peter Hylton (1990) – though he should not be blamed for my way of putting it.

4 Bradley (1883), *PL* p. x. Although he does not say so explicitly, the reference is probably to the claim that the rational and the real are one.

Bradley's rejection of this is made clear in a famous purple passage at the end of the same work (pp. 590–1); it is what produces the peculiar view of truth which we examined in Chapter 4.

5 We should notice that Moore and Russell may have read Bradley in the way that they did because it was easy to do so. I try to do justice to this fact below.

6 For an illustration of this disappearance, see the discussion of item 18 in Chapter 1, (pp. 17–18).

7 Manser (1983), p. 120; *idem*, 'Bradley and Internal Relations', in *Idealism Past and Present*, Royal Institute of Philosophy Lecture Series 13 (Cambridge: Cambridge University Press, 1982), p. 182. 'Bradley and Internal Relations' is only negligibly different from Chapter VII of Manser (1983). Manser is a welcome exception to the habit of treating Bradley's writings as exhibiting no change in view over time.

The symposium in question is in *Aristotelian Society Supplementary Volume* XIV, 1935.

8 For example, *ETR*, 239 and 312, from 1909c and 1911b respectively.

9 The theory of denoting concepts which we find in *The Principles of Mathematics* is an exception to this denial; but it is just that – an exception, brought in to deal with difficulties arising for the principal doctrine, as we saw in Chapter 5 (p. 111*f*) above.

10 This, too, is clearly what 'external' means on p. 488 of Bradley (1883). There are in *PL* other uses of the phrase 'external relation' that are more reminiscent of Bradley's later 'metaphysical' aspersions on externality, but these are hardly relevant to a claim to find a special logical doctrine of internality in that book.

11 One must also read the beginning of p. 27 to get absolutely clear about these. Another example, where one has to consider the footnote as well as the text to get the intended sense, is in Bradley (1911b) *ETR*, p. 326.

12 If additional confirmation is needed, it can be found in Manser's further remark on p. 127, 'It is not explicitly "relational" propositions that Bradley is talking about, but any possible proposition.'

13 'A place in analytical philosophy's pantheon'. This is my phrase, not Manser's. It should not, obviously, be interpreted as 'among the analytical philosophers', for on any plausible definition of the term, Bradley is not going to count as an analytical philosopher (any more than Hume, who most certainly has a place in the pantheon). A convincingly detailed demonstration of Bradley's contribution to debates characteristic of analytical philosophy can be found in Levine (1998).

14 For example, the admirable Bradley scholar James Allard at one stage not only accepted Manser's view of the treatment of internal relations in *The Principles of Logic*, but went on to use it as part of the basis for posing an 'antinomy' between Bradley's theory of judgment and his theory of inference, since, according to Allard, his theory of inference requires some judgments to contain more than one distinct idea while his theory of judgment requires that judgments all contain only one distinct idea. But Allard's own description of the problem reveals that it can be posed without bringing in the notion of internal relations at all, arising as it does from the conflicting requirements that judgments are to have no relations inside their content and that they are to have some such relations. See Allard (1985), p. 475,

and *idem* 1989 §2 especially nn. 8 and 12. The mistake is eliminated from Allard (2005).

Thomas Baldwin, in his elegant and insightful article 'Moore's Rejection of Idealism' (Baldwin 1984), finds in Bradley's thought a distinction in some respects analogous to Manser's, between essentialist and semantic holism, suggesting that the former is based on the doctrine of internality of relations and the latter on that of their unreality. I do not think the distinction so neat. There are some hints as to why in the final section of this chapter.

15 The complete text is reproduced in *CP6* pp. 349–51.

16 Though one must be careful here: the index entry reflects only one half of Bradley's considered view that all relations are both internal and external (1924, *CE* p. 641). One might suppose simply that there had been a change of mind between 1893 and 1924, were there not in the same index an exactly parallel phenomenon with the entry 'Idea is what it means'; for here we have again only one half of Bradley's considered – and this time already-formed – view (1883, *PL* pp. 6–7), and the references do not support the entry. As anyone who has seriously tried to use it can attest, Bradley was right to describe his own index as 'useless ... faulty and incomplete' (1897, *AR* p. 565).

17 See, for example, Bradley (1893) *AR* p. 1, and (1909c) *ETR* p. 239; the apparent conflict between this and his account of judgment in *The Principles of Logic* is merely apparent, for the account of judgment is an account of the status of those relations, as ideal not real. This is just another example of the perpetual difficulty encountered in giving any exposition of absolute idealism to a readership which does not share its assumptions, of saying what a denial of reality is if it is not to amount to a flat denial of existence. I have more to say about this in the next section, inspired by the most profound single remark on the subject, that of Wittgenstein (*Philosophical Investigations*, §402), which has informed my approach in this book and is quoted at the beginning as an epigraph.

18 In the final section of Chapter 2 above, we observed a closely related dispute showing similar characteristics, and its eventual negative significance for Bradley's metaphysics.

19 There are of course some terms which play a limited role of this sort in our language, like 'father', 'the current Premier of the State of Western Australia' and so on. But such terms are only partial redressings of the systematic linguistic shortcoming which Bradley is indicating, and of course they are relational. Neither should we forget that Bradley argued (1883), *PL* Ch. 1, that all language necessarily remains at the level of universals, and cannot without appeal to extra-linguistic resources enable the completely unambiguous designation of individuals. What I am saying about Bradley's procedure shows up a striking contrast (pointed out to me by Terry Diffey) between him and Collingwood:

> My reason for adopting this terminology is, chiefly, that it stands nearer than any other to everyday speech, and therefore begs fewer questions. The philosopher who tries to 'speak with the vulgar and think with the learned' has this advantage over one who adopts an elaborate technical vocabulary: that the use of a special 'philosophical language' commits the user, possibly even against his will, to accepting the philosophical doctrines which it has been designed to express, so that these doctrines

are surreptitiously and dogmatically foisted upon every disputant who will consent to use the language: whereas, if the language of every day is used, problems can be stated in a way which does not commit us in advance to a particular solution. This gives the user of common speech an advantage, if what he wants to do is to keep the discussion open and above-board and to get at the truth. For a philosopher whose aim is not truth but victory it is of course a disadvantage; he would be wiser to insist at the start upon using a terminology so designed that all statements couched in it assume the contentions he is anxious to prove. And this in effect is what those philosophers are doing who profess themselves unable to grasp the meaning of this or that statement until it has been translated into their own terminology. To insist that every conversation shall be conducted in one's own language is in men of the world only bad manners; in philosophers it is sophistry as well.

(Collingwood 1938, p. 174)

20 For example, by Baldwin (1990), p. 314 n. 34. It should be noted that Baldwin's page references to *Appearance and Reality* are to the old Allen & Unwin (formerly Swan Sonnenschein) edition, whose pagination is very different from the Oxford edition now more commonly used. The same is true of Wollheim (1959), but not of Wollheim (1969).

21 Hylton's more extreme suggestion, that 'Until he comes to defend himself against criticism, however, Bradley makes no real use of this distinction' (1990 p. 54), seems to me to need careful weighing against some of the remarks in Bradley (1893). (One would like to know what 'real' is being opposed to here.) But, as will become clear, in the end it hardly matters whether this commitment is merely a matter of appearance or not.

22 See Candlish (1978), §8.

23 See, for example, Bradley (1909c), *ETR* p. 237n.

24 As I noted previously, there are two occurrences of the phrase 'internal relation' on p. 26, but – as can be clearly seen by going on to read the first four lines of p. 27, if it is not already obvious – both reflect the pun we have already observed in *The Principles of Logic*.

25 I think that the idea of terms without any relation at all is hard for a present-day reader to keep in mind, because it is a question that for us seems not even to arise, so that it is easy to overlook Bradley's opposition to it. The clue to its occurrence in his writing is phrases like 'the mere "And"'. On the intelligibility of the idea itself, see Hylton (1990), p. 26.

26 In fact, the latter belief does emerge briefly at p. 513 of Bradley (1897), but is immediately swamped by concerns about externality. My suggestion that Bradley was confused in *AR* is borne out by one of his own later remarks concerning what seems to have been a dialectical form of the doctrine of internal relations in that book, where he says 'I have perhaps fallen in places into inconsistency' (1909c, *ETR* p. 224n).

27 'So Matter is in the same position as the gorgons and the harpies', said McTaggart (1906, p. 95), making a typical idealist point. As John Wisdom (1942), p. 439, said, remarking on Moore's appeal to this very passage, such people 'expect to shock us ... And they do shock us. They send a fear into our hearts.'

28 This idea that to be real is to be a substance is no passing fancy, as its frequent recurrence in Bradley's writings attests (1883), *PL* pp. 52, 71, 187; (1893), *AR* p. 9; (1909c), *ETR* p. 227n; (1911a), *ETR* pp. 289–90. It is worth mentioning here that it would be no use to try to turn Bradley's use of the notion of substance back on him by, for example, suggesting that no ordinary thing can be a substance either, for Bradley would of course accept that suggestion. For him, only the Absolute itself is substantial (the position he takes is comparable to that of Descartes, who also works with a conception of substance as independent when elaborating his dualism but finds that in the last analysis only God is absolutely independent), so that a successful attack of this kind would have to reject the legitimacy of the notion of substance itself.

Despite Russell's claim, cited in Chapter 5 (p. 132*f*) above, that use of the notion of substance depends upon the false belief that all propositions are, in the last analysis, of subject–predicate form, this possibility was not open to Russell himself, for his own views on particulars in 'The Philosophy of Logical Atomism' require that legitimacy, as we shall see in the next paragraph but one.

29 There is an interesting and entertaining attempt to spell out Wittgenstein's point by Nicholas Denyer (1991) pp. 118–26. It is criticized by Richard Gaskin (1998), §§1 and 2.

30 See especially *CP9* p. 173 (*LK* p. 336): immediately after quoting a Bradley criticism, without remarking that the criticism appeared in *Mind* 1910 and concerned *The Principles of Mathematics*, Russell says, 'With regard to external relations, my view is the one I have just stated, not the one commonly imputed by those who disagree.' It is hard to see this omission as not disingenuous.

31 It is easy for us to forget that this assumption is not obvious to those who have not received a twentieth century philosophical training. Here, for example, is Beatrice Webb's percipient comment on one of the forces behind the assumption:

> Bertrand Russell's nature is pathetic in its subtle absoluteness: faith in an absolute logic, absolute ethic, absolute beauty, and all of the most refined and rarefied type. His abstract and revolutionary methods of thought and the uncompromising way in which he applies these frightens me for his future and the future of those who love him or whom he loves. Compromise, mitigation, mixed motive, phases of health of body and mind, qualified statements, uncertain feelings, all seem unknown to him. A proposition must be either true or false; a character good or bad, a person loving or unloving, truth speaking or lying.
>
> (*Diaries*, ed. Norman and Jeanne MacKenzie, 4 vols, Cambridge, Mass.: Belknap Press of Harvard University Press, 1982–85; ii, pp. 252–3; quoted in Griffin 1992, p. 249)

32 For the argument for this, see Chapter 2 (p. 26*f*) above.

33 Russell (1959), pp. 56–7. He is quoting there from Russell (1907), *PE* p. 141.

34 Russell (1918): *CP8* p. 170, *LK* p. 190.

35 Quinton, after noting the 'remarkable number' of senior idealist philosophers who became university vice-chancellors [for North American readers, 'presidents'] as their metaphysics was overtaken by the views of

their younger colleagues, observes ironically, 'The Hegelian mode of thought, with its combination of practical realism and theoretical nebulosity, is a remarkably serviceable instrument for the holders of high administrative positions' (1971, p. 5). We shall see in Chapter 7 that this is not merely a joke, though these days holders of high administrative or managerial positions are more conveniently served by relativism about truth.

36 See, for example, Russell (1903), § 216, and (1919a), chapter 4.

37 The point is well-made by Mander (1994), pp. 108–9, though he sees Bradley as more consistent and systematic than I do.

38 A good proportion of the extensive additions in the second edition of *The Principles of Logic* arise from Bradley's concern with this notion. See Allard (2005), pp. 55–7 for an unusually clear account. The unfamiliar terminology disguises the fact that Bradley is dealing with the question of what Frege (or rather, his translators) called 'force'.

39 One reader of a draft of this book objected, 'I disagree with [Candlish's] understanding of the question "Are relations and their terms real?" as equivalent to "Are relations and their terms substances?" in as much as the second is an all-or-nothing question, while reality is for Bradley a matter of degree.' It should be clear from what I have just said that the answer to this objection is that, for Bradley, the question 'Are relations substances?' is, on this reading, itself one of degree.

40 Russell (1927), p. 263.

41 See, for example, Russell (1903), §99, and Wollheim (1969) p. 114, (1959), p. 116.

42 The conventional wisdom on this matter became so entrenched that, for example, Nicholas Griffin felt able to write of Bradley's arguments concerning relations, without further explanation: 'The defects of these arguments are by now well-known' (Griffin 1983, p. 199). Compare, too, these remarks from Reinhardt Grossmann (1974), p. 67, where an at least plausible sentence is used as a licence for concluding a false one (I have italicized the revealing phrase): 'What Bradley's argument shows is, in the last analysis, that relations behave quite differently from non-relational entities when it comes to being related to something. Bradley, *needless to say*, is comparable to someone who concludes from our glue and board example that there simply can be no glue at all.' This conventional wisdom persists, in somewhat more vestigial form, in Linsky (1992), p. 273.

43 A telling example from another area of philosophy altogether is described by Rai Gaita (1991), p. 74.

44 For Wittgenstein's criticism, see the discussion by David Pears (1977). Russell's tendency to try to solve problems by introducing objects of acquaintance to do the job, and Wittgenstein's opposition to this, extends far beyond the analysis of the proposition. For other examples in a completely different context, see Candlish (1991).

45 Consider this, for example:

> Of course, all the ordinary objects of daily life are apparently complex entities ... For my part, I do not believe in complex entities of this kind ... The analysis of apparently complex things such as we started with can be reduced by various means, to the analysis of facts which are apparently about those things.
>
> (Russell 1918; *CP8* pp. 170–1, *LK* p. 190–2)

Simples ... are of an infinite number of sorts. There are particulars and qualities and relations of various orders, a whole hierarchy of different sorts of simples, but all of them, if we were right, have in their various ways some kind of reality that does not belong to anything else. The only other sort of object you come across in the world is what we call facts and facts are the sort of things that are asserted or denied by propositions, and are not properly entities at all in the same sense in which their constituents are. That is shown in the fact that you cannot name them. You can only deny, or assert, or consider them, but you cannot name them because they are not there to be named ...

(Russell 1918; *CP8* pp. 234–5, *LK* p. 270)

46 A point which, incidentally, shows the unfairness, at least on more recent conceptions of meaning, of Russell's charge (Russell 1900, p. 50n): 'Mr. Bradley, in attempting to reduce all judgment to predication about Reality, is led to the same view [i.e. that "substance remains, apart from its predicates, wholly destitute of meaning"] concerning his ultimate subject. Reality, for him, is not an idea, and is therefore, one must suppose, meaningless.'

7 Decline and Fall

1 A slightly different but fuller version of the foregoing account can be found in Pigden (2003).
2 The first quotation is from Moore (1919), p. 88, the second from p. 32 of Moore (1903). Bradley's unpublished notes reveal that he held Moore (as a philosopher) in contempt. Baldwin (1990) pp. 24–8 provides a useful and sympathetic brief study of Moore's relations paper and assesses its (still considerable, despite my strictures) achievement.
3 These articles, originally published in 1925 and 1939 respectively, were reprinted in G.E. Moore, *Philosophical Papers* (London: Allen & Unwin, 1959). They can now most easily be found in Baldwin (ed.), (1993), pp. 106–33 and 147–70.
4 For Russell's own difficulties in the same area, see Chapter 3 above.
5 For Russell's claim that 'philosophy, in our own day, is becoming scientific', see his 1914b, pp. 240–6. For good accounts of the visionary side of Bradley's metaphysics, see Blanshard (1984), p. 214 and Findlay (1984).
6 But see Part 3 of King-Farlow (1978), in which, among other unusual things, is sketched a monistic semantics for a recognizably Russellian calculus.
7 Griffin (ed.) (1992), p. 224. The quotation is from a letter to Helen Thomas, dated 30 Dec. 1901. For an excellent brief account of the complex logical relationships between the vindication of mathematics and the refutation of idealism, see Hylton (1990), pp. 167–70. (The account is developed at length in the subsequent pages.) My point here concerns not these relationships but historically effective causes.
8 Here I am greatly indebted to Fussell (1975); all otherwise unidentified quotations in this paragraph are taken from his chapter II, where the detailed evidence required for the demonstration of my claims is provided.
9 *Ibid.*, p. 63.

214 Notes to pp. 183–8

10 Spenser Wilkinson, *The Nation's Awakening* (London, 1896), quoted by Gollwitzer (1969), p. 155 (from which the two preceding quotes about the representatives of idealism are also taken); cf., too, Quinton (1971).

11 There are honourable exceptions, including Davidson himself, Gaskin (1997, 1998), Gibson (2004) and Read (2005). Typically these concentrate on one or other unity problem, though what is thought to need an account of its unity varies: for some it is facts, for others, propositions, for others again, sentences.

12 See, for example, Armstrong (1968), pp. 106–7. To be fair to Armstrong, he is a philosopher who always took Bradley seriously. In my experience (and this is part of the answer to the question posed in the opening paragraph of my Preface), it is those analytic philosophers who, unlike Armstrong himself, have been primarily logicians rather than metaphysicians who have taken Russell at his word and dismissed Bradley out of hand.

13 Donald Davidson (2005), p. 106, says:

> ... Bradley held that the [infinite regress] problem constituted a reductio of the thesis that there are such things as relations, while Russell continued to insist on the reality of relations despite the fact that he could not give a consistent account of the relations which unify a proposition. In this debate Bradley won, although Russell was on the right side.

Davidson's views here are expressed in just the kind of blurred language that it is important to avoid on this topic. This has not prevented him, however, from coming to precisely the wrong verdict in his final sentence.

14 As Sainsbury (1996), p. 144, points out, citing examples, theories apparently similar to Russell's multiple relation theory of judgment are 'being advanced, or at least taken seriously, by many influential contemporary writers'.

15 For illustrative argument, see Candlish (2002).

Bibliography

Apart from the lists of convenient abbreviations, in each case the citation date shown following the author's name is the date of original publication. A separate date is shown for the edition cited only where this differs from the original. Page references in footnotes are, unless otherwise stated, to the latest edition cited.

Bradley's writings

Abbreviations used for easy recognition below and in the main text

AR   *Appearance and Reality*, the so-called 'ninth impression'. Oxford: Clarendon Press, 1930 (see the Bibliographical Note on p. 224).

CE   *Collected Essays*. Oxford: Clarendon Press, 1935.

ETR   *Essays on Truth and Reality*. Oxford: Clarendon Press, 1914.

PL   *The Principles of Logic* (second edition, revised, with commentary and terminal essays). London: Oxford University Press, 1922.

WLM   *Writings on Logic and Metaphysics*, edited by James W. Allard and Guy Stock. Oxford: Clarendon Press, 1994.

Works cited

Bradley, F.H. (1883) *The Principles of Logic*. London: Oxford University Press, 1922.

— (1893) *Appearance and Reality*. Oxford: Clarendon Press, 1930.* [AR]

— (1897) Appendix, Index and Explanatory Notes to the second edition of *AR*.

— (1906) 'Introductory', in *ETR*: 1–28.

— (1907) 'On truth and copying', *Mind*, reprinted in *ETR*: 107–26 and in *WLM*.

— (1909a) 'On our knowledge of immediate experience', *Mind*, reprinted in *ETR*: 159–91 and in *WLM*.

— (1909b) 'On truth and coherence', *Mind*, reprinted in *ETR*: 202–18 and in *WLM*.

— (1909c) 'Coherence and contradiction', *Mind*, reprinted in *ETR*: 219–44 and in *WLM*.

— (1910a) 'On appearance, error and contradiction', *Mind*, reprinted in *ETR*: 245–73.

— (1910b) Supplementary Note to 1910a, *Mind*, reprinted as 'Supplementary Note II' in *ETR*: 276–88.

— (1911a) 'Reply to Mr. Russell's explanations', *Mind*, reprinted as 'Supplementary Note III' in *ETR*: 288–92. (This may also be found in *The Collected Papers of Bertrand Russell, VI: Logical and Philosophical Papers 1909–13*, London: Routledge, 1992, 394–97.)

— (1911b) 'On some aspects of truth', *Mind*, reprinted in *ETR*: 310–52.

— (1914) *Essays on Truth and Reality*. Oxford: Clarendon Press, 1968. [*ETR*]
— (1914a) 'A discussion of some problems in connexion with Mr. Russell's doctrine', in *ETR*: 293–309.
— (1914b) 'On Professor James's "Radical Empiricism"', in *ETR*: 149–58.
— (1914c) 'What is the real Julius Caesar?', in *ETR*: 409–27.
— (1922) 'Additional Notes' and 'Terminal Essays' in the second edition of *PL*.
— (1924) 'Relations', in *CE*: 629–76. [This uncompleted but important essay was not in fact published until 1935, but I have given the date of its final form as this is a better indication of when Bradley was writing: in 1935 he had been dead for more than ten years.]
— (1935) *Collected Essays*. Oxford: Clarendon Press. [*CE*]
— (1999) *The Collected Works of F.H. Bradley*, 12 volumes, edited and introduced by W.J. Mander and Carol A. Keene. Bristol: Thoemmes.

Russell's writings

Abbreviations used for easy recognition below and in the main text

CP1 *The Collected Papers of Bertrand Russell*, Vol. 1: *Cambridge Essays 1888–99*. London: George Allen & Unwin, 1983.

CP4 *The Collected Papers of Bertrand Russell*, Vol. 4: *Foundations of Logic 1903–05*. London: Routledge, 1994.

CP6 *The Collected Papers of Bertrand Russell*, Vol. 6: *Logical and Philosophical Papers 1909–13*. London: Routledge, 1992.

CP8 *The Collected Papers of Bertrand Russell*, Vol. 8: *The Philosophy of Logical Atomism and Other Essays 1914–19*. London: George Allen & Unwin, 1986.

CP9 *The Collected Papers of Bertrand Russell*, Vol. 9: *Essays on Language, Mind and Matter 1919–26*. London: Routledge, 1994 (reprint of Unwin Hyman edition of 1988).

EA *Essays in Analysis*, edited by Douglas Lackey. London: Allen & Unwin, 1973.

LK *Logic and Knowledge*, edited by Robert C. Marsh. London: George Allen & Unwin, 1956.

ML *Mysticism and Logic*. London: George Allen & Unwin, 1963; originally published 1917.

PE *Philosophical Essays*. London: George Allen & Unwin, 1966; originally published with somewhat different contents and different pagination 1910.

Works cited

Russell, B. (1893) 'On the foundations of ethics', in *CP1*: 208–11.
— (1894) 'Cleopatra or Maggie Tulliver', in *CP1*: 92–8.
— (1897a) 'Seems, madam? Nay, it is', in *CP1*: 106–11.
— (1897b) *An Essay on the Foundations of Geometry*. London: Routledge, 1996.
— (1900) *A Critical Exposition of the Philosophy of Leibniz*. London: Allen & Unwin, 1937.

— (1903) *The Principles of Mathematics*. London: Allen & Unwin, 1937.
— (1904a) 'Meinong's theory of complexes and assumptions', in *CP4*: 432–74 (also in *EA*).
— (1904b) Letter to Frege 12 December 1904, in G. Frege *Philosophical and Mathematical Correspondence*. Oxford: Basil Blackwell, 1980: 166–70.
— (1905a) 'The existential import of propositions', in *CP4*: 486–9.
— (1905b) 'On denoting', in *CP4*: 415–27 (also in *LK*).
— (1907) 'The monistic theory of truth', in *PE*: 131–46.
— (1908) 'Mathematical logic as based on the theory of types', in *LK*: 57–102.
— and Whitehead, A.N. (1910a) [See Whitehead].
— (1910b) 'On the nature of truth and falsehood', in *CP6*: 116–24 (also in *PE*).
— (1911) 'Knowledge by acquaintance and knowledge by description', in *CP6*: 148–61 (also in *ML*).
— (1912) *The Problems of Philosophy*. London: Oxford University Press, 1946.
— (1913) *Theory of Knowledge*: The 1913 Manuscript. London: Routledge, 1992.
— (1914a) 'The relation of sense-data to physics', in *CP8*: 5–26 (also in *ML*).
— (1914b) *Our Knowledge of the External World*, revised edition. London: George Allen & Unwin, 1926.
— (1918) 'The philosophy of logical atomism', in *CP8*: 160–244 (also in *LK*).
— (1919a) *Introduction to Mathematical Philosophy*. London: George Allen & Unwin.
— (1919b) 'On propositions: what they are and how they mean', in *CP8*: 278–306 (also in *LK*).
— (1921) *The Analysis of Mind*. London: George Allen & Unwin.
— (1924) 'Logical atomism', in *CP9*: 160–79 (also in *LK*).
— (1927) *An Outline of Philosophy*. London: George Allen & Unwin.
— (1937) 'Introduction to the second edition', *The Principles of Mathematics*. London: George Allen & Unwin.
— (1940) *An Inquiry into Meaning and Truth*. London: George Allen & Unwin (Pelican reprint, 1962).
— (1946) 'Philosophy for laymen', in *Unpopular Essays*. London: George Allen & Unwin, 1950: 35–49.
— (1959) *My Philosophical Development*. London: George Allen & Unwin.
— (1967) *The Autobiography of Bertrand Russell*, Vol. 1. London: George Allen & Unwin (single-volume edition, 1975).

Other writings

Acton, H.B. (1967) 'Bradley, Francis Herbert', in P. Edwards (ed.), vol. 1: 359–63.
Allard, J. (1980) 'Bradley's argument against correspondence', *Idealistic Studies*, 10: 232–44.
— (1984) 'Bradley's principle of sufficient reason', in A.R. Manser and G. Stock (eds): 173–89.
— (1985) 'Bradley's intensional judgments', *History of Philosophy Quarterly*, 2: 469–75.
— (1989) 'Bradley on the validity of inference', *Journal of the History of Philosophy*, 27: 267–74.
— (1996) 'Degrees of truth in F.H. Bradley', in W.J. Mander (ed.): 137–58.
— (2005) *The Logical Foundations of Bradley's Metaphysics: Judgment, Inference, and Truth*. New York: Cambridge University Press.

Armstrong, D. (1968) *A Materialist Theory of the Mind*. London: Routledge & Kegan Paul.

Arnauld, A. and Nicole, P. (1662) *The Art of Thinking* [The Port-Royal *Logic*]. Indianapolis: Bobbs-Merrill, 1964.

Audi, R. (ed.) (1995) *The Cambridge Dictionary of Philosophy*. Cambridge: Cambridge University Press.

Ayer, A.J. (1936) *Language, Truth and Logic*, 2nd edn. London: Gollancz, 1946.

— (1971) *Russell and Moore: The Analytical Heritage*. London: Macmillan, now Palgrave Macmillan.

— (1972) *Russell*. London: Fontana.

Bach, K. (1998) 'Content: wide and narrow', in E. Craig (ed.), *The Routledge Encyclopedia of Philosophy Online*. London: Routledge, http://www.rep.routledge.com/article/W040.

Baldwin, T. (1984) 'Moore's rejection of idealism', in R. Rorty *et al.* (eds): 357–74.

— (1990) *G.E. Moore*. London: Routledge.

— (1991) 'The identity theory of truth', *Mind*, 100: 35–52.

— (ed.) (1993) *G.E. Moore: Selected Writings*. London: Routledge.

Basile, P. (1999) *Experience and Relations: An Examination of F.H. Bradley's Conception of Reality*. Berne: Paul Haupt.

Baxter, D. (1996) 'The complex–unity problem', in W.J. Mander (ed.): 1–24.

Blackburn, S. (1984a) *Spreading the Word*. Oxford: Clarendon Press.

— (1984b) 'Is epistemology coherent?', in A.R. Manser and G. Stock (eds): 155–72.

— (1994) *The Oxford Dictionary of Philosophy*. Oxford: Oxford University Press, 1996.

— and Simmons, K. (eds) (1999) *Truth* (Oxford and New York: Oxford University Press).

Blanshard, B. (1984) 'Bradley on relations', in A.R. Manser and G. Stock (eds): 211–26.

BonJour, L. (1995) 'Coherence theory of truth' in R. Audi (ed.): 133.

Bosanquet, B. (1895) *The Essentials of Logic*. London: Macmillan, now Palgrave Macmillan.

— (1911) *Logic*, 2 volumes. Oxford: Clarendon Press.

Bradley, J. (ed.) (1996) *Philosophy after F. H. Bradley*. Bristol: Thoemmes.

Broad, C.D. (1933) *An Examination of McTaggart's Philosophy*, Volume I. Cambridge: Cambridge University Press.

Campbell, C.A. (1931) *Scepticism and Construction*. London: George Allen & Unwin.

Candlish, S. (1978) 'Bradley on my station and its duties', *Australasian Journal of Philosophy*, 56: 155–70.

— (1981) 'The status of idealism in Bradley's metaphysics', *Idealistic Studies*, 11: 242–53.

— (1982) 'Idealism and Bradley's logic', *Idealistic Studies*, 12: 251–9.

— (1984) 'Scepticism, Ideal Experiment and Priorities in Bradley's Metaphysics', in A.R. Manser and G. Stock (eds): 243–67.

— (1991) '"Das Wollen ist auch nur eine Erfahrung"', in R. Arrington and H-J. Glock (eds), *Wittgenstein's Philosophical Investigations: Text and Context*. London: Routledge: 203–26.

— (1998) 'The wrong side of history: relations, the decline of British idealism, and the origins of analytic philosophy', in G. Stock (ed.): 111–51.
— (1999a) 'A prolegomenon to an identity theory of truth', *Philosophy*, 74: 199–221.
— (1999b) 'Identifying the identity theory of truth', *Aristotelian Society Proceedings*, XCIX: 233–40.
— (2002) 'Russell and Wittgenstein', in R. Haller and K. Puhl (eds), *Wittgenstein and the Future of Philosophy. A Reassessment after 50 Years: Akten des 24. Internationalen Wittgenstein Symposiums*. Vienna: Hölder–Pichler–Tempsky: 19–27.
— (2003) 'Truth, identity theory of', in E. Zalta (ed.), *The Stanford Encyclopedia of Philosophy* (Winter 2003 Edition), http://plato.stanford.edu/archives/win2003/entries/truth-identity/. Stanford, CA: CSLI, Stanford University. First posted 1996, last revised 2003.
— (2004) 'Private Language', in E. Zalta (ed.), *The Stanford Encyclopedia of Philosophy* (Spring 2004 Edition), http://plato.stanford.edu/archives/spr2004/entries/private-language/. First posted 1996, last revised 2004.
— (2005) 'Truth, identity theory of', in E. Craig (ed.) *The Routledge Encyclopedia of Philosophy Online*. London: Routledge, http://www.rep.routledge.com/article/N124.
Cartwright, R. (1987a) 'A neglected theory of truth', in R. Cartwright, *Philosophical Essays*. Cambridge, MA: MIT Press: 71–93.
— (1987b) 'On the origins of Russell's theory of descriptions', in R. Cartwright, *Philosophical Essays*. Cambridge, MA: MIT Press: 105–33.
Chihara, C. (1972) 'Russell's theory of types', in D.F. Pears (ed.): 245–89.
Collingwood, R.G. (1938) *The Principles of Art*. Oxford: Clarendon Press.
Craig, E.J. (ed.) (1998) *The Routledge Encyclopedia of Philosophy*. 10 volumes. London: Routledge.
Cresswell, M. (1977) 'Reality as experience in F.H. Bradley', *Australasian Journal of Philosophy*, 55: 169–88.
— (1979) 'Bradley's theory of judgment', *Canadian Journal of Philosophy*, 9: 575–94.
— (1985) Review of Manser 1983, *Philosophical Review*, 94: 139–41.
Dancy, J. (1985) *An Introduction to Contemporary Epistemology*. Oxford: Basil Blackwell.
David, M. (2001) 'Truth as identity and truth as correspondence', in M. Lynch (ed.): 683–704.
Davidson, D. (2005) *Truth and Predication*. Cambridge, MA: The Belknap Press of Harvard University Press.
De Morgan, A. (1847) *Formal Logic: or, the calculus of inference, necessary and probable*. London: Taylor & Walton.
Denyer, N. (1991) *Language, Thought and Falsehood in Ancient Greek Philosophy*. London: Routledge.
Dretske, F. (1981) *Knowledge and the Flow of Information*. Oxford: Basil Blackwell.
Edwards, P. (ed.) (1967) *The Encyclopedia of Philosophy*, 8 vols. New York: Macmillan.
Engel, P. (2001) 'The false modesty of the identity theory of truth', *International Journal of Philosophical Studies*, 9: 441–58.
— (2002) *Truth*. Chesham: Acumen.
Field, H. (2001) *Truth and the Absence of Fact*. Oxford: Clarendon Press.

Findlay, J.N. (1933) *Meinong's Theory of Objects and Values*. Oxford: Clarendon Press, 1963.

— (1984) 'Bradley's contribution to Absolute-theory', in A.R. Manser and G. Stock (eds): 269–84.

Fogelin, R. (1976) *Wittgenstein*. London: Routledge & Kegan Paul.

Frege, G. (1892) 'On concept and object', in *Translations from the Philosophical Writings of Gottlob Frege*, translated and edited by Peter Geach and Max Black, 2nd edn. Oxford: Basil Blackwell, 1960: 42–55.

— (1918) 'Thoughts', in Frege, *Logical Investigations*, edited by Peter Geach. Oxford: Basil Blackwell, 1977: 1–30.

Fussell, P. (1975) *The Great War and Modern Memory*. New York and London: Oxford University Press.

Gaita, R. (1991) *Good and Evil: An Absolute Conception*. London: Routledge.

Gaskin, R. (1997) 'Russell and Richard Brinkley on the unity of the proposition', *History and Philosophy of Logic*, 18: 139–50.

— (1998) 'The unity of the declarative sentence', *Philosophy*, 73: 21–45.

— (ed.) (2001) *Grammar in Early Twentieth-Century Philosophy*. London: Routledge.

Geach, P.T. (1957) *Mental Acts*. London: Routledge & Kegan Paul.

Gibson, M.I. (2004) *From Naming to Saying: the Unity of the Proposition*. Oxford: Blackwell.

Gollwitzer, H. (1969) *Europe in the Age of Imperialism*. London: Thames & Hudson.

Grayling, A.C. (1982) *An Introduction to Philosophical Logic*. Brighton: Harvester.

— (1996) *Russell*. Oxford: Oxford University Press.

Griffin, N. (1983) 'What's wrong with Bradley's theory of judgment?', *Idealistic Studies*, 13: 199–225.

— (1985) 'Russell's multiple relation theory of judgement', *Philosophical Studies*, 47: 213–41.

— (1991) *Russell's Idealist Apprenticeship*. Oxford: Clarendon Press.

— (ed.) (1992) *The Selected Letters of Bertrand Russell*, i: *The Private Years (1884–1914)*. London: Allen Lane.

— (1993) 'Terms, relations, complexes', in A.D. Irvine and G.A. Wedeking (eds), *Russell and Analytic Philosophy*. Toronto: University of Toronto Press: 159–92.

— (1998, 2003) 'Russell, Bertrand Arthur William', in E. Craig (ed.), *The Routledge Encyclopedia of Philosophy Online*. London: Routledge, http://www.rep.routledge.com/article/DD059.

Grossmann, R. (1974) *Meinong*. London: Routledge & Kegan Paul.

Haack, S. (1978) *Philosophy of Logics*. Cambridge: Cambridge University Press.

Hamlyn, D.W. (1970) *The Theory of Knowledge*. Basingstoke: Macmillan, now Palgrave Macmillan.

Hardy, T. (1891) *Tess of the d'Urbervilles*. London: Macmillan, 1912, now Palgrave Macmillan.

Hobhouse, L.T. (1904) *Democracy and Reaction*. London: T. Fisher Unwin.

Hodges, W. (1977) *Logic*. Harmondsworth: Penguin.

Holdcroft, D. (1984) 'Holism and truth', in A.R. Manser and G. Stock (eds): 191–209.

Honderich, T. (ed.) (1995) *The Oxford Companion to Philosophy*. Oxford: Oxford University Press.

Horwich, P. (1998) *Truth*. 2nd edn, revised. Oxford: Clarendon Press.

Humberstone, I.L. (1995) 'Comparatives and the reducibility of relations', *Pacific Philosophical Quarterly*, 76: 117–41.

Hume, D. (1739) *A Treatise of Human Nature*. Oxford: Clarendon Press, 1888.

Hylton, P. (1984) 'The nature of the proposition', in R. Rorty *et al*. (eds): 375–97.

— (1990) *Russell, Idealism, and the Emergence of Analytic Philosophy*. Oxford: Clarendon Press.

Irvine, A. (2004) 'Bertrand Russell', in E. Zalta (ed.), *The Stanford Encyclopedia of Philosophy* (Fall 2004 Edition), http://plato.stanford.edu/archives/fall2004/entries/russell/. Stanford, CA: CSLI, Stanford University. First posted 1995, last revised 2004.

Jackson, F. (1977) *Perception: a representative theory*. Cambridge: Cambridge University Press.

Jeffrey, R. (1967) *Formal Logic: its Scope and Limits*. New York: McGraw-Hill.

Joachim, H.H. (1906) *The Nature of Truth*. London: Oxford University Press, 1939.

Johnston, M. (2005) 'Constitution', in F. Jackson and M. Smith (eds), *The Oxford Handbook of Contemporary Philosophy*. Oxford: Oxford University Press: 636–77.

Keene, C.A. (1999) 'Introduction', in W.J. Mander and Carol A. Keene (eds), *The Collected Works of F.H. Bradley*, Volume 4: *Selected Correspondence* edited by Carol A. Keene. Bristol: Thoemmes: xiii–xxxii.

Kilmister, C.W. (1996) 'A certain knowledge? Russell's mathematics and logical analysis', in R. Monk and A. Palmer (eds): 269–86.

King-Farlow, J. (1978) *Self-Knowledge and Social Relations*. New York: Science History Publications.

Kirkham, R.L. (1992) *Theories of Truth*. Cambridge MA: MIT.

— (1998) 'Truth, coherence theory of', in E.J. Craig (ed.), Vol. 9: 470–2.

Kneale, W.C. and Kneale, M. (1962) *The Development of Logic*. Oxford: Clarendon Press.

Kripke, S.A. (1980) *Naming and Necessity*, revd edn. Oxford: Basil Blackwell.

Lacey, A.R. (1976) *A Dictionary of Philosophy*. London: Routledge & Kegan Paul.

Leibniz, G.W. (1686) *Discourse on Metaphysics*, translated and edited by Peter G. Lucas and Leslie Grint. Manchester: Manchester University Press 1953, reprinted 1961.

Levine, J. (1998) 'The what and the that: theories of singular thought in Bradley, Russell and the early Wittgenstein', in G. Stock (ed.): 19–72.

Lewis, D. (1981) 'Introduction', in D. Lewis, *Philosophical Papers*, Vol. I. New York and Oxford: Oxford University Press: ix–xii.

Lewis, H.A. (ed.) (1991) *Peter Geach: Philosophical Encounters*. Dordrecht: Kluwer.

Linsky, L. (1992) 'The unity of the proposition', *Journal of the History of Philosophy*, 30: 243–73.

Locke, J. (1706) *An Essay Concerning Human Understanding*, 5th edn. London: Dent, 1965.

Lotze, H. (1874) *Logic*, translated by Bernard Bosanquet. Oxford: Clarendon Press, 1888.

Lowe, E.J. (2006) 'Metaphysics', in D. Moran (ed.), *Routledge Companion to Twentieth-Century Philosophy*. London: Routledge.

Lynch, M. (ed.) (2001) *The Nature of Truth*. Cambridge, MA, and London: MIT Press.

MacIntyre, A. (1984) 'The relationship of philosophy to its past', in R. Rorty *et al*. (eds): 31–48.

Mackie, J.L. (1973) *Truth, Probability and Paradox*. Oxford: Clarendon Press.
Magee, B. (1971) *Modern British Philosophy*. London: Secker & Warburg.
Makin, G. (2000) *The Metaphysicians of Meaning: Russell and Frege on sense and denotation*. London and New York: Routledge.
Mander, W.J. (1994) *An Introduction to Bradley's Metaphysics*. Oxford: Clarendon Press.
— (ed.) (1996) *Perspectives on the Logic and Metaphysics of F.H. Bradley*. Bristol: Thoemmes.
Manser, A.R. (1983) *Bradley's Logic*. Oxford: Blackwell.
— and Stock, G. (eds) (1984) *The Philosophy of F.H. Bradley*. Oxford: Clarendon Press, reprinted with corrections 1986.
McDowell, J. (1994) *Mind and World*. Cambridge, MA: Harvard University Press.
McTaggart, J.M.E. (1906) *Some Dogmas of Religion*. London: Edward Arnold, 1930.
Mill, J.S. (1843) *A System of Logic*. London: Longmans, Green, 1900.
Monk, R. (1996) *Bertrand Russell: The Spirit of Solitude*. London: Jonathan Cape.
— and Palmer, A. (eds) (1996) *Bertrand Russell and the Origins of Analytical Philosophy*. Bristol: Thoemmes.
Montague, R.D.L. (1964) 'Wollheim on Bradley on idealism and relations', *Philosophical Quarterly*, 14: 158–64.
Moore, G.E. (1899) 'The nature of judgment', in T. Baldwin (ed.): 1–19.
— (1903) 'The refutation of idealism', in T. Baldwin (ed.): 23–44.
— (1919) 'External and internal relations', in T. Baldwin (ed.): 79–105.
— (1925) 'A defence of common sense', in T. Baldwin (ed.): 106–33.
— (1939) 'Proof of an external world', in T. Baldwin (ed.): 147–70.
Noonan, H. (1996) 'The Gray's Elegy argument – and others', in R. Monk and A. Palmer (eds): 65–102.
Oaklander, L.N. (2005) 'Negative facts', in E. Craig (ed.), *The Routledge Encyclopedia of Philosophy Online*. London: Routledge, http://www.rep.routledge.com/article/N118.
O'Connor, D.J., and Carr, B. (1982) *Introduction to the Theory of Knowledge*. Brighton: Harvester.
Oliver, A. (1999) 'A few more remarks on logical form', *Aristotelian Society Proceedings*, XCIX: 247–72; reprinted (slightly adapted) in R. Gaskin (ed.) 2001: 142–62. Page references in text to original.
Palmer, A. (1988) *Concept and Object*. London: Routledge.
Passmore, J.A. (1957) *A Hundred Years of Philosophy*, 1st edn. London: Duckworth.
— (1969) 'Russell and Bradley', in R. Brown and C.D. Rollins (eds) *Contemporary Philosophy in Australia*. London: George Allen & Unwin: 21–30.
Paton, H.J. (1956) 'Fifty years of philosophy', in H.D. Lewis (ed.), *Contemporary British Philosophy* (3rd series). London: George Allen & Unwin: 335–54.
Pears, D.F. (1967) *Bertrand Russell and the British Tradition in Philosophy*. London: Collins.
— (ed.) (1972) *Bertrand Russell: A Collection of Critical Essays*. New York: Doubleday.
— (1975) 'Wittgenstein's Treatment of Solipsism in the *Tractatus*', in D.F. Pears, *Questions in the Philosophy of Mind*. London: Duckworth: 272–92.
— (1977) 'The relation between Wittgenstein's picture theory of propositions and Russell's theories of judgement', *Philosophical Review*, 86: 177–96.

Pigden, C. (2003) 'Bertrand Russell: moral philosopher or unphilosophical moralist?', in N. Griffin (ed.), *The Cambridge Companion to Bertrand Russell*. Cambridge: Cambridge University Press: 475–506.

Proops, I. (2001) 'Logical syntax in the *Tractatus*', in R. Gaskin (ed.): 163–81.

Quine, W.V.O. (1940) *Mathematical Logic*, revd edn. New York: Harper & Row, 1951.

—— (1953) *From a Logical Point of View*. New York: Harper & Row, 1961.

—— (1966) 'Russell's ontological development', *The Journal of Philosophy*, LXIII: 657–67. [Reprinted in R. Schoenman (ed.), *Bertrand Russell: Philosopher of the Century*. London: Allen & Unwin, 1967: 304–14; and in Pears (ed.): 290–304.]

Quinton, A. (1971) 'Absolute idealism', *Dawes Hicks Lecture on Philosophy*, British Academy. Oxford: Oxford University Press, 1972.

Ramsey, F.P. (1927) 'Facts and propositions', in F.P. Ramsey, *The Foundations of Mathematics*. London: Routledge & Kegan Paul, 1931: 138–55.

Read, S. (1995) *Thinking about Logic*. Oxford and New York: Oxford University Press.

—— (2005) 'The unity of the fact', *Philosophy*, 80: 317–42.

Rescher, N. (1973) *The Coherence Theory of Truth*. Oxford: Clarendon Press.

Richards, T.J. (1978) *The Language of Reason*. Sydney: Pergamon Press.

Rorty, R. (1967) 'Relations, internal and external', in P. Edwards (ed.), vol. 7: 125–33.

——, Schneewind, J.B. and Skinner, Q. (eds) (1984) *Philosophy in History*. Cambridge: Cambridge University Press.

Sainsbury, R.M. (1979) *Russell*. London: Routledge & Kegan Paul.

—— (1991) *Logical Forms*. Oxford: Basil Blackwell.

—— (1995) *Paradoxes*. 2nd edn. Cambridge: Cambridge University Press.

—— (1996) 'How can we say something?' in R. Monk and A. Palmer (eds): 137–53, reprinted in R.M. Sainsbury (2002).

—— (2002) *Departing from Frege: Essays in the philosophy of language*. London and New York: Routledge.

Searle, J.R. (1958) 'Proper names', *Mind*, 67: 166–73.

Smiley, T. (1982) 'The schematic fallacy', *Aristotelian Society Proceedings*, LXXXIII, 1982/83: 1–17.

Sorensen, R.A. (1992) *Thought Experiments*. New York: Oxford University Press.

Sosa, E. (1993) 'Epistemology, realism, and truth: the first Philosophical Perspectives lecture', *Philosophical Perspectives*, 7, Language and Logic: 1–16.

Sprigge, T.L.S. (1993) *James and Bradley: American Truth and British Reality*. Chicago and La Salle: Open Court Publishing Company.

—— (1995) 'Bradley, Francis Herbert' in T. Honderich (ed.) 1995: 100–2.

Stevens, G. (2003) 'The truth and nothing but the truth, yet never the whole truth: Frege, Russell and the analysis of unities', *History and Philosophy of Logic*, 24: 221–40.

—— (2004) 'From Russell's paradox to the theory of judgement: Wittgenstein and Russell on the unity of the proposition', *Theoria*, 70 (1): 28–61.

Stock, G. (ed.) (1998) *Appearance versus Reality*. Oxford: Clarendon Press.

Stout, G.F. (1911) 'Real being and being for thought', in G.F. Stout, *Studies in Philosophy and Psychology*. London: Macmillan, 1930: 335–52.

Stove, D. (1985) 'Cole Porter and Karl Popper: the jazz age in the philosophy of science', in D. Stove 1991b: 1–26.

— (1991a) 'Idealism: a Victorian horror-story (Part One)', in Stove 1991b: 83–133.
— (1991b) *The Plato Cult.* Oxford: Blackwell.
Strawson, P.F. (1959) *Individuals: An Essay in Descriptive Metaphysics.* London: Methuen.
— (1974) *Subject and Predicate in Logic and Grammar.* London: Methuen.
Stroud, B. (1979) 'Inference, belief, and understanding', *Mind,* 88: 179–96. Reprinted in B. Stroud, *Meaning, Understanding, and Practice.* Oxford: Oxford University Press: 33–51.
Walker, R.C.S. (1985) 'Spinoza and the coherence theory of truth', *Mind,* 94: 1–18.
— (1989) *The Coherence Theory of Truth.* London: Routledge.
— (1998) 'Bradley's theory of truth' in G. Stock (ed.): 93–109.
— (2001) 'The coherence theory', in M. Lynch (ed.): 123–58.
Warnock, G.J. (1958) *English Philosophy Since 1900.* London: Oxford University Press.
Watling, J. (1970) *Bertrand Russell.* Edinburgh: Oliver & Boyd.
Weiss, B. (1995) 'On the demise of Russell's multiple relations theory of judgement', *Theoria,* 61: 261–82.
White, A.R. (1967) 'Coherence theory of truth', in P. Edwards (ed.), vol. 2: 130–3.
— (1971) *Truth.* New York: Anchor.
Whitehead, A.N. and Russell, B. (1910) *Principia Mathematica.* Cambridge: Cambridge University Press.
Whyte, J.T. (1990) 'Success semantics', *Analysis,* 50: 149–57.
Wilson, F. (1996) 'Moore's refutation of idealism', in P. Coates and D. Hutto (eds), *Current Issues in Idealism.* Bristol: Thoemmes: 23–57.
Wisdom, J.A.T.D. (1942) 'Moore's technique', in P.A. Schilpp (ed.), *The Philosophy of G. E. Moore.* La Salle, Illinois: Open Court: 421–50.
Wittgenstein, L. (1913a) Letter to Russell of June 1913, in L. Wittgenstein, *Letters to Russell, Keynes and Moore.* Oxford: Basil Blackwell, 1974: 23.
— (1913b) 'Notes on Logic', Appendix I of *Notebooks 1914–1916.* Oxford: Basil Blackwell, 1961: 93–106.
— (1919) Letter to Russell of 19 August 1919, in L. Wittgenstein, *Letters to Russell, Keynes and Moore.* Oxford: Basil Blackwell, 1974: 71–3.
— (1921) *Tractatus Logico-Philosophicus.* London: Routledge & Kegan Paul, 1933. [1921 is the date of publication of the original *Logisch-philosophische Abhandlung.*]
— (1953) *Philosophical Investigations.* Oxford: Basil Blackwell.
Wollheim, R. (1959) *F.H. Bradley,* 1st edn. Harmondsworth: Penguin.
— (1969) *F.H. Bradley,* revd edn. Harmondsworth: Penguin.
Woozley, A.D. (1949) *Theory of Knowledge.* London, Hutchinson.
Wright, C. (1995) 'Critical Notice of *The Coherence Theory of Truth – Realism, Antirealism, Idealism,* by Ralph C.S. Walker, *Synthèse,* 103: 279–302.

Bibliographical Note: The Publishing History of *Appearance and Reality*

Both the first (1893) and second (1897) editions of *Appearance and Reality* were published by Swan Sonnenschein (later taken over by the firm of George Allen, which subsequently became George Allen & Unwin), publishers of Muirhead's Library of Philosophy. It has always been rumoured that the book had originally been offered to, and rejected by, the Clarendon Press. On receipt of information from the Press, Richard Wollheim attempted to scotch this rumour in the revised edition of his *F.H. Bradley* (Wollheim 1969, p. 228). After reporting accurately that the book had been submitted to the Clarendon Press but withdrawn from consideration by Bradley himself, Wollheim continues, 'The Delegates complied with this request, regretfully we must assume, since they informed Bradley that they had formed "a very high opinion of its merit and interest".' Wollheim draws some conclusions: 'In consequence, the story retailed, for instance, by J.H. Muirhead that the book had been turned down is without foundation. Indeed, the most likely explanation of Bradley's new course of action is that he wanted to accommodate Muirhead, who was editor of the new Library of Philosophy.' This suggests that Muirhead was not only mendacious but irrational, in that he was prepared falsely to advertise the contents of his own Library as rejected material. Muirhead actually said ('Bradley's Place in Philosophy', *Mind*, vol. 34, 1925, pp. 173–84), 'The Delegates of the Clarendon Press of that time refused to be sponsors for it, ostensibly on account of what seemed to be its negative attitude to religion' (pp. 178–9). This is not completely accurate either. But two things are clear from the Bradley correspondence. One is that Muirhead claimed to have the story of the rejection from Bradley himself. The other is that it was important to Bradley's literary executors, in their (eventually successful) legal battle with Stanley Unwin over the transfer of the book from Allen & Unwin to the Clarendon Press as part of the (never-completed) project of publishing a collected edition, to establish that the Press had not rejected the original manuscript. And indeed the Press's records showed no such rejection. This, however, is not evidence that Muirhead's story is 'without foundation', since according to a letter from Bradley to an unnamed publisher (presumably Swan Sonnenschein), he says quite unequivocally that he had withdrawn the book prior to its official consideration by the Clarendon Press since he had been requested to do so by friends amongst the Delegates who told him that the book would be rejected, albeit with regret. According to Bradley's letter, they apparently found it 'controversial'.

A full-scale and uniform collected edition of Bradley's writings did not appear until 1999, with a different publisher (Thoemmes); volume 5 contains the correspondence relevant to this matter. But the Clarendon Press did for many years maintain in print most of Bradley's published work, including *Appearance and Reality*. Theirs is the 'ninth impression' most commonly found and used, which appeared in 1930. According to the printed information facing the title page, it is the ninth impression of the 1897 second edition. However, not only does this 'ninth impression' have a completely different pagination from that of the Swan Sonnenschein original, but the information is further misleading in that it does not reveal the existence of this earlier, different, publisher. What may be merely an oversight could, given the history of the book, easily be interpreted as reticence.

Index

Absolute, the, 7, 12, 21, 22–3, 132, 140, 179, 193n30
abstraction, 36, 42, 94–5, 153–4, 171
acquaintance, 62, 64, 65, 88, 103, 113, 114, 116–17, 119, 125, 127–8, 143
  as philosophical problem-solver, 71–2, 115, 117, 205n34
Acton, H.B., 13, 190n12
Alexander, Samuel, 193n29
Allard, James W., xvii, 82, 190n13, 192n12, 198n1, 198n4, 199n8, 199n15, 205n39, 208–9n14, 212n38
Almeida, Claudio de, 196n12
Amery, Leopold Stennett (1873–1955), 183
analysis, 115, 121, 203–4n21
  reductive and non-reductive, 113–14
  revelatory of logical form, 111, 120, 146
Apollo, 113
Armstrong, David Malet, xvii, 185, 214n12
Arnauld, Antoine, 29, 205n41
Asquith, Herbert Henry (1852–1928), 183
association of ideas, 190n2
atomism
  Bradley's hostility to, 34, 191n4
  logical, xiii, 16, 75–7
axiom (also doctrine, also dogma) of internal relations
  alleged bases of, 7, 11, 12–13, 142
  attribution to Bradley, 13–14, 15–16, 142, 151–2, 161, 193n29, 194n31
  Bradley's commitment to, 155–8
  Bradley's hostility to, 42–4, 139, 145, 158–9

connection with doctrine of unreality of relations, 155, 159–61, 165–6
  interpretations of, 14–15, 142, 150–4, 155, 161
  Manser on, 145–50
  Moore on, *see under* Moore, G.E.
  Russell on, 138–9, 151, 171
  of secondary significance, 167
  see also relations, reducibility of
Ayer, A.J., 3, 8, 15, 144, 158, 190n7, 202n8

Bach, Kent, 201n27
Baldwin, Thomas, xvii, 8, 17, 145, 160, 162, 198n1, 200n22, 209n14, 210n20, 213n2, 213n3
Basile, Pierfrancesco, 190n13, 198n1
Baxter, Donald, 24
beer, 21
behaviourism, 77, 188
being *vs* existence, 108
belief, *see* judgment
Berkeley, George, 21–2, 32, 143, 191n3
billiards, 37, 152–4
Blackburn, Simon, 14, 15, 190n11, 198n1
Blackwell, Kenneth, xvii
Blanshard, Brand, 13, 213n5
BonJour, Laurence, 190n10
Bosanquet, Bernard, 7, 28
Bradley, A.C., 2
Bradley, F.H., *see under topic entries*
Bradley, James, 189n4
Broad, C.D., 13
broad content, 104

Caesar, Julius, 111, 195n2
Cambridge, University of, xi, 2, 10, 175
  Apostles, 175
Campbell, C.A., 194n36

227